MGB ROADSTERS 1962-1980

Compiled by
R.M. Clarke

ISBN 1 869826 108

Distributed by
Brooklands Book Distribution Ltd.
'Holmerise', Seven Hills Road,
Cobham, Surrey, England

Printed in Hong Kong

BROOKLANDS BOOKS

BROOKLANDS ROAD TEST SERIES
AC Ace & Aceca 1953-1983
Alfa Romeo Alfasud 1972-1984
Alfa Romeo Alfetta Coupes GT. GTV. GTV6 1974-1987
Alfa Romeo Giulia Berlinas 1962-1976
Alfa Romeo Giulia Coupes 1963-1976
Alfa Romeo Spider 1966-1987
Allard Gold Portfolio 1937-1958
Alvis Gold Portfolio 1919-1969
American Motors Muscle Cars 1966-1970
Aston Martin Gold Portfolio 1972-1985
Austin Seven 1922-1982
Austin A30 & A35 1951-1962
Austin Healey 3000 1959-1967
Austin Healey 100 & 3000 Col No.1
Austin Healey 'Frogeye' Sprite Col No.1 1958-1961
Austin Healey Sprite 1958-1971
Avanti 1962-1983
BMW Six Cylinder Coupes 1969-1975
BMW 1600 Col. 1 1966-1981
BMW 2002 1968-1976
Bristol Cars Gold Portfolio 1946-1985
Buick Automobiles 1947-1960
Buick Muscle Cars 1965-1970
Buick Riviera 1963-1978
Cadillac Automobiles 1949-1959
Cadillac Automobiles 1960-1969
Cadillac Eldorado 1967-1978
High Performance Capris Gold Portfolio 1969-1987
Chevrolet Camaro & Z-28 1973-1981
High Performance Camaros 1982-1988
Chevrolet Camaro Col No.1 1967-1973
Camaro Muscle Cars 1966-1972
Chevrolet 1955-1957
Chevrolet Impala & SS 1958-1971
Chevrolet Muscle Cars 1966-1971
Chevelle and SS 1964-1972
Chevy EL Camino & SS 1959-1987
Chevy II Nova & SS 1962-1973
Chrysler 300 1955-1970
Citroen Traction Avant Gold Portfolio 1934-1957
Citroen DS & ID 1955-1975
Citroen 2CV 1949-1988
Shelby Cobra Gold Portfolio 1962-1969
Cobras & Replicas 1962-1983
Corvair 1959-1968
Chevrolet Corvette Gold Portfolio 1953 1962
Corvette Stingray Gold Portfolio 1963-1967
High Performance Corvettes 1983-1989
Datsun 240Z 1970-1973
Datsun 280Z & ZX 1975-1983
De Tomaso Collection No.1 1962-1981
Dodge Charger 1966-1974
Dodge Muscle Cars 1967-1970
Excalibur Collection No.1 1952-1981
Ferrari Cars 1946-1956
Ferrari Cars 1973-1977
Ferrari Dino 1965-1974
Ferrari Dino 308 & Mondial 1980-1984
Ferrari 308 & Mondial 1974-1979
Ferrair Collection No.1 1960-1970
Fiat-Bertone X1/9 1973-1988
Fiat Pininfarina 124 + 2000 Spider 1968-1985
Ford Automobiles 1949-1959
Ford Fairlane 1955-1970
Ford GT40 Gold Portfolio 1964-1987
Ford Falcon 1960-1970
High Perfomance Mustangs 1982-1988
Ford Cortina 1600E & GT 1967-1970
Ford RS Escorts 1968-1980
High Performance Escorts Mk1 1968-1974
High Performance Escorts Mk II 1975-1980
Honda CRX 1983-1987
Hudson & Railton 1936-1940
Jaguar Cars 1957-1961
Jaguar Cars 1961-1964
Jaguar Mk2 1959-1969
Jaguar E-Type Gold Portfolio 1961-1971
Jaguar E-Type 1966-1971
Jaguar E-Type V-12 1971-1975
Jaguar XKE Collection No.1 1961-1974
Jaguar XJ6 1968-1972
Jaguar XJ6 Series II 1973-1979
Jaguar XJ6 & XJ12 Series III 1979-1985
Jaguar XJ12 1972-1980
Jaguar XJS Gold Portfolio 1975-1988
Jaguar XK120.XK140.XK150 Gold Portfolio 1948-1960
Jeep CJ5 & CJ6 1960-1976
Jeep CJ5 & CJ7 1976-1986
Jensen Cars 1946-1967
Jensen Cars 1967-1979
Jensen Interceptor Gold Portfolio 1966-1986
Jensen Healey 1972-1976
Lamborghini Cars 1964-1970
Lamborghini Cars 1970-1975
Lamborghini Countach Col No.1 1971-1982
Lamborghini Countach & Urraco 1974-1980
Lamborghini Countach & Jalpa 1980-1985
Lancia Stratos 1972-1985
Land Rover 1948-1973 - A Collection
Land Rover Series II & IIa 1958-1971
Land Rover Series III 1971-1985
Land Rover 90 & 110 1983-1989
Lincoln Gold Portfolio 1949-1960
Lincoln Continental 1961-1969
Lotus and Caterham Seven Gold Portfolio 1957-1989
Lotus Elan Gold Portfolio 1962-1974
Lotus Elan Collection No.1 1963-1972
Lotus Elite 1957-1964
Lotus Elite & Eclat 1974-1982
Lotus Turbo Esprit 1980-1986
Lotus Europa 1966-1975
Lotus Europa Collection No.1 1966-1974
Lotus Seven Collection No.1 1957-1982
Marcos Cars 1960-1988
Maserati 1965-1970
Maserati 1970-1975
Mazda RX-7 Collection No.1 1978-1981
Mercedes 190 & 300SL 1954-1963

Mercedes 230/250/280SL 1963-1971
Mercedes Benz SLs & SLCs Gold Portfolio 1971-1989
Mercedes Benz Cars 1949-1954
Mercedes Benz Cars 1954-1957
Mercedes Benz Cars 1957-1961
Mercedes Benz Competition Cars 1950-1957
Mercury Muscle Cars 1966-1971
Metropolitan 1954-1962
MG TC 1945-1949
MG TD 1949-1953
MG TF 1953-1955
MG Cars 1959-1962
MGA Roadsters 1955-1962
MGA Collection No.1 1955-1982
MGB Roadsters 1962-1980
MGB GT 1965-1980
MG Midget 1961-1980
Mini Moke 1964-1989
Mini Muscle Cars 1961-1979
Mopar Muscle Cars 1964-1967
Mopar Muscle Cars 1968-1971
Morgan Three-Wheeler Gold Portfolio 1910-1952
Morgan Cars 1960-1970
Morgan Cars Gold Portfolio 1968-1989
Morris Minor Collection No.1
Mustang Muscle Cars 1967-1971
Oldsmobile Automobiles 1955-1963
Old's Cutlass & 4-4-2 1964-1972
Oldsmobile Muscle Cars 1964-1971
Oldsmobile Toronado 1966-1978
Opel GT 1968-1973
Packard Gold Portfolio 1946-1958
Pantera Gold Portfolio 1970-1989
Plymouth Barracuda 1964-1974
Plymouth Muscle Cars 1966-1971
Pontiac Tempest & GTO 1961-1965
Pontiac GTO 1964-1970
Pontiac Firebird 1967-1973
Pontiac Firebird and Trans-Am 1973-1981
High Performance Firebirds 1982-1988
Pontiac Fiero 1984-1988
Pontiac Muscle Cars 1966-1972
Porsche 356 1952-1965
Porsche Cars in the 60's
Porsche Cars 1960-1964
Porsche Cars 1964-1968
Porsche Cars 1968-1972
Porsche Cars 1972-1975
Porsche Turbo Collection No.1 1975-1980
Porsche 911 1965-1969
Porsche 911 1970-1972
Porsche 911 1973-1977
Porsche 911 Carrera 1973-1977
Porsche 911 Turbo 1975-1984
Porsche 911 SC 1978-1983
Porsche 914 Gold Portfolio 1969-1976
Porsche 914 Collection No.1 1969-1983
Porsche 924 Gold Portfolio 1975-1988
Porsche 928 1977-1989
Porsche 944 1981-1985
Range Rover Gold Portfolio 1970-1988
Reliant Scimitar 1964-1986
Riley 11/2 & 21/2 Litre Gold Portfolio 1945-1955
Rolls Royce Silver Cloud 1955-1965
Rolls Royce Silver Shadow 1965-1981
Rover P4 1949-1959
Rover P4 1955-1964
Rover 3 & 3.5 Litre 1958-1973
Rover 2000 + 2200 1963-1977
Rover 3500 1968-1977
Rover 3500 & Vitesse 1976-1986
Saab Sonett Collection No.1 1966-1974
Saab Turbo 1976-1983
Shelby Mustang Muscle Cars 1965-1970
Stubebaker Gold Portfolio 1947-1966
Stubebaker Hawks & Larks 1956-1963
Sunbeam Tiger & Alpine Gold Portfolio 1959-1967
Thunderbird 1955-1957
Thunderbird 1958-1963
Thunderbird 1964-1976
Toyota MR2 1984-1988
Triumph 2000. 2.5. 2500 1963-1977
Triumph GT6 1966-1974
Triumph Spitfire 1962-1980
Triumph Spitfire Col No.1 1962-1982
Triumph Stag 1970-1980
Triumph Stag Collection No.1 1970-1984
Triumph TR2 & TR3 1952-60
Triumph TR4-TR5-TR250 1961-1968
Triumph TR6 1969-1976
Triumph TR6 Collection No.1 1969-1983
Triumph TR7 & TR8 1975-1982
Triumph Vitesse & Herald 1959-1971
TVR Gold Portfolio 1959-1988
Volkswagen Cars 1936-1956
VW Beetle Collection No.1 1970-1982
VW Golf GTi 1976-1986
VW Karmann Ghia 1955-1982
VW Kubelwagen 1940-1975
VW Scirocco 1974-1981
VW Bus. Camper. Van 1954-1967
VW Bus. Camper. Van 1968-1979
VW Bus. Camper. Van 1979-1989
Volvo 120 1956-1970
Volvo 1800 1960-1973

BROOKLANDS ROAD & TRACK SERIES
Road & Track on Alfa Romeo 1949-1963
Road & Track on Alfa Romeo 1964-1970
Road & Track on Alfa Romeo 1971-1976
Road & Track on Alfa Romeo 1977-1989
Road & Track on Aston Martin 1962-1984
Road & Track on Auburn Cord and Duesenburg 1952-1984
Road & Track on Audi & Auto Union 1952-1980
Road & Track on Audi 1980-1986
Road & Track on Austin Healey 1953-1970
Road & Track on BMW Cars 1966-1974
Road & Track on BMW Cars 1975-1978
Road & Track on BMW Cars 1979-1983

Road & Track on Cobra, Shelby & GT40 1962-1983
Road & Track on Corvette 1953-1967
Road & Track on Corvette 1968-1982
Road & Track on Corvette 1982-1986
Road & Track on Datsun Z 1970-1983
Road & Track on Ferrari 1950-1968
Road & Track on Ferrari 1968-1974
Road & Track on Ferrari 1975-1981
Road & Track on Ferrari 1981-1984
Road & Track on Fiat Sports Cars 1968-1987
Road & Track on Jaguar 1950-1960
Road & Track on Jaguar 1961-1968
Road & Track on Jaguar 1968-1974
Road & Track on Jaguar 1974-1982
Road & Track on Jaguar 1983-1989
Road & Track on Lamborghini 1964-1985
Road & Track on Lotus 1972-1981
Road & Track on Maserati 1952-1974
Road & Track on Maserati 1975-1983
Road & Track on Mazda RX7 1978-1986
Road & Track on Mercedes 1952-1962
Road & Track on Mercedes 1963-1970
Road & Track on Mercedes 1971-1979
Road & Track on Mercedes 1980-1987
Road & Track on MG Sports Cars 1949-1961
Road & Track on MG Sprots Cars 1962-1980
Road & Track on Mustang 1964-1977
Road & Track on Peugeot 1955-1986
Road & Track on Pontiac 1960-1983
Road & Track on Porsche 1961-1967
Road & Track on Porsche 1968-1971
Road & Track on Porsche 1972-1975
Road & Track on Porsche 1975-1978
Road & Track on Porsche 1979-1982
Road & Track on Porsche 1982-1985
Road & Track on Porsche 1985-1988
Road & Track on Rolls Royce & B'ley 1950-1965
Road & Track on Rolls Royce & B'ley 1966-1984
Road & Track on Saab 1955-1985
Road & Track on Toyota Sports & GT Cars 1966-1984
Road & Track on Triumph Sports Cars 1953-1967
Road & Track on Triumph Sports Cars 1967-1974
Road & Track on Triumph Sports Cars 1974-1982
Road & Track on Volkswagen 1951-1968
Road & Track on Volkswagen 1968-1978
Road & Track on Volkswagen 1978-1985
Road & Track on Volvo 1957-1974
Road & Track on Volvo 1975-1985
Road & Track - Henry Manney at Large and Abroad

BROOKLANDS CAR AND DRIVER SERIES
Car and Driver on BMW 1955-1977
Car and Driver on BMW 1977-1985
Car and Driver on Cobra, Shelby & Ford GT 40 1963-1984
Car and Driver on Corvette 1956-1967
Car and Driver on Corvette 1968-1977
Car and Driver on Corvette 1978-1982
Car and Driver on Corvette 1983-1988
Car and Driver on Datsun Z 1600 & 2000 1966-1984
Car and Driver on Ferrari 1955-1962
Car and Driver on Ferrari 1963-1975
Car and Driver on Ferrari 1976-1983
Car and Driver on Mopar 1956-1967
Car and Driver on Mopar 1968-1975
Car and Driver on Mustang 1964-1972
Car and Driver on Pontiac 1961-1975
Car and Driver on Porsche 1955-1962
Car and Driver on Porsche 1963-1970
Car and Driver on Porsche 1970-1976
Car and Driver on Porsche 1977-1981
Car and Driver on Porsche 1982-1986
Car and Driver on Saab 1956-1985
Car and Driver on Volvo 1955-1986

BROOKLANDS PRACTICAL CLASSICS SERIES
PC on Austin A40 Restoration
PC on Land Rover Restoration
PC on Metalworking in Restoration
PC on Midget/Sprite Restoration
PC on Mini Cooper Restoration
PC on MGB Restoration
PC on Morris Minor Restoration
PC on Sunbeam Rapier Restoration
PC on Triumph Herald/Vitesse
PC on Triumph Spitfire Restoration
PC on VW Beetle Restoration
PC on 1930s Car Restoration

BROOKLANDS MOTOR & THOROGHBRED & CLASSIC CAR SERIES
Motor & T & CC on Ferrari 1966-1976
Motor & T & CC on Ferrari 1976-1984
Motor & T & CC on Lotus 1979-1983

BROOKLANDS MILITARY VEHICLES SERIES
Allied Mil. Vehicles No.1 1942-1945
Allied Mil. Vehicles No.2 1941-1946
Dodge Mil. Vehicles Col. 1 1940-1945
Military Jeeps 1941-1945
Off Road Jeeps 1944-1971
Hail to the Jeep
US Military Vehicles 1941-1945
US Army Military Vehicles WW2-TM9-2800

BROOKLANDS HOT ROD RESTORATION SERIES
Auto Restoration Tips & Techniques
Basic Bodywork Tips & Techniques
Basic Painting Tips & Techniques
Camaro Restoration Tips & Techniques
Custom Painting Tips & Techniques
Engine Swapping Tips & Techniques
How to Build a Street Rod
Mustang Restoration Tips & Techniques
Performance Tuning - Chevrolets of the '60s
Performance Tuning - Ford of the '60s
Performance Tuning - Mopars of the '60s
Performance Tuning - Pontiacs of the '60s

BROOKLANDS BOOKS

CONTENTS

ACKNOWLEDGEMENTS

In September 1962 the Abingdon coded project EX205 developed into the MGB, a model that became the worlds most popular sportscar and remained in production for eighteen years.

It has been my practice to write in the introduction a few paragraphs on the history of the car in question. It is however unnecessary in this instance as our final story is an excellent Classic and Sportscar 'Profile' by Mark Hughes and Mike Walsh which incorporates all that one could wish to know, and I commend it to you.

We are indebted once again to Classic and Sportscar this time for our cover illustration which depicts Roger Jerram's beautifully preserved 1967 model in full flight. It is perhaps not surprising that Rogers car is in such pristine condition as he has been associated with the MG Sprite & Midget, B,C V8 Centre in Richmond for many years.

Brooklands Books are produced in small numbers by enthusiasts for enthusiasts and their availability is due solely to the generosity and understanding of the original magazine publishers. We are sure MGB owners and restorers will wish to join with us in thanking the management of Autocar, Autosport, Car & Car Conversions, Car and Driver, Classic and Sportscar, Modern Motor, Motor, Motor Sport, Motor Trend, Road Test, Road & Track, Sports Car Graphic, Sports Car World and the World Car Catalogue, for allowing their copyright articles once again to be included in this series.

R.M. Clarke

JOHN BOLSTER TESTS

THE M.G.B

THE world of the sports car is changing fast. We used to admire the type of two-seater that was all engine and performance, and precious little else. Most people still imagine that they would enjoy this sort of machine, but when it comes to signing a cheque they always go for something less spartan. A sports car must still have superior performance and handling qualities but it is now expected to have all the creature comforts of a luxurious saloon, which means that noise, vibration, and hard suspension are out.

Such a car is the M.G.B. It starts off by being outstandingly good looking and it goes on by being practical and comfortable. It is faster, more flexible, and much quieter than the M.G.A, which it replaces, but although it seems "softer" than its predecessor, it can do everything just a little better than that car could.

The biggest difference between the two cars is the deletion of the separate chassis frame, which was a hefty, box-section structure. A lot of weight has been saved which has enabled such important things as winding windows to be incorporated,

the much better equipped new model being only a few pounds heavier than its forbear. The wheelbase is 3 ins. shorter, but a great deal of extra luggage space has been found, largely by moving the seats forward about 6 ins.

The new construction has enabled more room to be provided for the pedals, and indeed the shorter car supplies the driver and passenger with as much space as they could possibly need. The M.G.A luggage boot was always rather a joke, and while the M.G.B cannot transport a cabin trunk, it is more sensibly endowed with baggage accommodation. There are locks for the glove box, both doors, and the boot.

Mechanically, the design is very similar, though appreciably softer suspension has been adopted. In front, the wishbones have the lever-type dampers incorporated with the top pivots and the steering is by rack and pinion. Behind, the hypoid axle is on underslung semi-elliptic springs and lever-type dampers. An open two-seater, especially one with large doors, is a most difficult body form to translate into a rigid structure. The scuttle and instrument

panel are too often the weak points, so the bulkhead is shaped to constitute an extremely strong girder which, with the centre of the instrument panel, is united with the transmission tunnel. This central member, which is vital to the stiffness of the body-cum-chassis, is used both as a duct for the built-in heating system and to carry the radio speaker.

The engine is a further development of the B-series B.M.C. unit, but it is more than that. The original unit was of 1,489 c.c., which was increased to 1,622 c.c., when it became somewhat rough. The existing cylinder head has been given a new "bottom end". A 1,798 c.c. cylinder block has larger main bearings to accommodate crankshaft journals of $\frac{1}{8}$ in. greater diameter. The crankshaft webs are a little thicker at the expense of slightly narrower journals. The resulting crank is much sturdier and makes the engine far smoother in operation; although the stroke is the same as before, the larger bore of 80.26 mm., coupled with this new crankshaft, gives a better torque curve throughout the range.

The 1,800 c.c. engine develops 94 b.h.p.

5

at 5,500 r.p.m. It is coupled by an 8 ins. diaphragm-spring Borg and Beck clutch to a four-speed gearbox with synchromesh on the upper three ratios, and no remote control extension is necessary with the forward seating position. The hypoid axle now has a 3.9 to 1 ratio to allow for the smaller diameter of the 5.60-14 ins. tyres. Lockheed disc port brakes are used in conjunction with drums at the rear.

As I have said, the new M.G. has a most attractive appearance. The doors are easy to enter and the very low floor level allows the feet to sink to a natural position in relation to the seat. There is enough seat adjustment for a veritable giant. With the hood raised, the roof at first seems a little "beetle-browed", but in fact the view all round is good, greatly aided by the transparent panels in the hood. A most ingenious framework keeps the hood fabric taut and it does not flap at 100 m.p.h. speeds. The folding operation is straightforward but not especially rapid, the top being neatly concealed when furled.

The gear lever is ideally placed and very light in action. The brakes demand appreciable pedal pressure but they do not fade and are constant in response. The steering is light and "quick", and if it feels a little "spongy" at first, the sensation is soon forgotten.

On the road, the M.G.B at once impresses by its smooth, quiet running and flexibility. It accelerates strongly from less than 20 m.p.h. in top gear and there is none of the "thump" that one associates with a big four-cylinder engine. On the gears, there is a marked reduction in the level of mechanical noise as the rev counter approaches 6,000 r.p.m. There is one small vibration period at 4,500 r.p.m.

The acceleration of this car is very lovely up to 90 m.p.h., which is a good cruising speed. A genuine 100 m.p.h. is always available, with a bit more to come on the longer straights. The gears are very easy to handle, except for an occasional reluctance to engage first speed at rest. The ratios are sufficiently close to allow 30, 50, and 80 m.p.h. to be achieved on the three indirect gears, to the considerable benefit of the acceleration times on the data panel.

Though the ride is soft for a British sports car it is still appreciably firmer than that of a typical saloon. There is some roll during hard cornering but this is not excessive, and does not obtrude during normal road driving. There is an almost total absence of axle tramp during wheelspin, which is rare, and though one can feel the axle bouncing on very bumpy corners the general impression is that the roadholding has not been allowed to suffer in obtaining a flat and comfortable ride. Deserving of the highest praise is the remarkable stability in gusty side-winds, which proves that the new body shape has other attributes than mere beauty of line.

This stability also proves that the inherent handling characteristic is just on the understeering side of neutral. Any energetic driving methods, however, will translate this to oversteer with an ultimate rear-end breakaway. This is the type of response at which most British sports car designers aim, and so there is nothing new to learn for the man who first takes over an M.G.B.

An oil radiator is mounted ahead of the water radiator. This keeps the oil temperature within bounds at all times, which is just as well, for the smooth, quiet engine encourages one to use full power whenever possible. In an entirely different context, the large space behind the seats is ideal for the carriage of parcels when her ladyship is at the wheel. With the hood raised, there is plenty of room for a child to travel on quite long journeys.

It will be noticed that all the performance figures are considerably better than those of the M.G.A. Weather conditions were far from ideal throughout my tests, and I am sure that I could have beaten the maximum speed and the acceleration times on a still summer's day. However, these are the unavoidable penalties of winter testing. Nevertheless, the virtues of this car cannot be read in the performance graph. With its winding windows, efficient heating and ventilation, complete equipment, and quiet running, it is a thoroughly practical machine by any standards. Indeed, it would be fair to say that many people who are tired of the rougher type of sports car, or even those who have previously only considered a saloon, would be very happy indeed as owners of the new M.G.B.

These cold and practical virtues will not be the deciding factor in some cases. Wherever I parked the car, I heard the most flattering comments on its appearance, and the interior appointments and instrument panel layout complement the attractive exterior. As a popsy-catcher, I award the M.G.B ten marks out of ten, which may not interest you at all but is certainly no disadvantage.

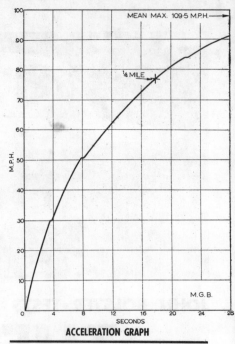

ACCELERATION GRAPH

MEAN MAX. 109·5 M.P.H.

M.G.B

SPECIFICATION AND PERFORMANCE DATA
Car Tested: M.G.B sports two-seater, price £834 6s. including P.T. Extras on test car: Oil radiator, radio, heater, wire wheels.
Engine: Four-cylinders 80.26 mm.×89 mm. (1,798 c.c.). Push-rod-operated overhead valves. Compression ratio 8.8 to 1. 94 b.h.p. at 5,500 r.p.m. Twin SU carburetters. Lucas coil and distributor.
Transmission: 8 ins. Borg and Beck diaphragm-spring clutch. Four-speed gearbox with synchromesh on upper three gears and short central lever. ratio 3.91, 5.37, 8.65, and 14.21 to 1. Open propeller shaft. Hypoid rear axle.
Chassis: Combined body and chassis. Independent front suspension by wishbones and helical springs. Rack and pinion steering. Rear axle on semi-elliptic springs. Lever-type dampers all round. Knock-on wire wheels (extra) fitted 5.60×14 ins. tyres. Lockheed hydraulic brakes with 10¾ ins. discs in front and 10 ins. × 1¾ ins. drums behind.
Equipment: 12-volt lighting and starting. Speedometer. Rev counter. Oil pressure, water temperature, and fuel gauges. Flashing indicators. Extra: Heater and radio.
Dimensions: Wheelbase 7 ft. 7 ins. Track (front) 4 ft. 1 in.; (rear) 4 ft. 1¼ ins. Overall length 12 ft. 9¼ ins. Width 4 ft. 11⅞ ins. Turning circle 32 ft. Weight 18 cwt. 1 qtr.
Performance: Maximum speed 109.5 m.p.h. Speeds in gears: 3rd, 86 m.p.h., 2nd, 51 m.p.h., 1st, 30 m.p.h. Standing quarter-mile 18 secs. Acceleration 0-30 m.p.h., 3.6 secs.; 0-50 m.p.h., 7.6 secs.; 0-60 m.p.h., 11.4 secs.; 0-80 m.p.h., 19.4 secs.
Fuel Consumption: Driven hard, 25 m.p.g.

NEAT AND TIDY (below): The four-cylinder push-rod engine of 1.8 litres fits snugly into the under-bonnet space, and the dip-stick can be seen to be readily accessible for once! LEFT: An attractively laid-out cockpit has always been an M.G. feature, and the M.G.B "office" is functionally arranged.

MGB 1800

WHEN I WENT TO THE STATES for the first time, at the end of 1948, a little English car called the MG TC was just starting its career and incredulous people were looking at this strange bug with wide eyes. "What kind of furrin job is that?" "Does it have an engine?" "What happens to that thing in a big wind?" et cetera. Imperturbable, the few proud owners of the TCs carried on bravely, unshaken, except for the fact that in reality and in retrospect, they were pretty well shaken up by the ride and the quick steering reaction of their uncomfortable but endearing TC. Quite quickly the MG TC became a success, and quite quickly, also, it became a sort of classic as its relatively brief career ended with the appearance of a "ridiculously modern" MG TD, which even had solid wheels instead of wire ones. "How could they have ruined the MG like this?" was heard everywhere among that group of aficionados, which included a certain young and coming driver, and TC owner, Phil Hill.

But, solid wheels or not, the TD was there to stay. It had a better ride, was more comfortable and had slightly better performance. Thousands upon thousands were sold and it was really this model which made the name of MG so famous in America. The MG TD was still going strong several years later when the TF arrived upon the scene. This was still a classic looking sports car which went well, especially when it was fitted with the 1500 cc engine.

Then, in 1955, the MG "A" came out. Once more there were loud outcrys when this modern looking sports car took the road, but with its pleasant lines the MGA had no difficulty in establishing itself on the world market. Constant ameliorations, the last one being the Mark II model, kept its sales alert and its owners generally happy. In fact, when its life ended this summer, 100,000 MGA's had been built — a resounding reception and a unique one in sports car history.

Filling the place of such a successful car is no easy task, but BMC has a fine chance of renewing its success, and perhaps of even bettering it, with their latest creation, the MG "B." How new and different is the MGB? Very much so. First, the body is entirely new and so is the interior. It is a very attractive design with smooth, clean lines, with a front resembling the MG Midget a bit. It has a new semi-wrap-around windshield, and it looks very pretty whether the top is up or down. The cockpit of the car is all new and is roomier than that of the MGA. The leather covered seats are very comfortable, there is plenty of leg room, as well as a good amount of space for head and shoulders. The dash board, which includes a glove compartment which can be locked, is functional but cleverly designed in that all the instruments are readable in a flash, all the switches handy to reach and the section including the speedometer and rev counter are in a rectangular cup preventing reflected glare. Special attention has even been given to the rear view mirror, which is on a thin rod in the center of the windshield so that it can be adjusted in any position on the rod. Roll-up windows, a welcome feature, have been added. There is quite a bit of room in the back seat, enough anyway to accommodate a couple of kids on a trip or at least to be used for extra baggage room. Incidentally, the trunk of the car is surprisingly roomy for a sports car, and this will be welcome, too. The driving position is excellent, with the stick gear shift ideally placed. The three-spoked steering wheel is typically MG, and I personally would replace it with a Nardi wooden one, which would fit in very well with the style of the cockpit.

As for the dimensions and weight, the MGB is quite different, too. Its wheelbase is 91 inches, instead of 94 for the MGA, while its overall length is 153.9 inches instead of 156. In height the car is roughly the same but it is one inch wider. The ground clearance is two inches lower, while front and rear tracks, with the wire wheels fitted on, are now 49.5 inches instead of 47.5 and 48.75 inches before. This more compact car weighs 1920 pounds instead of 2,000 pounds, an appreciable weight savings due to its shorter dimensions and the use of an aluminum hood.

"Improving the Breed" again, it's a highly successful replacement for the popular MGA.

Basically the same, solid MG powerplant, the "B" engine is bored out to 80.26 mm, increasing its size to 1798 cc. We found it quiet and strong, well able to pull the taller gearing. The new power provides it with a startlingly un-MG-like exhaust note.

In the bottom photos Cahier is shown busily testing the new car at the Charlegrove track in England. He concluded it is the best MG ever built. Our tests here at the main office, in the dry, showed it to be an excellent handler and we heartily concur with Bernard. The "B" has a relaxed understeer handling and improvements have been made in its stopping.

A wider, more usable luggage compartment is a feature of the new car with a welcome addition — an outside latch.

At right, the wide door reveals that the driver is no longer buried well beneath the dash. Access is much better.

The excellent detail finish and design is apparent in right photos. Transportable radio is standard on West Coast.

The independent front suspension, below, remains the same but the difference in tread, wheelbase make improvement.

MGB 1800

Under this hood sits the new power plant which is no less than the faithful old four-cylinder BMC 1600 brought up to 1798 cc, this increase being accomplished by enlarging the bore from 76.2 mm to 80.26 mm. The head remains basically the same, with a compression ratio of 8 to 1. Twin SU carburetors are used as in the past. Thanks to the bigger engine displacement, the horsepower has been brought up to 94 DIN, with the torque of the engine significantly improved from 97 lb/ft at 4,000 rpm to 107 lb/ft at 3,500 rpm. An oil temperature cooler radiator is now standard equipment.

Independent front suspension, by means of wishbones and coil springs, and rear suspension with semi-elliptic springs controlled by hydraulic shock absorbers, are basically the same as on the MGA. Fourteen-inch wheels are now used, rather than 15-inch ones, with a tire size of 5.60. The gearbox is the same old faithful four-speed forward, a sturdy rather "unrefined" unit still using an un-synchronized first gear. Gear ratios are the same except that the final drive ratio is 3.9 instead of 4.1. The brakes remain the same, with 11-inch discs in front and 10-inch drums on the rear. As you can see, many significant changes have been made, inside and out, changes which have almost completely altered its comportment on the road.

Some dry but mostly wet weather followed me during my day of testing, and this was very good as it gave me the opportunity of seeing the MGB at work under various conditions. As soon as you are on the road you realize that the new MGB has broken away from the traditional MG type in many ways. Comfortably installed at the wheel you are quickly taken by the fact that you are driving a very refined sort of sports car. The engine is very smooth and quiet. There is a marked absence of wind noise with the top up, an unusual feature for the average sports car. The steering is direct and pleasant. The gearbox seemed, for some reason, much nicer to operate, and the brake pedal required a minimum of pressure. Driving through the outskirts of Oxford in traffic, I enjoyed the pleasure of the wonderful flexibility of the engine which would accelerate smoothly from 1000 rpm up. This meant that you could go down as low as 20 mph in top gear and the car would accelerate briskly and without protest, all the way up.

Behind all this smoothness the new power plant has a lot of punch and go, a feeling which was fully confirmed by the figures taken later on during the acceleration test. Once on the open road I could try the car at high speeds, discovering how steady it was at 100 mph plus, while an 80 mph cruising speed (which incidentally, is only 4,500 rpm) seemed to be a pace you could maintain all day long with a maximum of comfort, a feeling of safety and a very low level of engine and wind noise. Abrupt stops at that speed were done in a very short distance and several consecutive stops did not seem to alter the efficiency of the brakes nor their balance. The handling on curves was another pleasant surprise, with the MGB going very steadily through them with what felt like little body roll and a behavior which I would call neutral. Of course, when pushing it really hard, I encountered some oversteering. It was not at all a vicious type of oversteering, and I felt the car to be easily controlled, even when literally thrown around corners, where the extra power and torque of the new engine were a handy factor for controlling and straightening out the car. Going up through the gears the revs would go very quickly to 6,200 rpm, which was the red line I used, although I believe that it wouldn't hurt to bring it for short moments to 6,500 rpm. My test drive finally took me to one of my favorite BMC testing grounds, the Charlegrove airport, where I was able to take all the acceleration figures.

These figures were rewarding, as I was able to record zero to 40 mph in 6 seconds, zero to 50 in 8.5 seconds, zero to 60

CONTINUED ON PAGE 23

VEHICLE ....MG	MODEL ....B "1800"
PRICE (as tested) ...$2649 POE L.A. Estimated	OPTIONS ....Radio, hardtop, wire wheels

ENGINE:

Type	4 cylinder, in-line, water-cooled
Head	Removable cast iron
Valves	Overhead valves, pushrod/rocker actuated
Max. bhp	94 @ 5500 rpms
Max. Torque	106 lbs./ft. @ 3500 rpms
Bore	3.16 in. 80.26 mm.
Stroke	3.5 in. 89 mm.
Displacement	109.6 cu. in. 1798 cc.
Compression Ratio	8.8 to 1.
Induction System	Twin SU carburetors, type HS4
Exhaust System	Cast manifold to single pipe and muffler
Electrical System	12-V Lucas

CLUTCH:
Borg & Beck (Diaphragm spring) dry single plate
Diameter ....8 in.
Actuation ....Hydraulic

TRANSMISSION:
4 speed forward, synchro top three
Ratios: 1st ....3.64 to 1
2nd ....2.21 to 1
3rd ....1.37 to 1
4th ....1.00 to 1
Reverse ....4.76 to 1

DIFFERENTIAL:
Hypoid
Ratio ....3.909 to 1
Drive Axles (type) ....enclosed, semi-floating

STEERING:
Rack & Pinion
Turns Lock to Lock 2.9
Turn Circle ....32 ft.

BRAKES:
Front — Disc Diameter .....10¾ in.
Rear — Drum Diameter ....10 in.
Swept Area ....346 sq. in.

CHASSIS:

Frame	Conventional box type frame
Body	Steel, bolt-on, aluminum hood
Front Suspension	Independent, coil springs and wishbones
Tire Size & Type	560 x 14 Dunlop Gold Seal

WEIGHTS AND MEASURES:

Wheelbase	91 in.	Ground Clearance	5 in.
Front Track	49¼ in.	Curb Weight	1960 lbs.
Rear Track	49¼ in.	Test Weight	2320 lbs.
Overall Height	49⅜ in.	Crankcase	4 qts.
Overall Width	59 in.	Cooling System	5½ qts.
Overall Length	153 in.	Gas Tank	12 gals

PERFORMANCE:

0-30	3.5 sec.	0-70	16.0 sec.
0-40	6.0 sec.	0-80	19.8 sec.
0-50	8.5 sec.	0-90	28.2 sec.
0-60	11.6 sec.	0-100	35.0 sec.

Standing ¼ mile ....18.5 sec. @ 78 mph
Top Speed (av. two-way run) ....107.5 mph

Speed Error	30	40	50	60	70	80	90
Actual	30	40	50	60	69	79	88

Fuel Consumption: Test ....24 mpg   Average ......26/28 mpg
Recommended Shift Points
Max. 1st ....32 mph   Max. 3rd ....80 mph
Max. 2nd ....53 mph   RPM Red-line ....6,200 rpm
Speed Ranges in gears:
1st .... 0 to 35 mph   3rd ....15 to 80 mph
2nd .... 5 to 52-55 mph   4th ....20 to 107 mph

Brake Test: No Fade encountered on many stops, at 80 mph±; tests were done on a straight level road. No test made in mountain type roads.

REFERENCE FACTORS:

BHP per Cubic Inch	0.858
Lbs. per BHP	20.8
Piston Speed @ Peak rpm	3208 ft./min.
Sq. In. Swept Brake area per Lb.	0.176

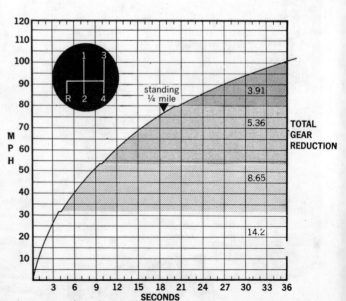

Mr. John Christy, Editor
Sports Car Graphic
5959 Hollywood Boulevard
Los Angeles 28, Calif.

Dear John:

Here is our brand new MGB. It represents the first all-out MG change
since the MGA series made its debut seven years and more than 100,000
vehicles ago. Everything is new but the Octagon. Production of our new
thoroughbred is now in full swing.

The B is designed to appeal to:

PRACTICAL GUYS who like wind-up
windows with adjustable side
vents, a wrap-around windshield
and wide opening doors with
outside handles and locks.

AESTHETIC GUYS who flip their
lids over subtly sculptured,
aerodynamic lines and magnificent
trim and finish.

HEEL AND TOE GUYS who revel in
supple suspension, cyclonic
acceleration and on a dime braking.

AND GALS.

Body styling? A picture is worth a thousand words.

Fade free, disc brakes up front are competition proved.
Pads are shielded from sludge and grit.

You couldn't wish for better cockpit comfort and
layout. Everything's there! Even the pedals are
spaced for size twelves.

There are two
The standard,
completely, st
Optional is an
into the carpe
this generous
shopping, extr

Choice of disc or wire wheels.

The new MGB front office is all
business. Displacement has been
increased to 1800 c.c. resulting in
more horses, quicker acceleration and
better top speed in all four forward
gears. Oil cooler is standard.

trunk? You said it.

es of vinyl soft tops.
t pack-away top, can be removed
in the trunk or left at home.
ched folding top which lowers
rea back of the seats. Incidentally,
will accommodate a lot of
gage or an occasional passenger.

For your technically minded readers here are the specs.

Kindest regards.

Yours sincerely,
HAMBRO AUTOMOTIVE CORPORATION

Tony R. Birt
Advertising Manager

P.S. First shipments have arrived. Some lucky BMC dealers already have them. Others will have them any day.

ENGINE: Four cylinder-O.H.V. operated by push-rods from 3-bearing camshaft with roller-chain drive and automatic chain tensioner. 3-bearing, counter-balanced crankshaft with renewable bearing liners. Solid-skirt, aluminum-alloy pistons with one scraper and three compression rings. Connecting rods with renewable, steel-backed, lead-indium bearings. Bore 3.16 in. Stroke 3.5 in. Capacity 1798 c.c. High compression engine develops 94 B.H.P. at 5,500 R.P.M. Compression ratio 8.75:1. Maximum torque 107 lb. ft. at 3,500 R.P.M.

CARBURETION: Twin S.U. semi-downdraught carburetors fed from rear mounted S.U. H.P.-type electric fuel pump. Air cleaner fitted to each carburetor. Tank capacity 12 U.S. gallons.

LUBRICATION: Full-flow external oil filter with renewable element. Oil cooler.

IGNITION: Oil-filled coil. Automatic advance and retard with centrifugal and vacuum control.

COOLING SYSTEM: Pressurized radiator with impeller pump and fan. Circulation thermostatically controlled.

TRANSMISSION: Borg and Beck single-plate dry clutch with hydraulic actuation. Four-speed gearbox with synchromesh on second, third, and top gears, giving overall ratios of first 14.21, second 8.65, third 5.37, top 3.90, and reverse 18.58 : 1. Central remote control floor gear change lever. Hardy Spicer propeller shaft with needle bearing universal joints. Three quarter floating rear axle with hypoid final reduction gears. Axle ratio 3.909 : 1. Road speed at 1000 R.P.M. in top gear: 17.9 M.P.H.

STEERING: Direct rack and pinion with large diameter, spring-spoke clear-view steering wheel, 3 turns lock to lock.

SUSPENSION: Front: Independent by coil springs and wishbone-type links controlled by hydraulic dampers. Rear: Semi-elliptic springs controlled by hydraulic dampers.

BRAKES: Lockheed hydraulic system employing discs at front and drums at rear. Front disc diameter 10¾ in. Rear drum diameter 10 in. Cable-operated, centrally positioned hand brake lever actuating brakes on rear brake-shoes.

ROAD WHEELS: Well-base disc-type wheels with 4-stud fixing fitted with 5.60—14 nylon tires with tubes. Spare wheel housed in trunk.

ELECTRICAL: Twin 6-volt batteries mounted in balanced position behind the seats: suppressor equipment; belt-driven generator; compensated voltage control; single-pole, positive-ground wiring system; ignition and starter switch; twin horns; self-parking, twin-blade windshield wipers; twin stop and tail lamps incorporating flashing direction signals and rear reflectors; sealed beam unit headlights; foot-operated dip switch; sidelights integral with flashing direction signals.

INSTRUMENTS: Large speedometer with dead-beat reading; oil pressure, fuel and water temperature gauges. Headlight high-beam warning light; large tachometer with ignition warning light; map-reading light switch; windshield wiper switch; manual choke; lighting switch; combined starter and ignition switch; panel light switch with rheostat; direction indicator lever on steering column with warning lights on instrument panel; windshield washer control; horn button in steering wheel center.

COACHWORK: Two-door, two-seater sports car of all-steel mono-construction; cold air ventilation to cockpit from grille in front of windshield away from exhaust fumes; adjustable bucket-type seats; occasional rear-seating; leather upholstery with leathercloth on non-wearing parts; fitted carpet over gearbox tunnel; Vinyl coated rubber mats on floor; one-piece hood hinged at rear; enclosed trunk with locking lid; curved laminated windshield; fully wind-down door windows with hinged quarter lights; windshield washers; waterproof stowaway top with large rear transparent panel; wide, rear-opening doors fitted with outside handles and locks; front and rear overriders; rear-view mirror adjustable for height; spare wheel, tools, jack and starting handle housed in trunk; screw-type gas tank cap; provision for fitting radio. Anchorages for safety belts on front seats.

OPTIONAL EQUIPMENT: Heater and demister; road speed tires; white-wall tires; wire wheels; tonneau cover; anti-roll bar; folding top.

COLORS: Tartan Red with black or red upholstery and red top. Old English White with black or red upholstery and grey top. Chelsea Grey with red upholstery and grey top. Iris Blue with black or blue upholstery and blue top. Black with black or red upholstery and grey top.

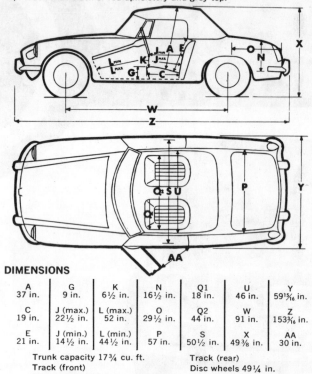

DIMENSIONS

A	G	K	N	Q1	U	Y
37 in.	9 in.	6½ in.	16½ in.	18 in.	46 in.	59¹⁵⁄₁₆ in.
C	J (max.)	L (max.)	O	Q2	W	Z
19 in.	22½ in.	52 in.	29½ in.	44 in.	91 in.	153³⁄₁₆ in.
E	J (min.)	L (min.)	P	S	X	AA
21 in.	14½ in.	44½ in.	57 in.	50½ in.	49⅜ in.	30 in.

Trunk capacity 17¾ cu. ft.
Track (front) Track (rear)
Disc wheels 49 in. Disc wheels 49¼ in.
Wire wheels 49¼ in. Wire wheels 49 in.
Ground clearance 5 in.

Specifications and colors subject to change without notice.

Product of **The British Motor Corporation Ltd.,** makers of MG, Austin Healey, Sprite, Morris and Austin cars.

New, chassisless MG B offers more en-gine, more comfort, but retains all the old zest, reports Bill Daly

GEE-WHIZ!

WHEN the late Jack Myers looked like being beaten by race handicappers, he would say "there's no substitute for inches," and forthwith bore the cylinders of his car out a fraction bigger.

Most of the time this formula worked successfully for Jack—just as it has for the just-released MG B.

Capable of 105 m.p.h. and offering every comfort for two people and their luggage, the latest version of this famous make has a bigger (1800c.c.) engine which, coupled with the car's new chassisless con-struction, makes it a delight to drive in town or country.

At 18½cwt., the B may be a little heavy for competition work—but it should certainly do better than the

NEW 1798c.c. engine develops 94 b.h.p., kicked test car to 105 m.p.h.

abortive twin-cam job of not so long ago. And it can accelerate this weight from rest to 90 m.p.h. in just over 32 seconds—or pull away smoothly from 15 m.p.h. in top gear.

The B's weightiness is justified by the provision of wide (36½in.) doors for easy entry, comfort-giving glass wind-up windows (just over two turns of the handle), a roomier cockpit with lots of elbow room, and all the leg-room adjustment any 6ft. 4in. midget might require.

Versatile Power-pack

Externally the new 1798c.c. engine appears unchanged—but it is, no doubt, the end of the line in the development of the 1½-litre B.M.C. unit, first produced in 1954 and progressively enlarged to 1588, then 1622c.c.

Bores have been enlarged once more, but there's no increase in stroke, although the casting has been altered internally to take the bigger bores; the inner wall of the tappet chest has been modified to retain adequate water passages.

Contact area between front and rear pairs of siamesed cylinders has been increased, and gudgeon-pin bosses now sport four holes instead of two, to give further internal cooling by oil spray. Crankshaft has been stiffened and main-bearing diameter increased by ⅛in. Minor head modifications round off the mechanical picture.

Under load, this enlarged, high-compression (8.8:1) version of the B series engine with twin SU carburettors has a much wider range of useful speeds than the B.M.C. touring vehicles, already renowned for smooth pulling power at low revs.

DASH (top right) is fully instrumented, gearshift a beauty. WELL behind seats (right) takes luggage or one small child. BOOT (below) loses much space to the spare wheel.

MAIN SPECIFICATIONS

ENGINE: 4-cylinder, o.h.v; bore 80.26mm., stroke 88.9mm., capacity 1798c.c.; compression ratio 8.8:1; maximum b.h.p. 94 at 5500 r.p.m.; maximum torque 107lb./ft. at 3500; twin SU semi-downdraught carburettors, SU electric fuel pump; 12v. ignition.
TRANSMISSION: Single dry-plate clutch, hydraulically operated; 4-speed gearbox, synchromeshed on top three; overall ratios—1st, 14.214; 2nd, 8.655; 3rd, 5.369; top, 3.901:1; reverse, 18.588:1; hypoid bevel final drive, 3.909:1 ratio. Road speed at 1000 r.p.m. in top gear, 17.9 m.p.h.
SUSPENSION: Front independent, by coil springs and wishbones; semi-ellip-tics at rear; hydraulic shock-absorbers all round.
STEERING: Rack-and-pinion; 3 turns lock-to-lock, 32ft. turning circle.
WHEELS: Centre-lock, knock-on wire wheels with tubed 5.60 by 14in. tyres.
BRAKES: Lockheed hydraulic; 10¾in. discs at front, 10in. drums at rear; total swept area, 350 sq. in.
CONSTRUCTION: Unitary.
DIMENSIONS: Wheelbase, 7ft. 7½in.; track, 4ft. 2in. front and rear; length 12ft. 9¾in., width 5ft. 2in., height (with hood up) 4ft. 1¼in.; ground clearance 5in.
KERB WEIGHT: 18½cwt.
FUEL TANK: 10 gallons.

PERFORMANCE ON TEST

CONDITIONS: Mostly wet; cold, no wind; two occupants, premium fuel.
MAXIMUM SPEED: 105.6 m.p.h.
STANDING quarter-mile: 18.4s.
MAXIMUM in indirect gears (to 6000 r.p.m.): 1st, 29.5 m.p.h.; 2nd, 48.0; 3rd, 78.0.
ACCELERATION from rest through gears: 0-30, 3.8s.; 0-40, 5.8s.; 0-50, 8.2s.; 0-60, 12.0s.; 0-70, 16.2s.; 0-80, 22.5s.; 0-90, 32.8s.
ACCELERATION in top (with third in brackets): 20-40, 7.5s. (5.0); 30-50, 7.4s. (5.2); 40-60, 8.0s. (6.8); 50-70 9.6s. (7.8); 60-80, 15.8s.; 70-90, 17.0s.
BRAKING: 29ft. 8in. to stop from 30 m.p.h. in neutral.
FUEL CONSUMPTION: 23.8 m.p.g. on test; 27.4 on normal running.
SPEEDOMETER: 2 m.p.h. fast at 30 m.p.h.; 5 m.p.h fast at 100 m.p.h.

PRICE: £1365 including tax

It enables the car to respond to your every mood: pottering along quietly and easily in top at low speeds; tractable as any town-bred saloon in city traffic, yet quickly overtaking most traffic when up-changes are made at around 3500 revs; or really stepping it out if you push the rev-counter needle up into the 5500-6000 region.

Acceleration from standstill is only fractionally quicker than that of the superseded MG A Mark II — but then the bigger, beefier new motor doesn't have to work so hard to achieve this result.

It is obviously detuned, as the 11 percent increase in capacity gives only about 5 percent more power,

helping to explain the smoother, quieter performance of the larger engine. At around 3000 r.p.m., torque increase is 17 percent.

At touring speeds the engine has a deeper, throatier rumble than any previous B.M.C. unit I can remember. At over 4000 revs, this note changes to a harder pitch.

Top-gear acceleration from slow speeds is one of the few "un-MG-like" features, being more in the "Dynaflash Fireball 8" class. Top-gear hill-climbing power can also be likened to the "D.F.8."

Our 1-in-4 test hill was tackled at 15 m.p.h. in second from the base. Accelerating all the way up, we crested the top at 45 m.p.h. — still accelerating. I was too amazed to think about changing up to third.

Fuel economy is in direct relation to the amount of lead contained in your right boot. Genteel motoring rewarded us with 27.4 m.p.g. — but high-speed tests naturally put a severe strain on fuel economy, reducing the overall figure to 23.8.

Since the MG B is a sports car, the 10-gallon fuel tank is a happy compromise, giving a reasonable range of about 250 miles (even with a fair proportion of high-spirited pedalling) without adding too much weight.

True MG Handling

With such big changes in construction and styling, I had expected to find some differences in behavior. Not so — ride and handling appear to be almost unchanged.

This is both a vice and a virtue. After 50 miles or so you realise the suspension is definitely "firm" —

yet it is this very firmness which gives the MG its sensitivity, allowing the driver to "feel" just what the car is doing in relation to the road surface.

Steering characteristic is still very definitely toward oversteer. But not at full chat on a good highway, where fast curves can be taken in a smooth arc — under these conditions steering is almost neutral.

It's on the tighter corners, where the lower cogs are hurriedly grabbed, that the old MG oversteer becomes evident. Altering tyre pressures made little difference.

On wet road surfaces, the steeper corners were, to put it mildly, excitingly "hairy" if taken with any gusto. However, steering correction alone (without applying extra power) was usually enough to straighten things out. Body roll was almost nonexistent.

Steering ratio is a fraction slower than on the MG A; all the better for it, and reassuringly responsive in front-wheel turning action — but I wish the steering wheel wasn't so stiff to turn in the column. It robs the system of much sensitivity.

Cockpit, Controls

This must be the first MG sports whose cockpit gives a feeling of spacious comfort, wooing you with attractively upholstered, comfortable seats, full-width carpeting, wind-up windows, a neatly cowled, fully-instrumented dash panel — even a lockable glovebox.

An improvement was noted in the gearbox synchro, the changes being noticeably smoother and easier. The shift lever is nicely positioned and just the right length to afford good

leverage, so you don't finish up with a sore palm after a day's motoring.

Thanks to the new chassisless construction, the pedal controls are no longer crammed together; but the accelerator is small, and set so far from the brake pedal that heel-and-toeing is almost impossible. An organ pedal would solve this problem.

It was also surprising to find a normal ratchet-type handbrake lever (positioned between driver's seat and transmission tunnel) instead of the traditional "fly-off" type. However, it proved eminently satisfactory, holding the car on one of the steeper pinches of the Silverdale hillclimb course.

The disc/drum footbrake layout worked like a charm. Despite the absence of a power booster, it called for moderate pedal pressure and stopped us in less than 30ft. from 30 m.p.h. in neutral. Braking was progressive, free from squeal and fade-free.

Disappointingly, the boot is only slightly roomier than the MG A's. If the spare wheel could be carried elsewhere, boot space would be vastly improved — but I can think of no more practical spot for it than right where it is: in a lockable boot.

The MG B cannot hope to please every sports-car enthusiast, but I'm willing to bet it will please the vast majority. It IS a genuine sports car, despite its "roadster" appearance, and it DOES have a true everyday usefulness — unlike many so-called sports cars you see transported to race meetings on trailers.

To this everyday usefulness you can add bags of performance, with refinement, comfort and economy thrown in for good measure. Fair value at £1365, I calls it. ● ● ●

The 1.8-litre M.G.-B

A Good All-rounder, Capable of over 110 m.p.h., with Adequate Acceleration and the Usual Sports-Car Amenities, Plus Improved Weather Protection

SUCCESSOR TO THE FAMOUS M.G.-A. —The revised appearance of the latest " big " sports M.G. is apparent from this photograph, taken on a disused runway adjacent to Blackbushe Airfield.

FROM the days of Cecil Kimber the M.G. has, in all its various guises, been primarily a sports car and always an excellent British export proposition. The famous Midget, weaned as the Minor-like M-type, has been developed out of all recognition and is today such a potent motor car in its own right that the engineering team at Abingdon, under the fatherly eye of John Thornley, decided last year that it was time the well-established M.G.-A grew up, taking on a new-found refinement and becoming endowed with even greater performance.

Consequently the well-known push-rod 4-cylinder engine was enlarged to 1,798 c.c. (80.3 × 88.9 mm.), developing a net maximum output of 94 b.h.p. at 5,500 r.p.m. This is accomplished on a c.r. of 8.8 to 1, and carburation is looked after by twin inclined type H4 S.U. carburetters.

This revised power unit is installed in a restyled unitary structure strengthened by box-section members below the doors and forming a body at once more modern, easier to enter and leave, and offering better-contrived weather protection (wind-up side windows and proper quarter-lights) than the A-series M.G. which the new B-type replaces. Although the acquired rigidity results in a comparatively heavy car, an axle ratio of 3.9 to 1 is specified, which, with overdrive, raises the topmost gear ratio to 3.135 to 1.

Every attempt has been made to render this open sports 2-seater a habitable car. The separate seats have pre-adjustable squabs and soft cushions formed of foam polyether plastic on a resilient rubber diaphragm mattress, upholstered in a combination of real and imitation leather. The wide screen affords maximum protection, the doors have the aforesaid glass windows, the body sides come up to shoulder level. Access to the restricted back seat is by folding forward the seat squabs but it is kinder to carry brief-cases or suitcases thereon than human freight. The doors have press-down plastic interior handles, set close up and forward, under the sills, and hinged " pulls " for closing them. There are exterior door locks. The centre of the screen is stayed to the scuttle sill and the high-set rear-view mirror does not impede forward vision.

Control arrangements are straightforward, simple and typical of a British sports car that does not change merely in recognition of the passage of time. The remote, very rigid central floor gear-lever protrudes from the pronounced propeller-shaft tunnel and has a rubber draught-excluding gaiter. It is set rather high but is easy to operate and has a sensibly small knob, engraved with the gear positions. A conventional central floor handbrake lever nestles between tunnel and driver's seat cushion, rather closely, and gone is the once-much-appreciated fly-off action, the usual knob at the lever's extremity having to be depressed to free it.

The 3-spoke sprung steering wheel has a hub-knob sounding the horn and there is a r.h. stalk for the direction-flashers. Rather small pendant pedals are used. Rubber mats cover the floor. The facia layout, on a matt black surface, again, is simple and

practical. A hooded nacelle before the driver carries a Jaeger 120-m.p.h. speedometer having trip with decimal and total mileometers, matched by a Jaeger tachometer reading to " 70," with yellow warning area from 5,500 to 6,000 r.p.m. and the danger area from 6,000 to 7,000 r.p.m. There are conventional warning lights for dynamo charge (in the tachometer dial), main beams (in the speedometer dial) and direction indicators (arrows inset into the black moulded facia panel). To the right of the nacelle is a quite worthless fuel gauge, the needle of which swings from " empty " to " full " as the car corners regardless of how much petrol is in the 10-gallon tank. To the left of the nacelle there is a combined water-temperature/oil-pressure gauge (normal readings : 50 lb./sq. in. and 170°F.). The flick-switches favoured by B.M.C. and rather large knobs look after the various electrical services, and there are two large heater control knobs with a rotary action, borrowed from bigger B.M.C. models. Fresh air can be admitted from the scuttle-located grille by a control on the facia having three positions.

Before the passenger there is a lockable but too-small cubby-hole, the lid of which has to be locked with the key, otherwise it falls open. As the lid is cranked it does not form a shelf when down. The driver's door could not always be opened with the sharp-edged exterior pull-out handle and its interior handle functioned stiffly. Panel lighting is brought in by a knob between the main instruments and there is a map-reading lamp with its own switch-knob on the extreme left of the facia on r.h.d. cars. The aforesaid flick-switches look after lamps (foot-dipper), wipers and heater fan, additional flick-switches on the underside of the facia controlling the fog and pass-lamps, if fitted. A knob above the oil gauge is depressed to operate the screen-washers. The release-control for the rear-hinged bonnet panel is below the facia on the driver's side.

The luggage boot will take small cases or squig-bags but it is largely occupied by the horizontally-accommodated spare wheel. The lid locks but, like the bonnet-panel, has to be manually propped open. The hood is the usual snug affair, clipping to the screen and behind the seats, and supported on a divided, folding-hoop frame.

It will be appreciated from the foregoing that the M.G.-B, while of handsome, much improved appearance, marred only by a rather short bonnet, bath-like cockpit, and recessed headlamps that could collect liberal quantities of snow, remains a sports car in the best British, rather antiquated tradition.

This extends to the specification. The engine has a long stroke, piston speed at peak revs. being as high as 3,150 ft./min. The valves are vertical in an iron head, and push-rod prodded. The drive goes through an 8-in. Borg & Beck clutch with spring diaphragm to a gearbox having synchromesh on the upper three forward ratios. An open one-piece propeller shaft connects this to a hypoid-bevel rigid back axle sprung on ½-elliptic leaf springs

The 1,798-c.c. engine of the M.G.-B. Note the twin S.U. carburetters with their drum-type air cleaners.

THE M.G.-B SPORTS 2-SEATER

Engine : Four cylinders, 80.3×88.9 mm. (1,798 c.c.). Push-rod-operated overhead valves. 8.8-to-1 compression ratio. 94 (net) b.h.p. at 5,500 r.p.m.
Gear ratios : 1st, 14.21 to 1; 2nd, 8.65 to 1; 3rd, 5.37 to 1; overdrive 3rd, 4.30 to 1; top, 3.90 to 1; overdrive top, 3.13 to 1.
Tyres : 5.60×14 Dunlop Gold Seal C41 on bolt-on steel disc wheels (but see text).
Weight : Maker's figure : 17 cwt. (unladen).
Steering ratio : 2.9 turns, lock-to-lock.
Fuel capacity : 10 gallons. (Range : approximately 252 miles.)
Wheelbase : 7 ft. 7 in.
Track : Front, 4 ft. 1 in. Rear : 4 ft. 1¼ in.
Dimensions : 12 ft. 9³⁄₁₆ in.×4 ft. 11¹⁰⁄₁₆ in.×4 ft. 1⅜ in. (high —hood up).
Price : £690 (£834 6s. 0d., inclusive of p.t.).
Makers : The M.G. Car Company Ltd., Abingdon-on-Thames, Berkshire, England.

damped by Armstrong lever-arm shock-absorbers. Front suspension is by coil springs and unequal-length wishbones, likewise Armstrong damped.

Rack-and-pinion steering is used and there is an option of disc wheels shod with 5.60×14 Dunlop C41 "Gold Seal" nylon tyres or, at an extra charge, centre-lock wire wheels with 5.90×14 Dunlop RS tyres.

Fuel feed is by an S.U. electric pump, the engine sump holds 7½ pints of oil, the gearbox 4½ pints, the back axle 2¼ pints. Ignition advance is 10° b.t.d.c., the sparking plugs Champion N5.

Driving Characteristics

On the road the M.G.-B is a typical M.G., responsive, very accelerative, hard sprung but not uncomfortable, and very docile even in o/d. top gear, in which it will poodle along at 20 m.p.h. The seating position is low, which is not entirely conducive to good visibility, but the seats are commendably soft and comfortable. It is just, but only just, possible to make "heel-and-toe" gear changes. The rather high-set gear-lever works well, in a "mechanical feel" sense, but was rather stiff on the test car, which was apparently only about 3,000 miles old. Reverse is obtainable by slapping the lever beyond 2nd-gear location. The clutch is moderately heavy and some slight judder was noticeable on rapid take-offs. There is a ledge on which the left foot can be rested clear of the pedal.

The steering, with its helical gear, is free from kick-back but very slight vibration is transmitted to the wheel, for, although the new form of unitary construction adopted for the M.G.-B is commendably rigid, some slight tremours are noticeable in the region of the scuttle. There is adequate castor-return action and this is sensibly high-geared steering (2.9 turns, lock-to-lock), yet it is not unduly heavy. As expected of rack-and-pinion mechanism, there is no lost motion. The steering column, incidentally, incorporates a universal joint.

The Lockheed brakes, 10¾ in. dia. discs at the front, 10 in. dia. drums at the back, providing a total friction area of 310 sq. in., kill the performance reasonably well—and there is very considerable performance, as the following figures, electrically recorded on a test track, show :—

Acceleration :

0-30 m.p.h. ..	3.3 sec.	0-70 m.p.h. ..	16.9 sec.
0-40 ,, ..	6.1 ,,	0-80 ,, ..	22.5 ,,
0-50 ,, ..	8.8 ,,	s.s. ¼-mile ..	18.5 ,,
0-60 ,, ..	12.8 ,,		

Maximum speeds : 1st : 30 m.p.h.; 2nd : 50 m.p.h.; 3rd : 80 m.p.h.; top : 106 m.p.h.

Overdrive is selected by a conveniently-placed flick-switch on the extreme right-hand corner of the facia and operates in 3rd and top gears. It is worth the extra £60 8s. 4d. charged, because

the normal low top gear limits the maximum speed potential. First and 2nd gears are also low, and present an unfortunate gap between the "take-off" gears and 3rd, in which 80 m.p.h. is obtainable. The makers ask that 100-octane fuel is used and that crankshaft speed is not taken above 6,000 r.p.m. Fast cornering results in a small degree of oversteer and slight body lean.

The test car had a Radiomobile radio in the centre of the facia panel, with an aerial that extended to a considerable height, and a speaker between the transmission tunnel and the facia.

I took over the M.G.-B during Marples' futile 50-m.p.h. speed-limit, which curbed my sporting ambitions and gave a range of 252 miles from a full fuel tank. Driving it as this car is intended to be driven, petrol consumption of 100-octane fuel was found to equal exactly 24 m.p.g. After 470 miles 1½-pints of oil were necessary to restore the sump level. The horizontal filler cap on the back panel of the body is unsecured.

The engine has plenty of space under the bonnet, so is commendably accessible, including plugs and dip-stick. An unusual item of detail concerns float-chamber vent pipes to drain off surplus fuel. The twin S.U.s have neat, separate Coopers air-cleaners.

Old-fashioned this latest 1.8-litre M.G. may be, but it provides very fast, enjoyable, predictable fresh-air motoring for two keen people. All manner of extras are available, such as heater, ashtray, tonneau cover, oil-cooler, front bumper, over-riders, head-lamps flasher (which I would like to see as standard on such a fast car), anti-roll bar, luggage-grid, etc. With all these the price is somewhat high, but most people will settle for the normal trim, when an M.G.-B can be bought for £834 6s., inclusive of p.t.

There were aspects of the car calling for mild criticism, including door rubbers all too easy to kick-off when getting out of the car. On the whole, however, the British Motor Corporation again offers notable value-for-money with this 110-m.p.h. sports M.G., and those who have long been staunch advocates of "Safety Fast" motoring will not be disappointed by the M.G.-B.—W. B.

MGB 1800

The MG hooked the American public on sports cars to begin with, and it's still casting the same ol' spell nearly 20 years later

There is a claque of automotive enthusiasts which still subscribes to the legend that a genuine sports car must be uncomfortable. Loyalty to such folklore involves a certain amount of frustration, because most contemporary vehicles have become too civilized to buffet passengers with wind, cramp and broil their legs, and flagellate their kidneys.

Only the Morgan remains from a bygone era to re-assure the believers that stiffness equals stability and discomfort equals desire fulfilled. There was a time when the MGs and Triumph TRs provided similar refuges from advanced automotive design, but both marques have given way to a growing demand for cars that handle properly and go fast with style and grace. The MGB 1800, for example, has roll-up windows and better weather protection than any of its predecessors. It goes faster, thanks to more displacement, and it generally radiates a chicness that was absent in the A-series.

But it is still an MG and the traditionalists need not despair completely.

The ride remains rather harsh (though spring rates have been lowered 25 percent from the A) and the live rear axle is located solely by longitudinal leaf springs. The resultant handling is fine on smooth pavement, but rough surfaces plunge the driver into reminiscences of bucking HRGs and Frazer-Nashes. There are a number of full-sized domestic cars that will get through a fast, rough corner with less bother than the MGB— and with British Motor Corporation's proved talent for making vehicles with excellent handling (viz the MG 1100) there is reason to assume that the MGB's inherent harshness will soon be eliminated.

There is a strong movement at BMC to break with the aged design traditions that created such great sales successes as the Austin-Healey and the MG Magnette and to move into the absolute vanguard of automotive engineering. The magnificent Mini, the first of the new breed, was followed by the MG 1100 and very soon a bigger engine version of that amazing vehicle will be introduced. Additionally, a radically updated Healey is in the works. The MGB is a step or two behind the company's pace-setters in a pure engineering sense, but it likewise is eons ahead of some of the other so-called sports cars that are presently available.

The appearance of the MGB is unchanged since its introduction in 1962 and it is a pleasing sight to behold. The styling maintains a sound connection with past members of the marque and there is no angle from which the MGB's identity is in question. The body panels mate nicely and the overall finish of the car is a cut above what might be expected in an under-$3000 sports car. Very rough roads can cloud this premise, because the entire structure tends to shake more than might be anticipated, but this might be blamed more on the rigid suspension than on any body looseness.

The bumpers remain dainty for scrimmage in American parking lots, but little improvement could be effected without ruining the appearance of the car. Both the hood and trunk lids are hinged without any sort of counter-balancing, which requires them to be held open by those metal rods that gas station attendants like to bend into peculiar shapes.

The initial impression of the cockpit is one of quiet, leathery opulence coupled with fighter plane efficiency. A few miles of travel uncover some minor irritations that blunt the total enjoyment of the car but in no way seriously diminish its overall quality. For example, the only interior storage space exists behind the locked door of the glove box. Opening this requires the trunk key—which most drivers carry on the same ring as its counterpart for the ignition. The ignition key cannot be removed while the switch is turned on, so that one who wants something from the glove box while the car is in motion must first pull over to the side of the road and turn off the engine, or try to wrestle the trunk key off the key ring.

The instrumentation is just fine, as it has been with MGs for many years. The dial faces are numbered in a clear, straightforward fashion and the switches open and shut precisely and without bother. It is particularly pleasant to note the absence of walnut trim on the dash and in its place a black crackle finish. Most British manufacturers of small cars cling to the notion that a few square inches of wood glued to the dash smacks of so much overt luxury that the passengers will forget they are not riding in a Bentley Continental.

Though the seats are really not high enough to provide maximum support across the shoulders or long enough to hold the driver's legs in place, they are adequately comfortable, well-upholstered and durable. In fact, all the interior appointments in the MGB are of quality and radiate good sense.

The top can cause headaches. There is a roof strut that runs laterally above the seats and a good bump can launch both driver and passenger into a skull-cracking collision with this length of iron. To anyone six feet or more, this is a genuine hazard, even with a seat belt tightly cinched. Though hardly in a class with the revered Porsche Speedster—which had about as much visibility as a sleeping bag—the MG's top also forms a rather formidable barrier for viewing the land-scape. Large drivers and passengers will find it necessary to hunch over in order to see what's going on from beneath this covering. The ease with which it can be put up and down may be exaggerated, but the operation can hardly be described as difficult. Once in place, coupled with the car's roll-up windows, it provides a properly airtight refuge from the elements.

The pendulum pedals are too high off the floor for efficient operation and we found the car devilishly hard to heel-and-toe. Additionally, there seemed to be an excess of travel in the throttle linkage, though the action was smooth and positive.

Excellent four-speed transmissions are no novelty today, and it must be difficult for BMC to justify the continued use of the present unit. It is unsynchronized

PHOTOGRAPHY: DAVE GITTENS

21

MGB 1800

Importer: BMC/Hambro Automotive Corp.
734 Grand Avenue,
Ridgefield, New Jersey

ACCELERATION

Price as tested: $2658 POE NY

Zero to	Seconds
30 mph	3.2
40 mph	4.8
50 mph	7.7
60 mph	11.0
70 mph	13.2
80 mph	19.8
90 mph	30.0
100 mph	42.0
Standing ¼-mile	76 mhp in 18.3

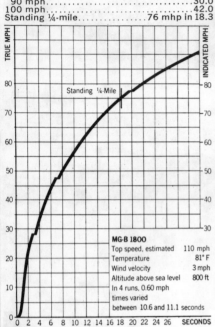

MG-B 1800
Top speed, estimated 110 mph
Temperature 81° F
Wind velocity 3 mph
Altitude above sea level 800 ft
In 4 runs, 0.60 mph times varied
between 10.6 and 11.1 seconds

ENGINE

Water-cooled V-four-in-line, cast iron block, 3 main bearings
Bore x stroke......3.16 x 3.50 in, 80.3 x 89 mm
Displacement..............109.6 cu in, 1798 cc
Compression ratio..................8.8 to one
Carburetion....................Two SU H-4
Valve gear...Pushrod-operated overhead valves
Power (SAE)...........98 bhp @ 5400 rpm
Torque.............110 lbs-ft @ 3000 rpm
Specific power output..0.89 bhp per cu in, 54.3 bhp per liter
Usable range of engine speeds 1000-6000 rpm
Electrical system...12-volt, 51 amp-hr battery
Fuel recommended..................Premium
Mileage...................20-28 mpg
Range on 12-gallon tank.......240-335 miles

DRIVE TRAIN

Clutch...................8-inch single dry plate
Transmission......4-speed, non-synchro first.

Gear	Ratio	Over-all	mph/1000 rpm	Max mph
Rev	4.75	18.59	—3.8	—23.5
1st	3.64	14.21	4.9	29.5
2nd	2.22	8.66	8.1	48.5
3rd	1.41	5.37	13.1	79.0
4th	1.00	3.91	17.9	110.0

Final drive ratio..................3.91 to one

CHASSIS

Wheelbase......................91 in
Track...............F 49 R 49.25 in
Length.....................153.75 in
Width.......................62.0 in
Height.....................49.25 in
Ground clearance................4.5 in
Dry weight..................1975 lbs
Curb weight.................2030 lbs
Test weight.................2315 lbs
Weight distribution front/rear.....53/47%
Pounds per bhp (test weight).......23.65
Suspension: F Ind., unequal-length wishbones and coil springs.
R Rigid axle and semi-elliptic leaf springs.
Brakes..Lockheed 10.75-in discs front, 10-in drums rear, 310 sq in swept area
Steering......................Rack and pinion
Turns, lock to lock..................3.0
Turning circle...................32 ft.
Tires...................5.60 x 14
Revs per mile...................920

CHECK LIST

ENGINE
Starting	Good
Response	Fair
Noise	Fair
Vibration	Poor

DRIVE TRAIN
Clutch action	Good
Transmission linkage	Good
Synchromesh	Fair
Power-to-ground transmission	Good

BRAKES
Response	Good
Pedal pressure	Good
Fade resistance	Good
Smoothness	Good
Directional stability	Good

STEERING
Response	Good
Accuracy	Good
Feedback	Fair
Road feel	Good

SUSPENSION
Harshness control	Poor
Roll stiffness	Good
Tracking	Good
Pitch control	Good
Shock damping	Good

CONTROLS
Location	Excellent
Relationship	Good
Small controls	Fair

INTERIOR
Visibility	Fair
Instrumentation	Good
Lighting	Good
Entry–exit	Fair
Front seating comfort	Fair
Front seating room	Good
Rear seating comfort	—
Rear seating room	—
Storage space	Poor
Wind noise	Good
Road noise	Good

WEATHER PROTECTION
Heater	Good
Defroster	Good
Ventilation	Poor
Weather sealing	Good
Windshield wiper action	Good

QUALITY CONTROL
Materials, exterior	Good
Materials, interior	Good
Exterior finish	Good
Interior finish	Good
Hardware and trim	Good

GENERAL
Service accessibility	Good
Luggage space	Good
Bumper protection	Fair
Exterior lighting	Good
Resistance to crosswinds	Good

in first gear, which automatically places it somewhere below the pinnacle of accomplishment in this field. Though the linkage is smooth and shifts can be made up and down through the range with a minimum of groping, second gear is much too low for normal driving. With a ratio of 2.22, it will not get you to 50 mph, and that is far too restricted for contemporary motoring. In fact, the 3.64 first gear, with a maximum speed of about 30 mph, is also on the low side. We found this particular gear rather difficult to get into while the car was at rest and finally were able to eliminate the graunching sounds only by sliding into second and then through the gate into first.

After a few miles of driving, the transmission tunnel gets extremely warm. This can be a source of comfort in winter weather, but summertime conditions can raise the temperature in the driver's leg to dizzy heights. We have heard of some MGB owners covering the tunnel with reflective aluminum foil in an effort to reduce the heat transfer, but additional factory-installed insulation is the only real key. Cockpit ventilation, which is practically nonexistent, would also help keep the driver and passenger comfortable.

There is an atmosphere that permeates the car that says "MG." No enthusiast can climb into the machine without being instantly aware that this is an MG. This impression gets massive reinforcement once the engine is turned on. There it is, the same exhaust note and virile mechanical clatter that has wooed enthusiasts since those giddy days following the war.

The engine began life in 1955 as a 1500cc unit and went through periodic expansions in displacement (1588cc, then 1622cc) until reaching its present level of 1798cc. This latest increase in size was reached by enlarging the bore to 3.16 in. while leaving the stroke at 3.50 in. Previous MG engines, particularly in the 1588cc trim, never established a widespread reputation for bottom end strength and therefore BMC increased the main bearing diameter from 2 in. to 2⅛ in. when the "B" was introduced. This, plus ¹⁄₁₆ in. thicker main bearing webs, seems to have corrected the problem.

The engine is smooth and flexible, and seems to be more robust below 3000 rpm than previous MGs. It is as good as a pushrod, long stroke powerplant can be expected to be and its 98 horsepower pulls the MGB around with suitable British pluck and enthusiasm.

Wheel size was reduced from 15 in. to 14 in. when BMC switched from the "A" to the "B" and this forced a slight reduction in the diameter of the front disc brakes. The Lockheed units were cut in size from 11 in. to 10¾ in. to fit in the smaller wheels, but there is no discernible loss of braking efficiency. The MGB is about 30 lbs. heavier than its predecessor, but the brakes do an excellent job of stopping from all speeds without any trace of fade.

The steering retains the rack and pinion design that has garnered BMC a reputation for producing some of the most perfect-steering automobiles in the world. The "B" points obediently on any sort of surface and does not seem to be seriously affected by cross winds. In fact, the car's excellent steering and brakes really encourage rapid travel over poor roads and come very close to nullifying the effects of the rear suspension. The MGB should maintain a strong position in the American sports car market for a number of years to come. It is an obvious next step for the youth who has learned his lessons on a Sprite or Spitfire, and is seeking greater power and speed, but prefers tradition to more comfort or engineering sophistication. At under $3000 complete, the car will continue to attract members of this crowd in profitable numbers.

There was considerable variance of opinion among the staff members concerning the possible effect of the sporty versions of the Mustang, Barracuda and Corvair on the MGB and Triumph TR-4 markets. Several felt the extra room, comfort and performance available in the domestic trio will cut deeply into the sales of these two British imports. Others disagreed strongly, claiming the MGB and the TR-4 are more perfectly suited to the purist segment of the public that restricts its choices to two-seat roadsters, preferably imported, and therefore are neatly insulated from the giant sales impact of the three domestics.

This is probably the case, though Detroit pressures, in the form of all-synchro transmissions, whopping horsepower and proper handling for relatively meager amounts of money —and of course the potent new Sunbeam Tiger—may ultimately force MG into developing a more powerful engine, a new transmission and an improved rear suspension. With these components fitted into the chassis that MG is making available today, the car's position in the enthusiast's market would be absolutely unchallenged.   C/D

in 11.6 seconds, and zero to 80 in 19.8 seconds, while the standing quarter of a mile was done in the excellent time of 18.5 seconds. Compared to its predecessor, the MGA Mark II, these figures are a noticeable improvement, as two seconds are gained on the standing quarter of a mile, while zero to 60 mph are covered in 1.5 seconds less. In top speed we recorded an average of 107 mph, which must be a good four miles an hour quicker than the Mark II. During all those acceleration runs I particularly noticed the fact that even at maximum revs the engine did not feel strained, and the smoothly operated clutch did not seem to mind my series of hard take-offs. Gear ratios were good, with 1st going to 32 mph, 2nd to 53 mph, and 3rd to a hair over 80 mph.

Soon after these acceleration tests were completed rain started to fall and that gave me the opportunity of seeing how the new top withstood the rain. Incidentally, at the beginning of my day I was shown how the top worked and I found it to be very easy to maneuver. Once up it gives a maximum of visibility in the back, which is not always the case with convertible tops. When the rains came I soon discovered that, although the top itself seems quite waterproof, there was quite a bit of water leaking in around the windshield pillars. This was certainly not pleasant and when asked about it the MG people told me that it is, in fact, a defect they had discovered in the early production models like mine, but that it is being taken care of. Let's hope so anyway.

At Charlegrove, where no one is really concerned about leaving the road, I did some rather quick laps on a very wet track. In doing so I found the MGB to be very outstanding on the wet, this undoubtedly due to the basically remarkable handling of the car coupled with the Dunlop Gold Seal tires, which seem to be just what the doctor ordered for that sort of weather. This does not mean that the car drove as if on rails. It would slide on corners, but not viciously, and I never found it on the point of spinning, although it was sometimes well out of shape. In regards to the ride of the car itself, I found it to be excellent on the smooth type English roads, but on some of the rougher parts of the Charlegrove testing grounds, I felt the car to be still on the firm side, even though there is a noticeable improvement over that of previous MGs.

As I am writing these lines I do not know what the price of the car will be, but if BMC can maintain the price at that of the MGA model, this new MGB will be a real buy for the money. Let's face it: it is the best MG yet made. I truly enjoyed driving it, being particularly impressed by its new design, refined features, general performance and handling. It is a well-finished car which will stand comparison with much more expensive models.

—*Bernard Cahier*

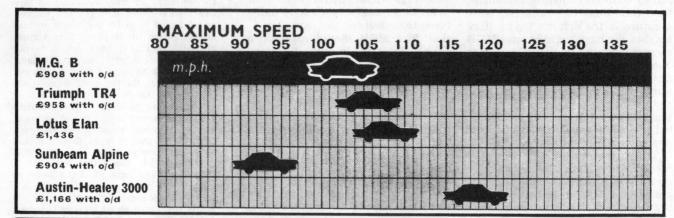
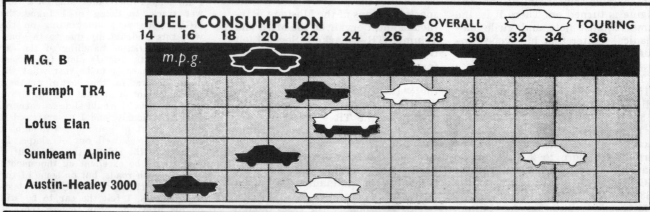
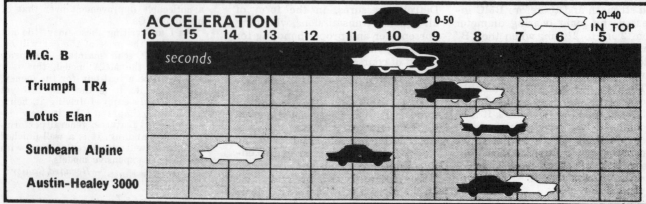

Gateway to fun: the M.G. B is the sort of car you can enjoy driving solo.

WITH saloons continually becoming faster and handling so much better, and in the main being relatively easy to insure, a sports car needs something more than the label to justify its purchase, especially when it is only a two-seater—even with large luggage space. The M.G. B's traditional virtues of "safety-fast" and the highly rated ability to take the roof off make it a very popular sports car—a car which, like others of its ilk, tends to be more related to the grand tourer than to the harsh, stark two-seaters of former years.

Since we last tested an M.G. B in October, 1962 overdrive has become an extra and the engine has been given five main bearings and a crankcase filter, without changing the performance specification; other reasonable extras fitted to our test car include Dunlop RS5 tyres, an oil cooler, safety belts, radio, de luxe hood and a pair of extra lights. Less reasonable items listed as extras, although they are almost essential, are the heater, headlamp flasher and tonneau cover; without them the car would be unrefined and almost unacceptable in an intemperate climate such as ours.

Although one needs all round independent suspension to get the best of the two worlds of ride and handling, a developed conventional system can offer a good compromise at a more economical price. On the M.G. B, the roadholding is traditional M.G. with predictable oversteer setting in at fairly high cornering speeds; the roll now associated with this limit arises from the use of relatively soft springs to give a well damped, comfortable ride. Interior seating comfort is well catered for within the limits of expense, providing reasonable adjustment for all sizes.

Performance and economy rarely come together, and full use of the M.G.'s acceleration (it is capable of 0-50 m.p.h. in nine seconds and has a maximum of 106·5 m.p.h.) will increase the consumption to below 25 m.p.g. Less strenuous driving, with liberal use of the overdrive, will record nearer our touring consumption of 30·1 m.p.g.

Although better attention could be paid to detail, with door sealing and slight leaks in the bare uncarpeted boot, the M.G. B justifies its world-wide popularity as a contemporary mixture of grand tourer with sports car lines and the ability to cruise effortlessly around the 100 m.p.h. mark.

Performance and economy

With the same nominal power as the original unit— 95 b.h.p. from 1,798 c.c.—the five-bearing engine which first appeared in the Austin 1800 is very smooth; its perform-

ance has dropped a little, possibly due to extra bearing friction. Although the yellow and red sectors on the rev counter still start at 5,500 and 6,000 r.p.m. respectively, it feels much more natural to use full revs in normal motoring (6,000 r.p.m. is the stated limit) for there is no trace of roughness right up to our maximum speed in direct top gear—106·5 m.p.h. and 6,000 r.p.m.

It comes as a pleasant surprise that a car which feels lacking in performance "kick" should record such figures as 0-50 m.p.h. in 9·0 sec., 0-80 m.p.h. in 21·2 sec. and have a maximile figure comfortably over 100 m.p.h. Its consistent acceleration steps in the gears are less surprising, since it just surges gently onwards from 10 m.p.h. in top. The recipe for such a docile engine has been used by M.G. for years—twin S.U. carburetters breathing into a carefully developed cylinder head but with a touring camshaft for greater tractability.

Unusually, this recipe has not produced a first time starter, particularly in wet weather. It needs several seconds of churning on full choke before firing and some choke thereafter until the temperature gauge has left its bottom stop at 90°F—before the engine will pull smoothly from rest. At this stage, the oil will not be anywhere near warm, particularly if an optional oil cooler is fitted—a reasonable precaution against losing viscosity on long motorway journeys in hot weather with the car cruising around its happy 90-100 m.p.h. gait in overdrive top.

Using overdrive makes 5 m.p.g. difference at a steady 30 m.p.h., but has less effect at higher speeds, and indeed our overall consumption at 21·3 m.p.g. is negligibly worse than that obtained with the non-overdrive test car two years ago. A more likely fuel consumption for ordinary main road motoring will be near our touring figure of 30·1 m.p.g., cruising gently in overdrive. Given a consumption of 25 m.p.g., a range of over 200 miles should be within the reach of most drivers on a 10-gallon tank. The handbook recommendation to use 100-octane fuel is justified by our experience of running-on (but not pinking) with a cheaper grade. Obviously the engine can be tuned with the lower compression or retarded ignition for countries without such fuel.

Transmission

It is a pity that the M.G. B didn't borrow its ratios from its younger brother the Midget. An unsynchronized first gear, which is becoming less acceptable as other manufacturers drop it, is noisy and hard to engage cleanly both at rest and on the move despite double de-clutching; it provides

M.G. B

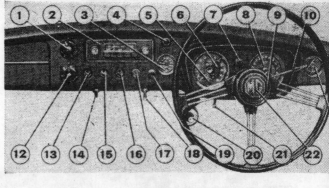

very easy starting on a 1 in 3 hill. The low second gear is unnaturally far from third, which itself could be higher; in fact, the ratios are far from sporting, although anyone who feels sufficiently strongly about this can fit the optional close ratio set.

A rigid gear lever emerging directly from the box without a remote extension allows great sensitivity and with the slight resistance of the synchromesh easing when the gears are synchronized this can be one of the smoothest changes possible with a progressively gripping clutch. The lever tends to stick and needs a firmer pull if hand and clutch movements do not coincide exactly and sometimes a fast change can beat the synchromesh, but mostly it is very pleasant to use with the lever sitting quite high on the tunnel conveniently close to the facia.

The overdrive switch, on the top right-hand end of the facia, is too short; in direct drive it is difficult to grab quickly, and almost impossible with a gloved hand. The ratio itself is ideal, providing a very relaxing 22·2 m.p.h. per 1,000 r.p.m. Although this is too high to give any increase in maximum speed over direct drive it is a useful ratio for fast cruising and allows the engine to take advantage of any downgrades without overstressing. An inhibitor controlled by manifold pressure prevents the overdrive being engaged or released on a trailing throttle.

Handling and brakes

Traditional M.G. enthusiasts, including M.G. A adherents, will initially be surprised at the lack of suspension tautness —once complementary to good handling—but the success of the compromise between handling and a good ride will soon dispel doubts. Although softer springs than the M.G. A have led to higher roll angles, which can be tempered with an optional anti-roll bar, the characteristics of final oversteer are still there but in a less tail-happy fashion. On fast corners the steering wheel can be gradually unwound as roll oversteer sets in and the tail begins to move pre-

You sit well down in the high-waisted, low-floored cockpit which is tailored for two only. The seat positions show range of adjustment.

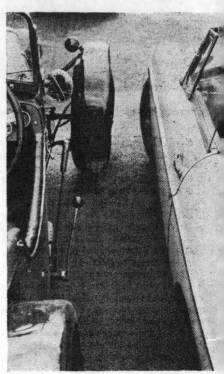

I, temperature control. 2, radio (extra). 3, water thermometer and oil pressure gauge. 4, windscreen washer. 5, main beam warning light. 6, speedometer. 7, panel light rheostat. 8, rev counter. 9, ignition light. 10, direction indicators. II, overdrive. 12, air distribution. 13, heater fan. 14, and 18, extra lights. 15, wipers. 16, lights. 17, ignition/starter. 19, choke. 20, dip (on floor). 21, trip reset. 22, horn. 23, petrol gauge.

The M.G. B's flush sides and winding windows reflect the change in style since the 1936 TT replica Fraser Nash.

Performance

Test Data: World copyright reserved; no unauthorized reproduction in whole or in part.

Conditions: Weather: Cold and dry, no wind (Temperature 32°-34°F, Barometer 29·60-29·70 in. Hg.). Surface: Tarmacadam, damp in patches. Fuel: Super premium (101 octane R.M.).

MAXIMUM SPEEDS

Mean of four opposite runs (direct top)	106.5 m.p.h.
Best one way ¼-mile	107.2
O/d 3rd gear (at 6,000 r.p.m.) ..	97.0
3rd gear	78.0
2nd gear	47.0
1st gear	28.5
"Maximile" Speed: (Timed quarter mile after I mile accelerating from rest)	
Mean	102.8
Best	103.4

ACCELERATION TIMES

0-30 m.p.h.	4.7 sec.
0-40	7.1
0-50	9.0

I, radiator filler cap. 2, coil (far side). 3, oil filler cap. 4, crankcase breather valve. 5, distributor. 6, dipstick. 7, starter solenoid. 8, voltage regulator box. 9, hydraulic fluid reservoirs. 10, oil cooler (extra). 11, SU carburetters. 12, heater. 13, overdrive inhibitor switch. 14, windscreen washer bottle.

dictably and progressively round; Dunlop RS5 tyres (optional to the standard C41s) contribute much to good manners. They are as good in the wet, allowing quite high cornering speeds, but the inside wheel will easily spin when accelerating hard on slower corners. Curiously the tyres squeal slightly as they wipe the surface dry. Steering, which is rather heavy at parking speeds and when cornering fast on sharp corners, despite low gearing and a large wheel, becomes increasingly sensitive as speed rises.

With wider rims on the optional wire wheels, giving rather more weight at the axle extremities, there is less of the live axle hop than is usual with simple leaf spring layouts. It only betrays itself by axle tramp on fast take-offs.

The disc/drum brake combination, despite the lack of servo, is reasonably light and extremely powerful. At no time did we experience any fade or lack of confidence in their ability to stop the car consistently from high speeds. The handbrake held the car on a 1 in 4 but reached the limit of its travel on the 1 in 3 hill.

Comfort and control

It might seem incredible that two cars, the M.G. A and the M.G. B, with an identical suspension layout should produce such a contrast in rides. The unitary construction of the latter provides considerable rigidity and freedom from scuttle shake; the ride is pleasantly firm and heavily damped but insulates the occupants well from individual bumps, and rough roads can be traversed in surprising comfort without the wheels leaving the ground.

Quite a range of adjustment is provided for the seating position; as well as sliding fore-and-aft, the backrest angle can be varied with a spanner on a simple stop. However, most people felt that there was not enough thigh support and very little lateral support, but still plenty of leg room for tall people. Our tallest staff member, at 6 ft. 5 in., complained that the window winder fouled his knee. Small passengers have to sit far forward to be able to reach the toe board. A rather cumbersome steering wheel seemed unnecessarily large as it limited the quick movements sometimes dictated by rather low gearing.

Pedals are well placed and you can operate brake and accelerator simultaneously (although not strictly heel-and-

The spare wheel reduces the boot's effective volume to 3·5 cu. ft. (right hand pile of boxes) but an additional 4·2 cu. ft. will fit behind the seats inside.

0-60	..	..	..	..	12.6
0-70	..	..	..	..	16.1
0-80	..	..	..	..	21.2
0-90	..	..	..	..	30.9
Standing quarter mile		..		..	18.8

			O/d		
			Top	Top	3rd
m.p.h.			sec.	sec.	sec.
10-30	..	..	—	10.0	6.1
20-40	..	..	14.9	9.4	6.1
30-50	..	..	14.8	9.0	6.0
40-60	..	..	14.6	9.2	6.5
50-70	..	..	14.3	9.3	7.3
60-80	..	..	16.2	10.8	12.6
70-90	..	..	26.8	14.8	—

HILL CLIMBING

At steady speed			lb./ton	
Top	..	..	1 in 8.2 ..	Tapley 270
3rd	..	..	1 in 5.5 ..	400
2nd	..	..	1 in 2.9 ..	600

SPEEDOMETER

30 m.p.h.	..	..	..	Accurate
60	..	..	..	1½% slow
90	..	..	..	5% slow
Distance recorder	..	..	4% slow

FUEL CONSUMPTION

Touring (consumption midway between 30 m.p.h. and maximum (68.2 m.p.h.) less 5% allowance for acceleration) .. 30.1
Overall 21.3
    m.p.g.=13.27 litres/100 km.
  Total test distance = 1,480 miles
Tank capacity (maker's figure) 10 gal.

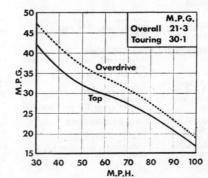

	M.P.G.
Overall	21·3
Touring	30·1

BRAKES

Pedal pressure, deceleration and equivalent stopping distance from 30 m.p.h.

lb.	g	ft.
25	37	81
50	69	43½
75	90	33½
85	100	30
Handbrake 35		86

STEERING

Turning circle between kerbs:

					ft.
Left	..	..	..	..	31¾
Right	..	..	..	..	29½
Turns of steering wheel from lock to lock	..	..	..	..	2.9

WEIGHT

			cwt.
Kerb weight (unladen with fuel for approximately 50 miles)	..	..	18.75
Front/rear distribution		..	53.5/46.5
Weight laden as tested	..	..	22.5

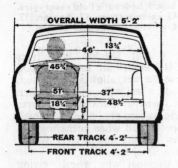

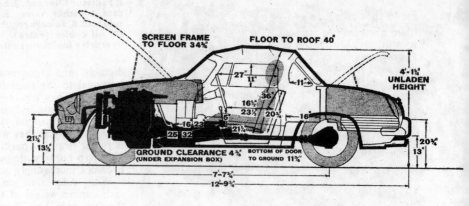

M.G. B

toe), but the dip switch is uncomfortably placed in front of and above the clutch pedal, requiring the heel to be clear of the floor.

With the hood up, visibility is hampered by the thick screen pillars needed for a firm hood anchorage, and by blind spots at the rear quarters; the shallow windscreen is inclined to prevent the top of traffic lights being seen. The wipers work well with rain but the extra friction when clearing dirty spray leaves an unswept area in the centre. Positive, squarish extremities make for easy parking. The hood itself is rigid and flap-free, tending to vibrate only over 80 m.p.h. or so; although it is leak-proof in heavy rain, poor door-sealing lets in draughts and some water. Raising and dismantling the hood takes time, particularly with the fixed hood frames on our car (there is a different one with removable hood sticks), as the fabric has to be carefully folded to preserve the transparent material.

The exhaust note is a little obtrusive without being unpleasant, and merges with general wind noise to make conversation difficult over 80 m.p.h. With the hood down, wind noise drowns all others in a healthy rush over one's head; keeping the side windows wound up makes this surprisingly draught-free.

Output from the heater/demister is woefully inadequate in the cold wet conditions experienced recently. It takes a long time to demist the screen and if it is raining the fan has to be kept on in stopping traffic—while the occupants' feet do without heat. Tortuous passages between heatbox and facia vents simply prevent a good blast getting through. Given a clear day, the interior will stay pleasantly warm, with warm air coming through flaps either side of the tunnel.

Fittings and furniture

Instruments on a crackle-finish black facia still give a sporting air and with the steering wheel spokes at twenty-to-four you can see all the instruments, but have to reach through for the panel rheostat. The switches are less clever and require an unusual degree of familiarity before one can correctly select the three in the centre controlling lights, wipers and heater fan—one needs to establish a reference point with, say, the thumb on the ignition key. Circular heater controls are likewise difficult to adjust with certainty, and are best left to the passenger. Door-operated courtesy lights are not fitted, but the map light on the left of the facia is useful and can safely be left on without disturbing the driver.

Luggage space is unusually capacious for a sports car; the boot takes a large suitcase on top of the spare wheel and more besides, while behind the seats is enough space for a portable cot or even two uncomfortable children sitting on the carpet. Lockable doors, together with winding windows, are fitted on the whole B.M.C. sporting range, but one would like to be able to open the passenger door before getting in oneself.

Safety padding is provided across the facia top but there are several hard edges, particularly hood frames; safety belts can be fitted.

MAKE M.G. ● MODEL B ● MAKERS M.G.
Car Co. Ltd., Abingdon, Berkshire

ENGINE

Cylinders	..	4
Bore and stroke	..	80·26 mm. × 89 mm.
Cubic capacity	..	1,798 c.c.
Valves	..	Pushrod o.h.v.
Compression ratio	8·8 : 1
Carburetters	..	2 HS4 SUs
Fuel pump	..	SU electric
Oil filter	..	Tecalemit, full flow
Max. power (net).	..	95 b.h.p. at 5,400 r.p.m.
Max. torque (net/ gross)	110 lb. ft. at 3,000 r.p.m.

TRANSMISSION

Clutch	..	Borg and Beck s.d.p. diaphragm spring
Top gear (s/m)	..	1 : 1 (overdrive, 1 : 0·803)
3rd gear (s/m)	..	1·372 : 1 (overdrive, 1·10 : 1)
2nd gear (s/m)	..	2·260 : 1
1st gear	..	3·64 : 1
Reverse	..	4·76 : 1
Overdrive	..	Laycock de Normanville
Final drive	..	Hypoid bevel, 3·909 : 1
M.p.h. at 1,000 r.p.m. in:—	
O/d top gear	..	22·2
Top gear	..	17·8
O/d 3rd gear	..	16·2
3rd gear	..	12·97

2nd gear	..	7·88
1st gear	..	3·74

CHASSIS

Construction	..	Unitary

BRAKES

Type	..	Lockheed hydraulic, disc front, drum rear
Dimensions	..	10¾ in. front, 10 in. rear
Friction areas	..	310 sq. in.

SUSPENSION AND STEERING

Front	..	Independent coil spring and wishbones
Rear	..	Live rear axle, leaf springs
Shock absorbers:	
Front and rear	..	Armstrong hydraulic lever arm
Steering gear	..	Rack and pinion
Tyres	..	5·60–14 tubed Dunlop Gold Seal

COACHWORK AND EQUIPMENT

Starting handle	..	No
Jack	..	Side lift, rotary handle
Jacking points	..	Socket under each door sill
Battery	..	12-volt
No. of electrical fuses	..	2

Indicators	..	Self-cancelling flashers
Screen wipers	..	Electric, single speed
Screen washers	..	Plunger, 2 jets
Sun visors	..	None
Locks:	
With ignition key	Both doors
With other keys	Dash locker, boot
Interior heater	..	Smiths 3½ kW. fresh air (extra)
Extras	..	Overdrive, hardtop, heater, folding hood, tonneau cover, anti-roll bar, oil cooler, wire wheels, road speed tyres
Upholstery	..	Leathercloth
Floor covering	..	Rubber matting and carpet
Alternative body types	..	None

MAINTENANCE

Sump	..	7½ pints S.A.E. 20W/30 or 10W/30
Gearbox	..	4½ pints S.A.E. 200W/30 or 10W/30
Rear axle	..	2¼ pints EP90 or EP80
Steering gear	..	EP90 or EP80
Cooling system	..	9½ pints (2 drain taps)
Chassis lubrication	Every 3,000 miles to 7 points
Ignition timing	..	10° b.t.d.c.
Contact breaker gap	..	0·014–0·016 in.
Sparking plug type	Champion N9Y
Sparking plug gap	0·024–0·026 in.
Tappet clearances (cold)	..	Inlet 0·38 in., Exhaust 0·38 in.
Front wheel toe-in	..	—³/₃₂ in.
Castor angle	..	7°
Tyre pressures	..	18 p.s.i. all round (24 p.s.i. at max. speeds)

Two convertible top styles are available: removable and folding. Fiberglass hardtop is also factory extra.

Rollup windows, no-draft vent make car weatherproof, comfortable.

Chrome rub strip is well placed to protect body paint.

Bumpers offer minimal protection in parallel parking situation.

Lack of wheel cutout flare causes rocker panel to be splattered.

Disc brakes are mounted at front, drum type are fitted at rear.

Knock-on hub wire spoke wheels are favorite option, cost $100 over stock disc type.

TO MGB OR NOT TO MGB?

The much-misused term 'sports car' would probably not be a part of our speech today had it not been for a squarecut, skinny wheeled rakish looking two-seater called the MG TC. This little machine which rode like a brick cart and was impossible to make weatherproof, made its debut here in 1948 as a regularly-imported item. It introduced bucket seats and road race competition to a new generation and inspired a breed of automobiles unlike anything Americans had been accustomed to.

It was a 'sports car' in the original sense, i.e., a vehicle designed for driving competitively or in the spirit of recreation with some exercise of skill. All-weather comfort was less of a requirement than classic styling and horsepower was secondary to precise handling.

From this 'hard' point the MG line began to soften. The TD, TF and MGA models were changed to follow 'modern' styling trends and to increase creature comforts. The TD was stylistically like the TC but with smaller wheels and coil spring front suspension. The TF was more streamlined and offered a heater and

radio. The MGA emerged with a full envelope body and proved to be the best seller of the lot. Some 100,000 were distributed in this country alone. Currently in production is the MGB, introduced in 1962.

The B has a great deal in common with its predecessors, particularly their sporty and competition flavor, but a number of further refinements practically eliminate the old hard ride, wind noise and discomforts which were long considered to be an integral part of the purist's sports car.

PRICE, PARTS, SERVICE

Although the base price is listed as $2,795, (West Coast Port of Entry), there are certain standard 'accessories' which are fitted to all cars as delivered to dealers. This increases the true base price somewhat but since they are items which are actually rather basic in themselves, the pricing arrangement is as equitable as the domestic manufacturer's method. The extras built into the MGB include: heater

($65), tonneau cover ($40), anti-sway bar ($20), seat belts ($17.50) and whitewall tires ($35). You might enjoy the car just as much without the rather expensive whitewalls, but the rest are necessities. Also included in the delivered price will be a get-ready and shipping charge which varies according to distance from the port of entry, but it is fair to assume that you will be looking at $3,000 for the car equipped with disc wheels.

The prime extra chosen by a great many buyers, is a set of wire wheels. These go for $100. Most cars are also sold with a radio ($89). The only remaining non-racing accessories likely to be selected are overdrive ($185) and a detachable hardtop ($235). With the full load an MGB could run up to $3,600 before taxes and license. However, the average car moves off the showroom floor at about $3,195.

At this figure, the dealer has approximately $550 profit margin, so there is very little, if any discounting. In shopping, ROAD TEST staff members didn't encounter any dealer who offered a discount and were able to get only slight over-allowances on trades. This is a pretty healthy situation in regard to an overall operation and is reflected in a generally amiable warranty and service attitude.

Since the MG has been sold here for going on 20 years, there is a good reservoir of know how and service experience which is reflected in lower shop costs when compared to some of the more exotic imported machines. The problem of parts scarcity, once a black mark against the BMC organization, now seems to be under control. Each dealer is required to stock $6,000 worth of spares for this model and, since few of them invest in body panels to any extent the six grand represents a fairly full house of the most-required components. Body damage is likely to tie any car up for a few days anyway, and these parts are available from the distributor's warehouse in a matter of hours, generally. A completely modern IBM inventory control method is used on the West Coast by British Motors (the distributors) and at the present time any part for an MGB can be had instantly. ROAD TEST is not familiar enough with the situation in other areas to assess it fully but contacts with scattered MG owners indicate that parts availability and service are wholly satisfactory. Certainly no other British car in this category has as much behind it as does the B.

DESIGN AND EXECUTION

The car is modern in concept and uses a unitized body construction throughout. Suspension is by coil springs at the front with wishbone type links controlled by hydraulic dampers. Semi-elliptic leaf springs with a conventional live axle are fitted at the rear. Body construction is of a high standard and there are few rattles in it. One of the faults, unfortunately common to many British cars is that the top level of the windscreen is too low for a tall driver. Anyone over six feet tends to adopt a crouching atti-

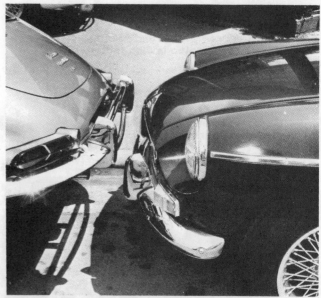
Low bumper and forward-jutting hood call for selective parking of MGB. Bumper overrides offer protection against other sports cars but big domestic cars and pickups are a threat.

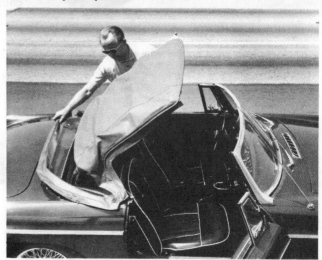
Folding soft top is easily handled by one person, disappears completely, uses up some of space behind seats.

Removable soft top is also one-man operation, stows in luggage compartment, frees more space behind seats.

Luggage space is restricted by spare and top, if removable type is carried. Small bags of soft variety can best be accommodated.

Headroom is adequate for six-foot driver, but top bow is close with seat fully shoved back. Removable hardtop offers better headroom.

Top frame of windshield is in line of sight of six-two driver. Seat rake can be adjusted and locked.

OTHER CARS IN THIS CATEGORY: Triumph TR-4A, Datsun Fairlady, Sunbeam Alpine, Fiat 1600 Roadster.

tude when driving with the top up.

The car is strictly a two seater, although there is space behind the seats suitable for small children or luggage.

There is a choice of two soft tops (at no extra charge) with the car and it is as well to evaluate both so that the buyer can decide which best suits his purpose. The "Folding Top" stays on the car and fits into the space behind the seats. When secured, there is space under it for small packages only but there is the benefit of having an empty trunk. The "Tuck-a-Way Top" is totally removed and then rolled and stowed in a bag in the trunk. The supporting bows are also stowed in a bag and both items take up about a quarter of the available space. However, the space behind the seats is completely available and if it is intended to carry youngsters, then this must be the model to buy. One can always leave the top at home in the garage but this calls for a fairly reliable weather forecast if any distance driving is contemplated.

Erecting and lowering the tops is not difficult but the nod must go to the folding top for speed. The tuck-a-way takes more time and patience. Changing it during a high wind or in a hurry in the rain can be pretty frustrating.

There is a minimum of chrome used on the car and what there is, is functional. Accessibility of the major components is good with the exception of the batteries (2 x 6V in tandem) which are located under the rear stowage space.

EXTERIOR & INTERIOR SIZE

The overall size of the car is 153 inches with a wheel base of 91 inches. The height with the top up is 49 inches and the width is 60 inches. Headroom is 37 inches and the leg reach is from 44½ inches to 52 inches which is generous by sports car standards. The distance between the doors is 50 inches and 46 inches of this is available for shoulder width, the actual width of the seat at shoulder level being 18 inches. Considering the overall size, the general feeling while sitting in the car is one of spaciousness.

The car weighs just over 1900 lbs. and sits on 5.60 x 14 tires. The general appearance is squat and solid.

Trunk space in sports cars is not normally noted for over generous room but the B comes off better than most. However, the spare tire lies flat on the floor and there is no way that it can be relocated to allow the full use of the floor width available. The spare is uncovered and care must be taken if light colored luggage is used.

CREATURE COMFORTS

The B has, with its various contemporaries, caught up with the modern trend in that it now has roll-up windows with quarter vents. Full weatherproofing is now the rule and the top fits snugly all round. The quarter windows provide good stability for the glass which is held firmly against the top even with the car being driven at high speed. It also cuts down on the rattles which are a common complaint with unsupported windows.

The individual seats are comfortable for a wide range of physical builds. They can be adjusted for rake, albeit with a wrench and the backs can be locked in a fixed position, again using a wrench. But when this is done entry and exit to the rear stowage space for bodies or luggage, with the top up, is extremely difficult. (The reason for locking the seat in the upright position is one of safety; to prevent jack-knifing in the event of a panic stop.)

The seats are upholstered in genuine leather and with an open car in hot climates, this will call for more maintenance care to prevent cracking over a period of time than if they were vinyl, as is the rest of the interior.

The heater is efficient for its size and provides an adequate amount of warm air to both passengers down to sub-freezing temperatures. There is a slight tendency for a draft to enter at the rear of the windows at shoulder level but this seems to be governed by how often the top is raised or lowered thereby causing it to lose some of its rigidity. It is not sufficient to give cause for despair.

By use of the vent behind the radio speaker mount, ambient air can be circulated around the passengers' feet in large amounts. This goes a long way toward eliminating the age old problem of overheating from the engine area which has plagued many British cars.

INSTRUMENTS & CONTROLS

Facing the driver, in a hooded cluster, are the electric tachometer, red-lined at 6500 RPM, and a 120 mph speedometer with a trip odometer incorporated. The tach is numbered every 500 rpm which tends to make it more difficult to read. To the right of this cluster is the combined oil pressure and water temperature gauge and above it, a button for the windshield washers. To the left, is the fuel gauge. The generator's operation is reflected by the conventional warning light on the tach face. In the center of the dashboard are three unmarked toggle switches which operate the lights, one-speed electric windshield wipers and fan for the heater system. The remaining portion of the dashboard is utilized by a lockable glove compartment. Everything is laid out in an orderly manner and is well within reach of small drivers.

The engine is basically the 91 cubic inch (1500cc.) unit of the MGA stretched out to 110 cubic inches

Bucket seats are upholstered in genuine leather, require more attention than rest of interior which is vinyl. All controls are well-placed for wide range of drivers.

Instruments include speedometer, tachometer, water temperature, oil pressure, fuel gage. Tach and speedo are always visible to driver of any height.

Oil cooler permits MGB engine to operate at peak output over long periods of time.

Handling of stock MGB is noteworthy; control is excellent. Car's forte is not high speed but cruising in relaxed fashion over difficult roads.

(1800cc.) with the addition of a five main bearing crankshaft. To compensate for the increased power, torque and higher RPM, an oil cooler is now fitted ahead of the radiator with hoses running back to the filter.

The engine produces its maximum torque of 110 lb/ft at 3000 rpm and revs happily well into the red zone. The rated hp is 95 at 5400 rpm. For performance on the track, quite a lot of extra power has been attained by conventional means but from the point of view of stretching the engine further for street use, there is little area where this can be done.

A look at the installation and the space available around it leaves one wondering when a bigger engine will be dropped in. The space almost begs for a small Ford V8 which seems to be the trend with British manufacturers these days. BMC has another twin overhead cam engine (one was tried six years ago) under development at the moment but whether it is scheduled for the B is difficult to say.

The four speed gear box is an extremely smooth-operating unit and has an impeccable synchromesh on second, third and fourth but none on first. Engagement of first while rolling can be achieved with practice but it is best considered only as a starting gear. Engine power is transmitted through a single-plate dry clutch which is hydraulically operated. The location of the gear lever is good and the throw through the gears is very satisfactory for the discriminating driver.

The satisfactory performance of the rear end system of live axle and semi-elliptic leaf springs is a good example of what can be done by trial and error with this type of suspension. But, if more horsepower is installed in the B, this will have to go by default because the transmission of additional power to the road could only then be achieved with independent axles. Now that the B's competitor, the TR4 has one, it should not be too far away.

CAR IN USE

For an average driver, male or female, the MGB handles in a very safe and pleasant manner. The rack and pinion steering is quick and responsive (2.9 turns lock to lock) and recentering action is good. The Lockheed front disc and drum rear brakes bring the car to a halt in a smooth manner with no appreciable fade, swerve or lack of control in repeated stops. For an experienced driver, the car can be driven hard, and will stand up to this treatment without complaints. The cornering characteristics are good in the manner of a front-engined car and there is little axle hop. There is plenty of warning before the rear end breaks away, and this can be easily corrected, in the normal manner.

The MGB is a genuine 100 mph car but to get to that last ten mph takes a little time. For anything over 100, better be going down hill and have a following wind. The pleasure from driving the car is not at the top end but in the middle speed ranges. Combined with its good cornering characteristics and precise controllability, the B has enough power here to make touring enjoyably sporting.

Gas consumption is dependent on driving style. It generally falls in the 22 to 28 mpg range. With the 12 gallon tank, this gives a useful range of 250 to 300 miles.

SUMMARY

ROAD TEST rates the car as a good buy in its category and the national sales of the car tend to support this view. The buyer is assured of a well established service network and also a strong resale value at trade in time. Maintenance costs are low although there will be the inevitable annoying failures of items such as the electric fuel pump, the rubber on the wiper blades and the deterioration caused by the use of pure rubber, rather than synthetic, throughout. The battery is in an awkward space for checking readily and one has to trust the dealer to ensure that it receives regular service but is never overfilled. On the road, for touring purposes, a small kit including some of the above mentioned items is a good safeguard for remote area driving. Lubrication intervals are at 3,000 miles and oil changes should not be deferred much past this point. Ignition system checking is also recommended at this same interval and the SU carburetors need some adjusting at least twice a year. But with this maintenance schedule, a properly tuned MGB, operated strictly on premium (97-100 octane) fuel, seems to run happily forever.

Although the MGB will not be hailed as a Classic like the TC, (examples of which are selling for nearly as much as new cost), it will undoubtedly continue to be highly popular in used condition with neophyte sports car buyers, college girls and such just as the TD has been. This is probably the best reassurance the purchaser could have and it definitely distinguishes the B in this low-priced sports car category.

Bill Tuckey drives . . .

THE MGB 1800

It may be just fine for boulevard Romeos, but boy racers had better shop somewhere else.

WE would not be at all surprised if the British Motor Corporation wishes it had never had any truck with the name of MG. Ever since it produced the TD version it has been shot at by all and sundry for everything from badge engineering to bastardising a hallowed name. The MGA almost gave the aficionado apoplexy, and even now, mentioning the name MGB in certain company is an invitation to a punch up the throat.

It is true that the MG has drifted slowly and gently, under the pressures of mass production, demands of export markets, and the effects of soft living, from an uncompromisingly spartan sports car into a gentleman's fast touring roadster. Most of the complainants say that this has been caused by the American market, but sports cars generally have become more liveable and less lovable, no matter who makes them.

The current version of the Bee is very much a fast, comfortable touring roadster and very little a sports car; but while there is some truth in allegations that it is bought more as

a toy for the rich man's son than as an enthusiast's road rocket, it is still the best-selling sports car in Australia.

This latest version has gained five bearings for its four-cylinder, 1800 cc engine, a "stretched" version of the original B series block, and thus conforms with the increasing trend to supporting the crankshaft as much as possible. The new engine is much more flexible than its predecessor, with more torque and lugging ability low down and surprising smoothness under 3000 rpm; but it is also much noisier and will not spin anywhere near as freely. There is a positive vibration period at 5000 rpm, and, indeed, the engine seems to "dwell" at that point and be reluctant to go any further. The tachometer is red-lined at 6000 rpm but we rarely saw that figure, even though we spent more than 1000 miles with the car, because of its reluctance to rev over 5000 and the fuss it put up when it did.

This MGB is slightly slower everywhere than the old car, due no doubt to increased friction of the bearing surfaces. The test car

Good range of fore-and-aft seat adjustment gets good position for wheel and gearlever, but pedals are badly located. Seats are quite good.

had covered more than 4000 miles when we took delivery, but was still freeing up even when we took it back. Compared with our previous MGB test — which was a car fitted with a hardtop that gave slightly improved airflow — the top speed is down by almost 6 mph. The standing quarter-mile time is 18.7 secs against 18.35, and acceleration through the range is correspondingly slower. The speedometer on the test car was grossly fast, so wounded five-bearing MGB owners can now stop writing those letters insisting that they have seen 110 mph in comfort. The car will only just top the ton, and then with a lot of noise and fuss.

In Britain the Bee is available with optional overdrive, using the same 3.9 to 1 rear end, and this would cut down a lot on the fussiness of the engine at high speed. The car itself seems to demand an overdrive, but at the other end of the scale it is probably more flexible in top gear at town speeds than any other sports car in the business.

It starts easily, needing full choke for an instant, but then settling down to a comfortable idle with oil pressure steady at 60-70 psi no matter what the engine speed. An oil radiator is standard. Below 3000 rpm the engine spins evenly and very smoothly, with no "four-banger" lumpiness or noises and almost no carburettor suck or fan thrash. Over this, however, valve gear thrash starts to become obtrusive, together with a little gearbox whine. The gearbox is — as is traditional to BMC units — very noisy in reverse and sings to itself on overrun in third and second. The gearbox has not been changed, and still lacks synchromesh on first gear, which is a pity. However, its movements are crisp, if a bit stiff through the narrow gate and long fore-and-aft throws. The synchromesh can be beaten on second and third by grabbing for a gear in a hurry and reverse can also be touched between third and top. Neutral is occasionally hard to find.

The steering wheel is quite large for these times at 16½ ins. and while the steering is high-geared and very accurate, needing only small movements at the rim for big changes in direction, it almost completely lacks castor and gets heavy at parking speeds. Still, a smaller wheel would increase the loading at the rim, so it is hard to see what can be done. The wheel itself is the Blumels-type tri-wire-spoked affair, with the horizontal spokes canted downward to clear the line of sight to the instruments.

The gear ratios are quite well selected, al-

Hood mounts over old-fashioned (but very effective) collapsible framework. It is not easy to erect, but once up it never flaps at speed.

though first is — in the British tradition — a little low. However, the flexibility of the power unit is such that the car can be dawdled along on a closed throttle in second almost down to a standstill, yet this ratio will take it right up to 50 mph. This fact also minimises the lack of synchromesh on first. The clutch feels solid and progressive, and did not develop any signs of overheating or slip during the acceleration runs.

There is no change to the brakes, which are still the same 10¾ in. disc front, drum rear combination. Pedal pressures are higher than one would expect for a sedan, but quite acceptable for a car of this kind. They work extremely well at all speeds, except that on the test car the pedal travel was too long and varied according to the heat of the brakes. The handbrake, between the seats, is cranked to clear the seat cushion and is well-located and strong.

BMC has obviously decided to build a big

safety margin into the handling of the MGB, but in the process the car has lost a lot of its sensitivity. The lack of self-centring in the steering and the normal amount of understeer — accentuated in the test car by the Dunlop B7 tyres — combine to make the driver use short bites at the wheel rather than positive sweeps. This technique needs a little adjusting to be comfortable, but at high speed the steering gets progressively lighter and the understeer less, so that around 60-80 mph the car is very nicely balanced.

The car does not wander at all, and the high-geared steering makes it very easy to control in a straight line. The steering collects good "feel" from the road, and if the tail is provoked into sliding the driver can make a very neat opposite lock recovery with the smallest of movements. However, while the ride of the MGB is firm and sometimes choppy on good surfaces and the car feels very strong and

robust, it gets upset by bad roads. The rear axle will dither about on bumps, and we found after a while that the best technique when going hard over indifferent roads was to keep a light hold on the steering and let the car jump about where it wanted to. The fact that you can start severe axle tramp in standing-starts on dry bitumen — also hints that the live rear axle needs some more location.

Mostly, we felt that the Bee was more comfortable cruising at 70 mph than 80 mph, partly because of the noise factor but also for reasons of control. It has good "swervability" — for want of a better word — so that at this speed on, say, a Sydney-Melbourne dash the driver can relax and enjoy things knowing that he has the brakes and the pointing to extract the car from emergencies.

The test car was in red, with all-black interior trim, and with its interesting body lines looked most handsome, even with the hood raised. The standard of trim in this version has improved over the last model and the seating has also been re-shaped. We found the seats to be quite good. The rolls around the outer edges are quite soft, and there is enough length in both the cushion and the squab to hold both passengers properly.

Everything open: Boot and bonnet lids need prop-stays, while boot takes a lot of luggage for a sports car. Sack is for hood sticks.

However, the driving position came in for a bit of criticism. In relation to the steering wheel, the pedals are too far away, so that the very short and very tall drivers are relatively too close to the wheel or too far from the gear lever. The wheel, with a large octagon emblem in the boss, is set almost vertical, at a nice angle, although a little offset to one side. There is a big range of fore-and-aft seat adjustment and the passenger can adjust the left seat very accurately to get his feet properly placed on the toeboard. However, it is a little awkward to heel-and-toe the pedals, and there is no really comfortable place for the left foot. The dipswitch is mounted in an utterly ridiculous spot halfway up the toeboard on the side of the transmission tunnel; the clutch foot has to cover an arc of possibly 6 in. to dip the lights, and even then the ankle is at an awkward angle.

The dashboard is finished in charcoal crackle

CHASSIS AND BODY DIMENSIONS:

Wheelbase	7 ft 7 in.
Track, front	4 ft 1 in.
Track, rear	4 ft 1¼ in.
Ground clearance	5 in.
Headroom	NA
Turning circle	33 ft 6 in.
Turns, lock to lock	2.8
Overall length	12 ft 9¼ in.
Overall width	4 ft 11¾ in.
Overall height	4 ft 1½ in.

GENERAL INFORMATION:

Steering type	Rack and pinion
Brake type	Lockheed disc front, drum rear
Swept area	310 sq ins.
Weight (kerb)	19 cwt
Tyre size	5.60 by 14
Make of tyre on test vehicle	Dunlop B7
Fuel tank capacity	10 gals
Cruising range	180-230 miles
Fuel requirement	95 octane
Oil system capacity	8.5 pints

SUSPENSION:

Front	coils, wishbones
Rear	semi-elliptic leaf
Shock Absorbers	hydraulic lever arm

ENGINE:

Cylinders	four, in line
Bore and Stroke	80.0 mm by 81.5 mm
Cubic capacity	1798 cc
Compression Ratio	8.8 to 1
Valve operation	pushrod, overhead
Piston speed at maximum rpm	3150 ft/min
Maximum power	95 bhp at 5400 rpm
Maximum torque	100 lb/ft at 3000 rpm
Power to weight ratio	86.3 bhp/ton

All figures checked to 0.5 percent by Smiths electric tachometer.

Top Speed Average	100.4 mph
Fastest Run	101.6 mph
Maximum, first	27 mph (6000 rpm limit)
Maximum, second	50 mph (6000 rpm limit)
Maximum, third	76 mph (6000 rpm limit)

The tough, long-stroke 1800 engine now has five bearings. Motor is very easy to work on, stays fairly clean. Oil cooler is standard.

finish, with a black rubber cowl above it. A shrouded nacelle in front of the driver holds speedometer with tenths and trip odometer and the tachometer. At left is the combined oil pressure-water temperature gauge and at right the fuel gauge, which still flickers too much to be reliable and showed quarter-full when we ran out of fuel. A washer button is above the oil/water gauge and in the centre of the dashboard is a radio blank. To the left of this are two dummy plugs for extra switches, and below it a row of three tumblers — spare wipers, and headlights — as well as the ignition switch and the choke, sensibly placed next to each other.

Below this is a big radio speaker, which joins the dashboard to the central tunnel, and on the tunnel is a flip-lid ashtray. Between the two main dials is the rheostat control for the dash lighting, while at far left is a lockable glovebox and a map light wired into the parking light system.

The door trim is carried right up to the window sills with an extra ledge of padding on the sill that makes a nice rest for one shoulder. Unfortunately, the interior door handles are made of some black plastic flexible composition

that may be very safe but which make the already-stiff doors of the Bee very hard to open. We broke the shaft of one handle on the first day simply by trying to get out in a hurry. Rubber matting covers the floors, with a grooved insert for driver and passenger, and black tufted carpet the gearbox hump and the shelf behind the seats.

The car is very pleasant to drive with the hood down, as a lot of the slipstream goes over the top of the windscreen. Putting up the side windows improves this a little more, so that the cockpit is quite a snug place. It depends of course, on how far back you have the seats. With the hood up, a lot of the gearbox, valve gear and rear axle sounds are emphasised — even amplified — as in most sports cars. However, there is absolutely no hood flap, and this is very rare, although on the test car the hood did not fit well as the trailing bottom corners of the window glass let draughts in through there.

The hood is not difficult to erect, providing you study the handbook first. Two expanding frames are joined in the centre and the fabric — which is completely detachable — laid over them. Most of the fasteners are of the "lift-the-Dot" kind, the hood brow snap-locks to the windscreen, and the final tensioning is done simply by pushing the rear of the hood frame backwards. There is only fabric above the passengers' heads, so nobody gets an unwanted belt across the skull.

The boot lid sits open on a prop, and it will take a fair amount of luggage. Even if it cannot be closed properly, the lid can be laid on the luggage and tied in place without any worries. A hessian-lined case is provided for the folded hood sticks, but no tonneau. The engine (again the lid goes up on a prop) is marvellously accessible. Even the mixture screws on the bottom of the twin SUs can be got at and the motor should be very easy to tune.

Looking back, I find that I have probably been a little harsh on what is, after all, the country's top-selling sports car. But if its makers design it more for comfort and popularity than for performance, then they should pay more attention to sound-proofing, driving positions, ease of control, and hood-erection. After all the Japanese are not making sports cars just as a quaint Oriental exercise.   #

Standing quarter mile average		18.7 secs
Fastest run		18.4 secs
0-30 mph		4.0 secs
0-40 mph		6.1 secs
0-50 mph		8.9 secs
0-60 mph		12.8 secs
0-70 mph		16.8 secs
0-80 mph		23.7 secs
0-60-0 mph		17.8 secs

	Top	Third
40-60 mph	8.8 secs	5.8 secs
50-70 mph	8.8 secs	6.3 secs
60-80 mph	10.0 secs	7.4 secs
70-90 mph	11.4 secs	— secs
Fuel consumption, cruising		21-26 mpg
Fuel consumption, overall		24.4 mpg

TRANSMISSION:

Overall ratios —	
First	14.21
Second (synchro)	8.66
Third (synchro)	5.37
Fourth (synchro)	3.91
Final drive	3.91 to 1

Dashboard layout can be classed as good. Leg room is also very generous. and there is room for children behind the two thick buckets.

Les soixante-douze heures du Mans

How three near-standard M.G.B.s scored three finishes in three consecutive races

By Dennis May

IN this exciting Le Mans era of double century speeds on the Mulsanne Straight, full race averages exceeding two miles a minute, and record laps crowding 140 m.p.h., M.G. could expect to dine in, rather than out, on the story of their bit-part in the *Vingt Quatre Heures* drama. It's notorious, however, that "modest worth neglected lies" in this wrong-headed world, and here is a case in point.

Three years in a row, 1963/4/5, the single M.G.B in the Le Mans act has finished, hale and practically whole (wholly whole, indeed, twice out of thrice). The 1963 car, openly mothered by the factory but technically a private entry, won its class,

came 12th overall and averaged 92 m.p.h. In '64 a far higher race speed, 99.9 m.p.h., made a far lower score: nowhere in class, 19th overall, but with consolation in the form of the *Motor* Trophy for the highest place by a British-built, British-entered car. This year, by one of those apparent paradoxes involving Brand X's mortality rate, the score went up again in spite of a fall in speed: 11th overall, second in class, fourth GT finisher regardless, 98.2 m.p.h.

No one, least of all B.M.C., expected the M.G.B.s to set the Sarthe on fire. Object of the triennial exercise has been to demonstrate that an essentially standard sample, using performance-gingering parts and treat-

ments which anyone can buy at printable prices, is unfailingly reliable in twice-round-the-clock racing service. Well, they made their point. And if the dreaded "spirit of the regulations" identifies the initials GT with cars in which one might actually tour grandly, the M.G.B, with such aids to gracious living as interior trim, carpets and door handles all retained, certainly conformed. Incidentally, the 1964 car weighed 22 lb. more than the winning 3.3-litre Ferrari. This year the difference was reversed by a small amount.

By the slightly wishful interpretation of the term "unscheduled stop" adopted by pit manager Peter Browning, this year's unscheduled stops were the M.G.'s first in the triennial series. Browning, a consummate organizer and arithmetician, had set a target of 288 laps, to be split into nine 29-lap sessions and one (the first) of 27. This would have hurdled the 100 m.p.h. barrier for the first time, following 1964's 99.9 near-miss. As it developed, unscheduled stops cost the entry 25 minutes and set it back six laps to 282. Telescoped, the hard-luck chapter of the story goes like this:

7¼ hours stage: Nearside rear tyre punctures, Andrew Hedges runs off at Tertre Rouge, makes it to pit on rim; 3 min. lost changing wheel and repairing incidental damage to wing.

8 hours: Stewards order come-in to replace stop-lamp bulb broken in the Tertre Rouge incident. Another 3 min. lost.

A near-standard M.G. with better than standard drivers—Andrew Hedges and Paddy Hopkirk at the end of the '65 24-hours.

The M.G.B (No. 39) in the thick of things with two Alpines in front and Porsche prototype to the rear.

"Yes, but . . ." Pitside conference between (l to r) Peter Browning, Paddy Hopkirk, Oliver Speight (Dunlop) and Andrew Hedges.

Do-it-yourself department. M.G. chief designer Syd Enever suddenly changed his views on the necessary width of air intake slot, so who better to modify it?

16¼ hours: 5½ min. lost wiring up exhaust pipe reported grounding on right-hand corners . . . another pay-off of that puncture.

19¾ hours: Paddy Hopkirk called in and carpeted by stewards for allegedly baulking Ferraris at White House . . .

Just in case Paddy's Irish honour should require him to clip somebody on the jaw when the rebuking started, Browning dismounted him and put Andrew Hedges in. Actually, Paddy treated the whole thing as a big joke, which was creditable considering he was genuinely convinced that he hadn't baulked anybody. His denial made sense too, because he could just get through White House flat-out, whereas the Ferrari drivers obviously would be braking heavily on the approach. In fact, some eye-witnesses testified that Hopkirk visibly gained away from the very drivers he was supposed to be hindering there. Admittedly no Mach-buster in a straight line (without a tow, 126 m.p.h. was its best flying kilometre speed), the M.G.B just had to be cornered close to the limit: and Paddy, "by nature for frolic designed", like Boswell, certainly showed no reluctance to use its excellent cornering qualities.

If you choose to regard Le Mans 1965 as no more than a qualified success for M.G., the cause of the dilution is traceable to a sort of inverted Playing-Fields-of-Eton element. The car was never race tested be-

Look, no superchargers, extra carburetters nor extra cylinders, even.

Les soixante-douze heures du Mans

fore leaving England: due to those horrid little things called exigencies, there simply wasn't time. R6 tyres were used at Le Mans in '64 but these had become obsolete this year and Dunlop prescribed R7s, which are slightly fatter and spongier. The team took a five-wheel set of R6s to France, however, and these were in use during the early practice spasms which produced the car's qualifying laps—4 m. 50 s. by Hopkirk, 4 m. 51 s. by Hedges. Following a switch to R7s there was no point in hurrying because the car had qualified. Thus practice did not bring to light any incompatibility between the M.G.B and the R7 tyre. It was accepted by all concerned that the car would wear R7s in the race, and this it did.

But following the fateful puncture Hedges reported that he had both smelt and heard the nearside rear tyre fouling adjacent hardware on right-handers. From this it was concluded that the R7s' slight extra girth, coupled with rather restricted clearances in the wheel arches, had caused one deflation and might cause others. So at the next routine stop an all-wheels change was made to the only available set of R6s. These were fairly well on in life and accordingly both drivers were cautioned to ease off a bit and make sure they lasted. It was at this stage that the car's race average dipped from three figures into the 99 and 98 brackets, never again to recover.

Whether the M.G. did or didn't baulk a Ferrari or Ferraris, there isn't the slightest doubt that a Ferrari baulked the M.G. On the run-in to a corner, Hopkirk found himself almost irretrievably formated to shunt the Italian car up the bustle, wham, and stood on his brakes with a violence that incinerated what remained of his front

pads and broke a caliper piston seal. Thereafter, for the 3½ laps left to go, with nothing but his gearbox and a practically useless handbrake for retardation, Paddy went round in consistent five-twenties— 94 m.p.h. When Peter Browning and the two M.G. mechanics, Tommy Wellman and Gerald Whiffen, skipped out on to the course to welcome Paddy home at the finish, brandishing a bottle of champagne, the brakeless car almost ran them over (imagine the waste of champagne if it had!). They finally brought it to a halt by hanging on and dragging their feet.

This year's unscheduled stops were not, strictly speaking, the first and only ones in our triennial story. Early in last year's race, after Hedges had bounced off the Mulsanne sandbanks and almost immediately given up his seat to Hopkirk at a routine stop, Paddy detected a front-wheel vibration, came in on his own initiative and had the wheel changed.

Browning himself described the 1964 runner as "very much a 'same as you can buy' car, the standard model being modified in accordance with the Stage 5 tune described in the works tuning manual and using competition parts available to any M.G. owner". Well, he could say that again, and again, because it was equally true of the 1963 and '65 cars. In fact, apart from weight-cutting and wind-unjamming measures in the bodywork department, all were identical. One might add, moreover, that the continued use of a three-bearing crankshaft made the '65 engine obsolete, which had not been the case last year nor the year before.

Shorn of niggling detail, Stage 5 treatment adds up to this—**Engine:** Bored out

from 1,798 to 1,801 c.c., 10.4:1 compression, high-lift camshaft, single Weber 45DCOE twin-choke carburetter, oversize sump and complementary oil pump, oil cooler, free-flow exhaust system, balanced crankshaft and flywheel. **Transmission:** Close-ratio gearbox, competition clutch, 3.3:1 final drive ratio (22.5 m.p.h. per 1,000 r.p.m. in top). **Electrics:** Lightweight battery, high-duty dynamo, high-speed wiper motor, Lucas 100 by 100 vertical dip headlamp units. **Suspension:** Competition dampers all round. **Elsewhere:** Oversize fuel tank (20½ gal.), Microcell driver's seat, seat belts, roll-over bar built up inside normally available hardtop, wide-rim wheels, racing tyres, competition brake pads.

The extended and penetratingly contoured nose section of the body differs entirely from the standard prow, as the photographs show. Part of this nosepiece, incidentally, dates from 1963 and is the only component to have seen three Le Mans (or Le Men, as the late Nevil Lloyd used to say). It is formed in light alloy and was until this year the only non-ferrous body part in use. It is said to be worth 6 b.h.p., usefully supplementing the 130 horsepower (approx) developed by the engine at something in the 6000/6500 range. This year all of the body panelling was in light alloy, resulting in a car weight, including 20.5 gallons of fuel, of 2,081 lb. Overall fuel consumption was 13.3 m.p.g., a figure beaten only by the Rover-B.R.M. (13.5) and the Austin Healey Sprite (19.1).

Considering that the M.G.Bs have been about as far-in and on-beat, so to speak, as cars come in the modern Le Mans context, it was pretty ironical that the organizers, in all relevant documents, including the official programme, classified the 1965 sample as a prototype. If that was a prototype, so is a fourpenny stamp.

Three starts and three finishes in three consecutive years . . . an average overall placement of fourteenth in fields averaging 51.67 runners. Not bad, not bad at all, as the shade of Cecil Kimber in whose lifetime a *seven-fifty* M.G. once finished sixth overall, would no doubt concede. So what next? Four consecutive starts, with fingers crossed for four finishes? Unfortunately, no. With those big Fords teuf-teuffing along at 200-plus m.p.h. these days a car like the M.G.B, Stuart Turner regretfully allows, is becoming an anachronism, "modest worth" notwithstanding (or is it the Fords that are anachronistic?). So temporarily—until C succeeds B in the M.G. suffix alphabet?— it's probably farewell to the sign of the octagon at Le Mans. **M**

A quick look at the dip-stick and off again— this was a routine pit stop with driver change.

The end you won't see very often: Note the outside bonnet release knob and safety strap.

OUR recent series on tuning the M.G.B. couldn't end, we reckoned, on a better note than by having a go at a car tuned on exactly these lines, with no "funny business" whatsoever, to Stage 6 in the M.G.B. tuning booklet which, incidentally, you can get from B.M.C. Special Tuning Department without any more strenuous exercise than simply writing and asking for it. So we got on to Basil Wales, who manages the Department, and he in turn put us on to Stuart Turner, who is—as you all know—B.M.C.'s competitions boss. And Stuart turned up trumps with an M.G.B. tuned to exactly this specification and, what's more, one which had more or less come straight back from the Targa Florio, where you may remember the Abingdon entries did all right, as they say.

No funny business, we said, and in fact from outside it would take a pretty practiced eye to detect any difference between this and any other M.G.B. The tyres were different, of course, though not much different, and it wasn't on racing boots or anything hairy like that; it had a hard-top beneath which a good stout roll-over bar was installed, and the boot was rather more full of petrol tank than normally is the case. Oh yes, and it had damn great white roundels for racing numbers all over it. which did wonders for the old ego. There were a few different seats and a few different

WORKS (Group III) STAGE 6 M.G.B.

IDENTICAL TO THE M.G.B. WHICH WON ITS CLASS IN THE TARGA-FLORIO —WOW !

instruments around the place, but otherwise the thing was apparently standard. And indeed, there was nothing on the car which you couldn't have on yours—provided, of course, you happen to have an M.G.B. The car was virtually ready for a Group III G.T. meeting as it arrived from the Works, which meant that headlamp cowls which you may have seen in photographs weren't fitted as, according to the regs, they "add to the streamlining". Wide-rim wheels would normally be fitted, but since the Department had no tyres to fit them (yes, they have these problems too) it was on standard wire wheels. The bonnet was secured with straps—these don't, of course, make the car go any faster, but they do satisfy the regulations, which is a good start. So far as the engine is concerned, it had the latest 1¾ in. S.U.s installed on the standard inlet manifold—again as a matter of complying with the rules, and we are told that this set-up shows no loss of power when compared with the previous S.U. set-up on a special manifold.

The valve gear was modified to the extent of having competition double valve springs (C-AHH 7265 inner, C-AHH 7264 outer), special rocker shaft brackets (C-EAH 762 front, C-AEH 763 rear) and rocker shaft distanced pieces (C-AEH 765 and C-AEH 764). Strengthened tappet adjusting screws (C-AEH 766) and special valve spring top and bottom cups (C-AEH 760 and C-AEH 810) plus matching collects (C-AEH 761) to suit the nimonic alloy inlet and exhaust an valves (C-AEH 757 and C-AEH 758) were fitted.

The camshaft was the full-race pattern C-AEH 770, which has a lift of 0·315 ins. and timing of 50-80-75-45, used along with the steel camshaft gears (C-AEH 771). A competition cylinder head gasket (C-AEH 768) and a special distributor with an advance curve to suit the Stage 4 engine tune (C-BHA 4415) and a set of plus 0·040 in. flat-top pistons completed the work done on the top end.

Downstairs the story is even shorter. For a start the car had the five-bearing nitrided competition crankshaft (C-AEH 822) and racing-clearance main bearings (C-18G 8103). The special deep sump (C-AEH 832) and oil-strainer packing-piece (C-AEH 847) looked after any lubrication problems there might be.

So far as the transmission is concerned, the car was equipped with competition clutch driven plate and cover assembly (part numbers C-BHA 4519 and C-BHA 4541), and the gearbox had the close-ratio gears. So far as "our" car is concerned, this means a replacement first-motion shaft (C-22H 846), second speed gear (C-1H 3299); third gear, C-1H 3300 and large diameter lay-gear (C-22H 464).

Suspension and brakes were the other departments affected by the tune, and taking the brakes first the mods were limited to a set of DS11 pads for the front discs and VG/95/1 shoes for the rear drums, plus the conversion of the hand-brake to fly-off operation (C-AHH 7222 and C-AHH 7223). On the suspension, there was a competition-type anti-roll bar of ⅝ in. diameter (C-AHH 7593) and the parts necessary for fitting it (C-AJJ 3306) and a set of competition-setting shock-absorbers (C-AHH 7104, front; C-AHH 7105. rear, right-hand; C-AHH 7106 rear, left-hand.)

Apart from this the car was mechanically standard. Bodily, apart from instruments, a roll-cage and a bigger fuel tank there were no changes either—except in the manner of its going. Most of the dispensable items of equipment had

All the fuses are brought inside within easy reach of the driver or navigator.

been dispensed with in the interests of lightness, but a good many things can't be chucked out because of Group III regulations, and the thing was still complete with carpets, door-trim, dashboard and so on. All the bright bits inside were painted matt-black to eliminate dazzle, and there were cosy bucket seats to sit on for driver and co-driver/navigator/ passenger or what-have-you. (And what have you?) Having climbed in, you switched on and started her up—not with the key, but with a monster plunger-type switch. The car invariably started easily and promptly, hot or cold, and thereafter began to idle with the lumpiness you might easily expect from a wildish sort of cam. We didn't expect it to be a nice car to drive in traffic, and it darn well wasn't, either—below 2,000 r.p.m. absolutely nothing happened, and the fire might just as well have been out. Power started at about two-five, the lowest engine speed at which you could comfortably move off from, say, traffic lights, and with a sudden-death competition clutch this made the rush-hour in Oxford Street a good thing to keep out of. So we kept out of it. For the rest, town driving still wasn't all that nice. Not that the car was particularly noisy—it wasn't, and in fact didn't sound particularly hot—you only found out how hot when other M.G.B.'s, attracted by the roundels, tried something! In top gear, 2,000 r.p.m. represented about 35 m.p.h., below which you simply could not go in fourth— slower than this and you came down a cog or two.

Things really start to happen at upwards of three-five, when you get the full benefit of all those extra horses, and the lumpy camshaft becomes definitely worthwhile. The M.G.B. in standard form is a nice, sprightly (no pun intended) sort of car, but its best friends couldn't say that was anything of a flier. This was the difference—this thing went like a bat outa hell, if we may use the phrase (and we just have) and then simply went on going faster and faster until it ran out of revs. At least, it was the rev-counter which ran out of figures. It would go all round the clock in top gear, and once you get up around five-five it makes all the right noises. The suspension, which is set up to give a pretty choppy, hard ride at low speeds, takes hold and sticks the thing down with the proverbial glue-pot on each corner. It goes round all the

swerves with nobody roll at all, although the handling wasn't all it could be on the standard wheels. But as we said, bigger rims would normal have been fitted, and B.M.C. say— and we are quite prepared to accept—that this makes all the difference.

The stop-watch tells a pretty exciting story by M.G.B. standards. The Stage VI car is, to start with, up to twelve miles an hour faster than the standard job, is three seconds quicker to sixty and seven seconds better to ninety. It's top whack is 118·5 m.p.h., and we got a genuine 120 m.p.h. one way. From rest, you get to sixty in 8·2 seconds, the legal limit so far as this country is concerned (we hope only temporarily, but we fear the very worst) comes up in eleven and you get to eighty in just fifteen. In well under half-a-minute you are doing the ton—in fact, this car gets to 100 before the standard one reaches ninety, which isn't at all bad going because the standard M.G.B. is all that much of a slouch.

In the gears, you get 46, 68 and 88 m.p.h., which means that all four cogs are really usable ratios. The man in a real hurry will find himself cursing the lack of synchromesh on bottom gear for the slow corners, but that is life, and you just have to get good at double-declutching or something. Apart from this, a second gear which will show nearly seventy miles an hour before its time to change up is worth its weight in gold, and on the right road this car is something of an education to drive. It is completely responsive, and with the right wheels and tyres would undoubtedly be a very, very impressive sports car indeed. As it is, we have seldom enjoyed a road-test more. Although it is a racer and nothing more or less, it is an essentially practical racer because unless you run into really bad traffic it is a completely practicable idea to drive it on the road—it doesn't overheat or oil its plugs unless seriously provoked: the clutch is heavy, the tickover uneven and the camshaft wild, but once you're on the move this ceases to be of much importance except as a source of joy! After all, if its a shopping car you want you'd hardly pick a Stage VI M.G.B. Now would you?

Fuel consumption? Who the hell cares!

Cars on Test

M.G.B. Works Racer, Group III Stage 6

Engine: As standard M.G.B., except for modifications detailed in text.

Transmission: As standard M.G.B., except for modifications detailed in text.

Suspension: As standard M.G.B., except for modifications detailed in text.

Brakes: As standard M.G.B., except for modifications detailed in text.

PERFORMANCE

Standard M.G.B. performance figures in brackets

		m.p.h.					secs.
MAXIMUM SPEED		120	(111·2)	Acceleration	0–30	2·5	(4·0)
Mean of two ways		118·5	(108·5)		0–40	3·8	(6·0)
					0–50	6·0	(8·0)
Speeds in gears:	First	46	(30)		0–60	8·2	(11·3)
	Second	68	(50)		0–70	11·0	(15·2)
	Third	84	(88)		0–80	15·0	(19·9)
					0–90	20·5	(27·1)
					0–100	26·1	—

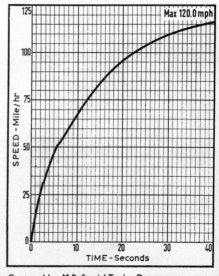

Car tuned by: M.B. Special Tuning Department, Abingdon

MGB

ENGINE CAPACITY 109.71 cu in, 1,798 cu cm
FUEL CONSUMPTION 25.4 m/imp gal, 21.2 m/US gal, 11.1 l × 100 km
SEATS 2 MAX SPEED 105 mph, 169 km/h
PRICE IN GB basic £ 747, total £ 919
PRICE IN USA $ 2,607

ENGINE front, 4 stroke; cylinders: 4, in line; bore and stroke: 3.16 × 3.50 in, 80.3 × 88.9 mm; engine capacity: 109.71 cu in, 1,798 cu cm; compression ratio: 8.8; max power (SAE): 98 hp at 5,400 rpm; max torque (SAE): 110 lb ft, 15.2 kg m at 3,000 rpm; max engine rpm: 6,200; specific power: 54.5 hp/l; cylinder block: cast iron; cylinder head: cast iron; crankshaft bearings: 5; valves: 2 per cylinder, overhead, push-rods and rockers; camshafts: 1, side; lubrication: eccentric pump, full flow filter; lubricating system capacity: 7.57 imp pt, 9.09 US pt, 4.3 l; carburation: 2 SU type HS 4 semi-downdraught carburettors; fuel feed: electric pump; cooling system: water; cooling system capacity: 10 imp pt, 12.05 US pt, 5.7 l.

TRANSMISSION driving wheels: rear; clutch: single dry plate, hydraulica controlled; gearbox: mechanical; gears: 4 + reverse; synchromesh gears: II, IV; gearbox ratios: I 3.636, II 2.214, III 1.373, IV 1, rev 4.755; gear lever: centr final drive: hypoid bevel; axle ratio: 3.909.

CHASSIS integral; front suspension: independent, wishbones, coil spring lever dampers as upper arms; rear suspension: rigid axle, semi-elliptic leafspring lever dampers.

STEERING rack-and-pinion; turns of steering wheel lock to lock: 3.

BRAKES front disc (diameter 10.75 in, 273 mm), rear drum; area rubbed by l ings: front 203 sq in, 1,309.35 sq cm, rear 107 sq in, 690.15 sq cm, total 310 sq 1,999.50 sq cm.

ELECTRICAL EQUIPMENT voltage: 12 V; battery: 58 Ah; generator type: namo, 22 Ah; ignition distributor: Lucas; headlamps: 2.

DIMENSIONS AND WEIGHT wheel base: 91 in, 2,311 mm; front track: 49 1,245 mm; rear track: 49.25 in, 1,251 mm; overall length: 153.40 in, 3,896 mm; width: 59.90 in, 1,521 mm; overall height: 49.37 in, 1,254 mm; ground clearanc 5 in, 127 mm; dry weight: 1,973 lb, 895 kg; distribution of weight: 54% front axle, 4 rear axle; turning circle (between walls): 32 ft, 9.8 m; tyres: 5.60 × 14; fuel tank pacity: 10 imp gal, 11.9 US gal, 45 l.

BODY sports; doors: 2; seats: 2.

PERFORMANCE max speeds: 34 mph, 54.7 km/h in 1st gear; 55 mph, 88.5 km in 2nd gear; 91 mph, 146.5 km/h in 3rd gear; 105 mph, 169 km/h in 4th gear; pow weight ratio: 20.1 lb/hp, 9.1 kg/hp; carrying capacity: 353 lb, 160 kg; acceleratic standing ¼ mile 18.7 sec, 0 — 50 mph (0 — 80 km/h) 8.5 sec; speed in direct dr at 1,000 rpm: 17.9 mph, 28.8 km/h.

PRACTICAL INSTRUCTIONS fuel: 98-100 oct petrol; engine sump oil: 6 imp pt, 8.24 US pt, 3.9 l, SAE 10W-20 (winter) 30 (summer), change every 3, miles, 4,800 km; gearbox oil: 4.50 imp pt, 5.50 US pt, 2.6 l, SAE 30, change ev 6,000 miles, 9,700 km; final drive oil: 2.25 imp pt, 2.75 US pt, 1.3 l, SAE 90, char every 6,000 miles, 9,700 km; greasing: every 3,000 miles, 4,800 km, 8 points; tap clearances: inlet 0.015 in, 0.38 mm, exhaust 0.015 in, 0.38 mm; valve timing: ir opens 16° before tdc and closes 56° after bdc, exhaust opens 51° before bdc a closes 21° after tdc; normal tyre pressure: front 19 psi, 1.3 atm, rear 22 psi, 1.5 a

VARIATIONS AND OPTIONAL ACCESSORIES wire wheels and knock-hubs; anti-roll bar on front suspension; oil cooler; front and rear brakes with in pendent circuits; hardtop; Laycock-de Normanville overdrive on III and IV, 0.802 tio; engine max power (SAE) 92 hp at 5,400 rpm, max torque (SAE) 105 lb ft, 1 kg m at 3,000 rpm, 8 compression ratio, 50.6 hp/l specific power.

The NICHOLSON-TUNED M.G.-B

Not for the road, unfortunately, is Nicholson's racing M.G.-B. The test car was in Stage 2 trim.

EVER since the M.G.-B was introduced it has been the subject of snide remarks from the competition fraternity on the score that it is too heavy to be anything but a quick touring car, and from the King's Road set because it looks too much like a Midget. Be that as it may, the " B " has endeared itself to thousands of owners for its unobtrusive performance, comfort and reliability, while a number of competition drivers have proved it to be a useful long-distance racing machine when tuned and lightened.

Bill Nicholson, one of the most successful drivers in M.G.s at the age of 48, started his own garage and tuning business in Northampton little more than a year ago and is now marketing a range of performance tuning kits, ranging from a Stage 1 cylinder head at £25 plus fitting to a £335 Stage 6 racing-engine conversion. For the purpose of our road test we drove a " B " with the £75 Stage 2 conversion consisting of a modified and flowed head plus an improved inlet manifold equipped with a pair of 1¾-in. S.U. carburetters (one size up from standard equipment). The car had overdrive and a 4.3 axle ratio, and suspension modifications to cope with extra performance consisted of lowered front and rear springs, a heavier (⅝-in.) anti-roll bar and adjustable rear shock-absorbers, the latter item not being needed unless the dampers are well worn.

The net power output is increased by some 12-14 brake to about 107 net, and although this has not been tested on a brake it appears to be a genuine estimate. In standard form the sports car accelerates rapidly but undramatically, while the Nicholson conversion introduces a keener edge to the pulling power and improves the top-end performance considerably. As an ex-development engineer with B.S.A. and Jaguar, the tuner is a past master at making engines breathe properly and his formulae work well on this unit.

In the prevailing cold weather the engine took several miles to warm properly and overcome its tendency to stalling, and as the water temperature fell below 160° F. on motorways also there is a clear indication that water-heated inlet manifolding is required. The selection of overdrive in the specification is a wise one, allowing better acceleration with the low axle ratio and more restful high-speed cruising. The speedometer was calibrated for a 4.1 axle, but allowing for the error we still found that the car could reach 60 m.p.h. from rest inside 11 sec. and achieve 100 m.p.h. within 30 sec., the time it takes an unmodified version to reach 90; maximum speed is raised from 109 m.p.h. to 117, comfortably inside the upper limit of 6,000 r.p.m.

So smooth was the five-bearing engine that it felt like a balanced unit, though this was not the case. In overdrive top the legal limit of 70 m.p.h. was reached with 3,500 r.p.m. on the tachometer, and it proved exceedingly hard to keep down to this speed—100 m.p.h. is a much more natural gait, cruising with 1,000 revs in hand. With a 9.5-to-1 compression ratio the car was on a diet of premium fuel, consumed at 24.3 miles per gallon, which can be considered a very reasonable figure. The electric fan installed was not needed during normal driving, when the temperature ranged from 150-185°, but once in a solid London traffic jam it was found necessary to switch the engine off for a few minutes.

The handling was quite substantially improved at the expense of the rather soft saloon-car ride that characterises M.G.s—reducing the tyre pressures from 30 lb. all round would have made it slightly better, and it might be a better compromise to soften the rear dampers and fit the ⅝-in. anti-roll bar at the front. The lighter anti-roll bar practically eliminated the roll oversteer tendency, and the heavier one should do so completely.

Before returning the car we met Bill Nicholson at Silverstone to try his four-year-old, but still immaculate, racing " B." With seven good wins to its credit last year the car is an exceptionally nice one to drive, having well-sorted handling that would make it an obvious choice for someone taking up *marque* racing. Surprisingly, the three-bearing engine has been retained, though not for much longer, and when we tried the car it was fitted with a new cylinder head designed to extend peak power up to 7,000 r.p.m. This it seemed to do most

successfully, pulling 122 m.p.h. on the straights without any fuss The output is likely to be around 140 b.h.p., not inconsiderable for a production-based 1,788-c.c. unit, and with two up to begin with we recorded a two-way 0-100 m.p.h. acceleration time of 19.9 sec.

Seemingly the car had no vices—we were given no instructions or warnings before setting out on the Grand Prix circuit—and there is sufficient adhesion to lift the inside rear wheel sometimes, indicating that a limited-slip differential could come in handy. Despite patches of frost on Woodcote and Club corners, severely restricting enthusiasm, Nicholson was able to lap consistently in 1 min. 56 sec., four seconds outside his own *marque* class record. The car has been lightened to around 17½ cwt., but £500 should go a long way toward preparing a replica such as that used by Jean Denton winning the Embassy Trophy in 1966.—M. L. C.

PERFORMANCE
Stage 2 modified M.G.-B

Speed, m.p.h.					sec.
0- 30	...	...	...	...	3.1
0- 40	...	...	...	...	5.3
0- 50	...	...	...	...	7.2
0- 60	...	...	...	...	10.6
0- 70	...	...	...	...	14.1
0- 80	...	...	...	...	18.8
0- 90	...	...	...	...	23.0
0-100	...	...	...	...	28.9
Speed in gears :					m.p.h.
1st	...	...	...	...	30
2nd	...	...	...	...	46
3rd	...	...	...	...	73
4th	...	...	...	...	99
4th overdrive	...	...	...	...	117

Fuel consumption : 24.3 m.p.g.
Cost of conversion as tested, including fitting : £113 17s.
Conversion by : Bill Nicholson Ltd., Wellingborough Road, Northampton.

A pair of 1¾-in. S.U.s with glass-fibre trumpets give a clue to 107-b.h.p. modifications.

MGB MK 2 - A SIX SPEED SMOOTHY

Now fitted with overdrive in the top two and syncromesh on first, the MGB has everything all others have — plus tradition to back it all up.

THE recent merger which brought into being the BLMC (British Leyland Motor Corporation) nametag must surely have something to do with it. Why else would BMC bring out the overdrive MGB nearly six months after Triumph with the six-cylinder (overdrive optional) TR5 PI?

Frankly, we can't answer that one, but we can answer the obvious question that's going to come from current and potential MGB owners; when will we see the MGC?

The answer is; you're not going to. At least not in the forseeable future in Australia.

Instead, BMC has now rolling off its new sports car assembly lines in Australia the MGB Mk2, basically a much-refined car compared with the earlier B, and featuring what is the equivalent of a six-speed gearbox with the overdrive on third and top.

In appearance, the Mk2 is the same car as ever, with the only external give-away being the reversing lights set into the rear body panel just beneath the bottom corners of the boot lid. And at the rear two extra nameplates have been screwed on, one reading "Mark 2", the other "overdrive".

Inside the cockpit small detailing procedures have been carried out, again to make the MGB more livable. Unlike we said in September 1965 "the MGB is becoming more livable and less loveable" . . . now we're sure much of that original love from dedicated enthusiasts will be back when they start to play the right tunes with six speeds and new features.

To be honest, the overdrive was optional in England when we tested the first of the five-bearing 1798 cc MGBs in 1965, and it only takes a little thought to realise that BMC only introduced the feature to Australia because of the growing murmur in the ranks regarding the MGC. The time had come for a change and the overdrive unit fitted the bill nicely.

We took delivery of our Mark 2 almost right off the production line. Naturally, waiting to have the car run in would have put us behind on schedule so the following morning we speared off into the central coast sunshine to log 1000 miles or so before having the car serviced and putting it to the test. Tight as it was, the run enabled us to live with the car for a while and really get to know what it was all about all over again. With a redline of 3000 rpm for the first 800 miles, we were looking forward to a rather dreary 10 grand miles — until we remembered that overdrive bit which gave us around 64 mph at the 3000 limit in fourth overdrive — or sixth gear,

The overdrive switch is fitted beside the fuel gauge on the extreme right of the facia. Only other extra is heater/demister switch beside glovebox.

Engine is unchanged from last model when the 5-bearing 1798 cc unit was installed. BMC plans to use these mechanicals in Australia for some time.

Spare wheel takes up a lot of the boot space, but there is still ample room for weekend luggage for small family. Vinyl bags are for hood bows.

if you like. Which meant it was easy keeping up with most of the highway traffic.

About 450 miles of roundabout driving in southern NSW brought us a few miles south of Canberra, so we headed for an overnight stay at Perisher Valley. Being just too late for the skiing season was fine with us, what we wanted was an uninterrupted day or so running through some rarefied air — which also unintentionally brought us onto a detour through over 50 miles of very dusty dirt roads which proved one thing we should have remembered about *any* sports car; retrace your steps at the detour sign or perish in hell with a quarter inch of dust on you.

We were surprised at the amount of dust the MGB collected in the boot. It was expected in the cockpit — there's no way around that one at all with a soft top — but the boot wasn't sealing as well as most BMC Australian-built cars normally do. We've done some pretty rugged cross-country work with BMC and never struck a boot as airy as this one. In fact, the engine compartment col-

lected hardly any dust — and we figured it should have been just the opposite.

While giving the car its due (it hadn't been road tested by BMC before we took delivery) the passengers door was impossible to open by a woman. Even a man's strength took some time to persuade it to unlatch, while on the other hand, the drivers door was a beauty. BMC has re-trimmed the doors, giving them a totally new appearance, and have fitted a new door catch system to the inside. Flush-fitting, the latches operate by pulling a flat handle out of the square groove toward you. A locking system also operates from the same square compartment, where another similar latch in the front of the door-opening one flips back across where your fingers would normally fit in. Until the lock-latch is flipped forward again (and this requires a deliberate movement; we couldn't manage to do it accidentally) it is impossible to open the door either from inside or out. We didn't like the window winders. The free-running knob is made of a very flexible rubber, and the water-sealing on the windows makes them slightly on the stiff side at the best of times, and you really had to put that little extra effort into winding the window down.

Interior-wise, everything is much the same. The only additions to the facia is the heater/demister switch which sits beneath the cigarlighter (or where it would go if it was fitted) alongside the lockable glove box. This is a four-stage electric-stove-type switch which is easily read and easy to use. On the other end of the facia right beside the driver's door and next to the fuel gauge is the toggle switch for the overdrive. Normal is up and overdrive is down. The unit cuts into overdrive with the smallest of pauses — but is instantaneous on flipping back to normal. Overdrive third gives you about 250 rpm up on normal fourth (or a drop of 500 rpm on third) — and overdrive fourth will drop you another good 500 rpm. You can use these top three all day in most circumstances if you want — and if you get the knack of switching it back from overdrive third to fourth normal the same time as you flip the gearlever from third to fourth. Really, it all depends on the length of the middle finger of your right hand. If you can work the switch with that while you're steering with your thumb and changing gear with your left hand at the same time . . . you've got it made. If you can't do it, you're going to lose out on the snob appeal of having six gears to twiddle as you pass the group by the local hamburger bar. Tough. Another nice touch is the fitting of syncromesh on first gear — a most welcome feature indeed.

If only Australians knew it, they really get a better MGB than does the home market in England. Standard in Australia are wire wheels one half inch wider than the four-stud pressed steel wheels in England. Standard also in the wheel department are Olympic GT radial tyres, whereas the British pressed steel wheels are fitted with Dunlop C41 — although both Australian standard features are on the home optional list.

Engine size has remained the same, and all mechanical features apart from the transmission are identical — as can be seen from the accompanying specification panel. Our figures are slightly down on what we ultimately expect from the car, as we still only had 1100 miles on the clock by the time we finished. We expect a full second less in the quarter mile and correspondingly better times right down the line.

Summing up — without becoming involved in unnecessary major detail changes — we think the MGB Mk2 is a credit to BMC Australia. Modifications against the English product are right in line with what is needed in this country, and dollar for dollar the car is still the best prepared, and soundest unit on the market today. #

SPECIFICATIONS

MAKE	MGB Mark 2
PRICE	$3325
ROAD TEST MILEAGE	1100 miles
OPTIONS	none

ENGINE:

Cylinders	four in line
Bore and stroke	80.26 mm x 88.9 mm
Cubic capacity	1798 cc
Compression ratio	8.8 to 1
Valves	push rod overhead
Carburettor/s	Twin SU semi-downdraught
Power	95 bhp at 5400 rpm
Torque	110 ft/lb at 3000 rpm

TRANSMISSION:

Type	four speed all-syncro
Clutch	B&B single plate hydraulic
Gear lever location	central floor

Overall ratios:

1st	13.446	3rd overdrive	4.43
2nd	8.470	4th overdrive	3.20
3rd	5.40	Reverse	12.098
4th	3.9	Final drive	3.9 to 1

CHASSIS AND RUNNING GEAR:

Construction	all-steel mono
Suspension front	independent, coils and w/bones
Suspension rear	semi-elliptic springs
Shock absorbers	hydraulic on all four
Steering type	rack and pinion
Turns lock to lock	2.9
Turning circle	32 ft
Brakes, type	disc front, drum rear
Dimensions	10¾ in. front, 10 in. rear

DIMENSIONS:

Wheelbase	91 in.
Track, front	49 in.
Track, rear	49¼ in.
Fuel tank capacity	12 gal
Tyres, size	165 x 14
Ground clearance	5 in.
Length	153 in.
Width	59½ in.
Height	49½ in.
Touring range	360 miles
Make on test car	Olympic GT
Weight (kerb)	1920 lb

PERFORMANCE

SPEEDS IN GEARS:

		Equivalent rpm
First	30 mph	6000 rpm
Second	50 mph	6000 rpm
Third	79 mph	6000 rpm
Third O/d	95 mph	6000 rpm

ACCELERATION THROUGH GEARS:

0-30 mph	3.0 sec	0-60 mph	11.1 sec
0-40 mph	4.5 sec	0-70 mph	14.3 sec
0-50 mph	7.4 sec	0-80 mph	21.0 sec

ACCELERATION IN GEARS:

		O/d	
	3rd gear	3rd gear	4th gear
30-50 mph	5.4	7.0	8.5
40-60 mph	5.9	7.1	7.9
50-70 mph	6.5	7.5	7.6

STANDING QUARTER MILE:

Fastest run	19.0 sec
Average of all runs	19.0 sec

FUEL CONSUMPTION:

Overall for test	27.5 mpg
Normal cruising	30.1 mpg

CALCULATED DATA:

Mph per 1000 rpm:
In 4th gear .... 18 mph;   4th O/d .... 22 mph

LUTE ELDRIDGE, LOCKHEED F-104 TEST PILOT

A SPECIAL BREED OF MAN

● MG drivers are a special breed among sports car enthusiasts. Their tradition of loyalty goes back to 1925, when the earliest models of these pace-setting little 4-bangers first rolled off a production line—all seven of them! ● In 1955, they watched the TF turn into the streamlined MGA and zoom ahead in both popularity and competitions. It became the first sports car to hit a production figure of more than 100,000, and it accumulated enough awards to crowd a badge bar. ● Today the style and engineering lessons of almost a decade have joined to create a spectacular new car—the MGB. New styling—based on an all-steel, unit-construction body. New power—from a larger engine. New safety—from bigger brakes. New feel to the wheel—because turns-to-lock have been raised from 2.6 to 2.9. And new comfort—wind-up windows, quick-stowing top, a smartly redesigned cockpit. With all these, the MGB retains all the basic good manners of its predecessors—exceptional cornering, no lurch or fade when braked, and a top speed of 100-plus without laboring. ● You can see why this distinctive breed of car appeals particularly to a special breed of man. Perhaps you're already a member of the MGB owners club. If you aren't, give yourself the thrill of driving one of these powerful, responsive new cars. You might just as well begin with the best.

Safety fast!

GORDON CHITTENDEN PHOTOS

ALL-SYNCHRO MGB

Yes, it really is true,
the MGB has a fully synchronized gearbox

THE MGB has been with us for over five years now and probably has two more years to go. Truly British, its character is now vintage. It has finally been updated by the substitution of an all-synchromesh gearbox (over chief engineer Alec Issigonis' dead body?), and this, plus certain changes necessitated by air-pollution and safety legislation in the U.S., offers the opportunity to give it a fresh evaluation. An automatic transmission model will be along

shortly too, and we will report on that when it is available.

The principal mechanical change is the new gearbox. It is marked visually by a straight gear lever instead of the bent one used before, and it sprouts from an opening farther back on the gearbox tunnel—perhaps a bit too far back, a criticism we almost never have to make. Shifting is much the same as before—a bit stiff and notchy, but wonderfully precise—and the new box not only eliminates the traditional 1st-

ALL-SYNCHRO MGB
AT A GLANCE

Price as tested	$2947
Engine	4 cyl, inline, ohv, 1798 cc, 92 bhp
Curb weight, lb	2220
Top speed, mph	104
Acceleration, 0–¼ mi, sec	18.7
Average fuel consumption, mpg	24.0

Summary: Strong performance, good durability . . . body, handling behind modern standards . . . synchro 1st gear, new indirect ratios big improvements . . . safety & emission changes not well worked out.

50

R&T ROAD TEST
ALL-SYNCHRO MGB

SCALE: 10" DIVISIONS

PRICE
Basic list $2810
As tested $2947

ENGINE
Type . . . . 4 inline, ohv
Bore x stroke, mm . . . . . . 80.3 x 89.0
 Equivalent in . . . . 3.16 x 3.50
Displacement, cc/cu in . . 1798/110.5
Compression ratio 8.8:1
Bhp @ rpm . . . . 92 @ 5400
 Equivalent mph 99
Torque @ rpm, lb-ft . . 110 @ 3000
 Equivalent mph 62
Carburetion . . . . two SU HS4
Type fuel required . . . . . . premium

DRIVE TRAIN
Clutch diameter, in 8.0
Gear ratios: 4th (1.00) 3.91:1
 3rd (1.38) 5.40:1
 2nd (2.17) 8.47:1
 1st (3.44) 13.45:1
Synchromesh . . . . on all 4
Final drive ratio 3.91:1
 Optional ratios . . . . none

CHASSIS & BODY
Body/frame: unit steel construction
Brake type: Girling; 10.8-in. disc
 front, 10.0 x 1.7-in. drum rear
Swept area, sq in 310
Wheels . . . . . wire spoke, 14 x 4½ J
Tires . . . . Dunlop C 41 5.60-14
Steering type . . . . . . rack & pinion
 Overall ratio 21.4:1
 Turns, lock-to-lock 2.9
 Turning circle, ft 32.0
Front suspension: unequal A-arms,
 coil springs, lever shocks, anti-
 roll bar
Rear suspension: live axle on multi-
 leaf springs, lever shocks

OPTIONAL EQUIPMENT
Included in "as tested" price: wire
 wheels, heater, tonneau cover,
 grille guard
Other: radio, folding top, overdrive,
 radial tires, chrome wire wheels,
 automatic transmission

ACCOMMODATION
Seating capacity, persons 2
Seat width . . . . 2 x 18.5
Seat back adjustment, deg 5
Driver comfort rating (scale of 100):
 Driver 69 in. tall 80
 Driver 72 in. tall 70
 Driver 75 in. tall 65

INSTRUMENTATION
Instruments: 120-mph speedometer, 7000-rpm tachomete , fuel
 level, oil pressure, water temperature
Warning lights: alternator, brake
 fluid loss, high beam, directional
 signals

MAINTENANCE
Engine oil capacity, qt 5.0
 Change interval, mi 6000
Filter change interval, mi 6000
Chassis lube interval, mi 3000
Tire pressures, psi 21/24

MISCELLANEOUS
Body styles available: roadster as
 tested, coupe
Warranty period, mo/mi: 12/12,000

GENERAL
Curb weight, lb 2220
Test weight 2590
Weight distribution (with
 driver), front/rear, % 54/46
Wheelbase, in 91.0
Track, front/rear 49.2/49.2
Overall length 153.2
 Width 59.9
 Height 49.8
Frontal area, sq ft 16.6
Ground clearance, in 4.5
Overhang, front/rear . . . 26.8/35.4
Usable trunk space, cu ft 2.9
Fuel tank capacity, gal 12.0

CALCULATED DATA
Lb/hp (test wt) 27.0
Mph/1000 rpm (4th gear) 17.6
Engine revs/mi (60 mph) 3410
Piston travel, ft/mi 1990
Rpm @ 2500 ft/min 4290
 Equivalent mph 77
Cu ft/ton mi 83.8
R&T wear index 68
Brake swept area sq in/ton . . . 239

ROAD TEST RESULTS

ACCELERATION
Time to distance, sec:
 0–100 ft 3.6
 0–250 ft 6.5
 0–500 ft 10.0
 0–750 ft 12.9
 0–1000 ft 15.6
 0–1320 ft (¼ mi) 18.7
Speed at end of ¼ mi, mph 73
Time to speed, sec:
 0–30 mph 3.9
 0–40 mph 6.0
 0–50 mph 8.4
 0–60 mph 12.1
 0–70 mph 16.7
 0–80 mph 23.2
 0–90 mph 32.8
Passing exposure time, sec:
 To pass car going 50 mph . . . 6.5

FUEL CONSUMPTION
Normal driving, mpg 21–27
Cruising range, mi 250–325

SPEEDS IN GEARS
4th gear (5650 rpm), mph 104
 3rd (6000) 79
 2nd (6000) 50
 1st (6000) 30

BRAKES
Panic stop from 80 mph:
 Deceleration, % g 72
 Control . . . . very good
Fade test: percent of increase in
 pedal effort required to maintain
 50%-g deceleration rate in six
 stops from 60 mph 17
Parking: hold 30% grade . . . . . . no
Overall brake rating . . . . good

SPEEDOMETER ERROR
30 mph indicated . . . . . actual 30.0
40 mph 40.0
60 mph 59.4
80 mph 79.2
100 mph 98.6
Odometer, 10.0 mi . . . . actual 9.85

ACCELERATION & COASTING

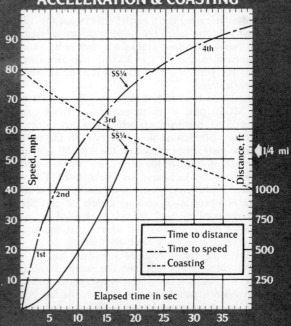

Legend:
— Time to distance
—·— Time to speed
- - - Coasting

Speed, mph / Distance, ft / Elapsed time in sec
(curves labeled: 4th, 3rd, 2nd, 1st, SS¼, ¼ mi)

ALL-SYNCHRO MGB

gear whine but improves general drivability by virtue of its better ratios. Specifically, 1st gear is taller than before (at 13.45 overall vs. 14.2) and so is 2nd (8.47 vs. 8.82); 3rd and 4th are essentially the same, and a cruising ratio can still be added by ordering overdrive at $175. In short, it's now possible to drive the MGB like any other car, and it's a pleasant change.

The manufacturer has taken the air-injection route to controlling exhaust emissions. By virtue of the concomitant changes to carburetion and timing, peak torque is slightly *up* from 107 lb-ft @ 3500 rpm to 110 @ 3000, and peak power is *down* from 98 bhp @ 5400 to 92 @ 5400. The performance figures reflect the changes exactly: acceleration times are generally a little better than the early model we tested, but top speed is down from 106 mph to 104. Fuel economy is down somewhat, from an average of 26 mpg to 24. The pleasant exhaust note turns into a burble-burble on deceleration but we got only one definite backfire during our 500-mi test. One common side effect of air injection, a tendency to return to idle slowly, was present in our test car to the extreme—it took 9 sec for the engine to get back to idle from 3000 rpm after releasing the throttle! Otherwise, the 1798-cc pushrod four is pretty much the same: mechanically smooth, now that it has a 5-bearing crankshaft, but noisy; and furnishing abundant torque for the 2200-lb car. An alternator has replaced the generator and the old rattling starter drive has finally been cured.

Safety legislation has resulted in an entirely new dash panel for the MGB, plus a rearrangement of most controls. There is a molded, padded facia which attaches to the existing sheet metal, eliminating the glove box on the right and forming a new instrument cluster on the left. All instruments are now directly in front of the driver, and smaller—but still readable—speedo and tach have been substituted. The vague, poorly marked heater controls are also relocated, and all dash switches are non-protruding rocking tablets. Wipers are now 2-speed, as required by law, and are controlled by a right-hand stalk on the steering column; where legal, the left-hand directional lever also works a headlight flasher.

For the first time in history an MG roadster has sun visors, again thanks to the safety regs, and the recessed inside door handles are a good solution. Over-the-shoulder belts come from the rear deck panel and fasten, with the lap belts, by means of Kangol magnetic latches which we found convenient to use.

The seating position bespeaks the vintage character of the

car perhaps as much as the high noise level. One sits very low in the car, on relatively soft seats; the steering wheel is huge (perhaps because the steering is so stiff), the pedals are close together, and tall drivers rest their right shins against the center console. The hood and door sills are high, the windshield header low—but overall vision isn't bad, thanks to the 3-piece rear window. Sealing of windows to the top is indifferent, and it's not difficult to see daylight beyond the door edges. There are no door stops to keep them open on a slope, and the roadster top (either the standard put-away affair or the optional folding one) is pure British blacksmithery—for an example of how a good roadster top is designed in AD 1968, see the Fiat 124 Spider. The trunk is an example of what a storage compartment ought not to be, unlined and mostly occupied by the spare wheel and tire. The reader should bear in mind that many of these criticisms don't apply to the MGB/GT—but it costs a few hundred dollars more than the roadster.

Handling, too, is vintage, but if one accepts the fact, it is still possible to enjoy driving the MGB hard. Steering is very heavy, presumably from lots of caster; stiff springing and a live rear axle mean some hopping about on rough roads, but on smooth surfaces one can enjoy the ease of breaking the rear end loose and the relatively flat cornering. Our car had the now-standard anti-roll bar, which helps keep the body flat and still doesn't add too much understeer to the picture; this used to be an option.

Braking, like steering, is heavy in the MGB—the initial half-g stop in our fade test took all of 60 lb pedal effort. The disc/drum brakes bring the B to a smooth, controllable stop at 23 ft/sec/sec (0.72-g) under panic conditions from 80 mph, and with the present friction material fade is a moderate 17% in our 6-stop test. The handbrake, however, won't hold the car on a 30% grade—an unusual failing in a car with drum rear brakes.

Against the rather outdated character of the MGB is an impressive record of reliability, plus minimum servicing requirements. In short, it is an unfussy car, one well sorted out by several years of production. If driven with any degree of skill and cared for decently it is economical and trouble-free, and mileages of 70,000 before overhaul are common. Earlier irritations such as engine vibration, rear-axle noise and electrical problems are in the past now. By modern standards the B is not a "refined" motorcar, but one must spend considerably more than the B's $2947 to get refinement in a car of comparable character.

MGB time

... another in our weekend mods series

As it was. The famous Nicholson 'B' has been developed since 1963 into one of the most immaculate, reliable winners on the circuits. It now features mag wheels, super-lightweight hardtop and some of the most beautiful flared alloy wings you ever did see.

"WHY don't you tell us what to do?" they said. Well, there's more of them than there are of us, so we listened politely while they expanded. "There you go with a load of weekend mods on family saloons forgetting, the while, that some people still run real, live, hairy-chested Men's cars like MG 'B's for instance." It was true, of course, and though the North Actoneers are as biased as the next bloke we just could not afford to neglect the 'B' brigade, so bare your hairy chests, lads, and out with the tool box.

For many people with any kind of pretension to automobile knowledge, the B in MG 'B' has for many moons stood for the Bill in Bill Nicholson, so what better place to go for advice than the boyo's own place in Wellingborough Road, Northampton? One tends to trip over MG 'B's while walking around the place, of course, but we were intrigued to see flocks of Fiats intermingled therewith. Bill has obtained a Fiat dealership and it is fairly obvious that he will be waving his magic wand over a model or two before very long — just stick with us for a full spread as and when. But back to the subject. First angle of attack for most cars is the suspension so prepare to descend on your B with a good, non-standard jack, two axle stands and a reasonable tool kit. One of the nice things about the B is its straightforwardness and you should find that no kinky, double-jointed thingies are required.

Firmer front springs — as available from Bill's goody store — do the front end a power of good for the modest outlay of £7 the two. After jacking the front end of the car to a reasonable working height, place the two stands under the front body members. A bottle jack is then a handy asset for placing under the pan of one or t'other front spring. When the bolts have been removed from the pan, lower away on the jack and the springs come out sitting on top of the pan. Then it's a straight swop for the firmer variety and reverse the procedure to get them back in position.

Much fiddling with jacks and stands (in the same weekend, even) should get the rear of the car pointing skywards ready to accept the go-firmer treatment on the blunt end. Under the accumulated gunge should lurk the bolts for the spring shackles and the shock-absorber mounting. Detach these in a sensible sequence and remove the springs. A pair of sensible springs can be obtained from a reputable stable (and the items from Bill are 13 gns. the two) and inserted forthwith. If time allows, this would be an ideal stage to pop a couple of adjustable rear shockers in, of course, which together with the springs are guaranteed to Transform your handlability. Nicholsons advise Armstrong Adjustarides here and sell them over the counter for £12 6s. per pair. These excellent devices have 22 'clicks'

and when doing the job himself, Bill puts them at 11 — his own preference for the road — and lets customers experiment from there.

Adjustable shockers are not available for the front end but for the road-going B man (same to you mate), the competition settings at £12 16s. a pair, again by courtesy of Armstrong, are the ones for which to go. We seem to have got round to the front again somehow, so while we're here and before we lose the literature, allow us to point out that a heavier anti-roll bar is another Nicholson nicety at a reesnable £2 13s. Just in case we have seduced some of the clean-hands brigade into reading our oil-impregnated weekend mod feature, they may be wondering how much Bill would charge to do all this with his own fair hands. The quick answer to that is £9 10s.

When talk centres on bringing any conventionally-braked car such as a B to a full stop, the stock advice seems to be DS 11s on the front and VG 95s on the back. Bill's long and successful circuit experience tells him otherwise, however. He reckons that constant hard use tends to heat up the VG 95s to such an extent that when you really have to stand on them, the rear wheels lock up. He therefore goes for MS 3s on the back end and for a detailed mod, $\frac{3}{4}$ in rear wheel cylinders as on the original Minis to balance up the braking. The later $\frac{5}{8}$ in cylinders are far too small, quoth he. This balancing of braking effort is, we would think, rather an individual preference thing so it would be as well to have a hard think about what set-up gives you most confidence if you intend to go into the topic in such great detail.

The fitting of a brake servo cannot, unfortunately, be regarded as a week-end mod for the purposes of this series and one apparently needs a thing called a flaring tool for the brake pipes and we can't expect even the groovy, switched-on readers of Triple C to have such an object kicking about in their average tool kits.

Before we start delving about in the engine room we'll go back a few lines of print to when we had the back end up in the air, remember? Well, if that diff of yours is a standard 3.89 and you have been out-dragged by hot Mins and things, one of the secret weapons which would even up the score could be a 4.3 or 4.1 replacement. Stop here anyone who has a GT model or a B with a tubed axle because this is not for you. Only the Bs with the Banjo-type axle qualify for this mod. To be precise, only those up to chassis Nos. 129287 WW and 132463 DW. Bill also prefers that the recipient vehicle should be fitted with overdrive, by the way.

A good first step in this operation is to drain the diff. This

MGB time

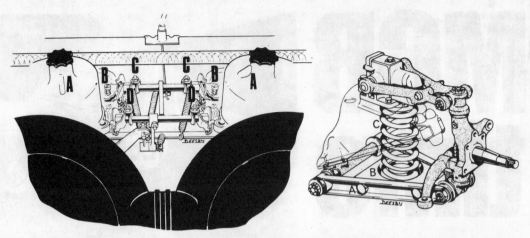

LEFT: The objective here is to get the two butterflies (lurking behind dashpots A) opening and closing at the same instant. Slacken off the throttle stops (B) with the butterflies closed and make the adjustments by the linkage clamp nuts (C). When this has been done, fine tuning is done by the throttle screws (D) acting on the cams shown. Right: Our artist has 'ghosted' the parts which prevent a full view of the coil spring (C), but this should locate easily at the top as shown. With the car in the air, jack under the pan (B) so that the four nuts and bolts (A) can be removed. B and C come away together and are returned simply by following the method in reverse.

may seem a stoopid point to mention, but Bill recalls painfully the time when he forgot and his B-diff showered him with hot oil as he struggled underneath it. Mind you, this was during a frantic operation on his own racer when he had only 15.8 minutes in which to do the job at a circuit, or something. Place your axle stands right at the forward end of the rear springs so that the ensemble is dropped on full rebound. Remove the brake drums and half-shafts and unfasten the prop shaft. Take out the ring of bolts in the nose-piece (keeping them all nice and tidy in an upturned hub-cap, if you still wear them) and fiddle it out, so to speak. And it probably will take some fiddling as you have to clear the battery casing so allow plenty of time for this operation and don't get too stroppy if it doesn't fall right first time. Again the return trip is simply a reversal procedure, terminated by the careful topping up of the fluid etc.

This 4.3 diff swop, plus Bill's Stage II conversion drops the 0-100 time from 52 secs to 28 to 29 secs. Need we say more? In fact — yes, because here we come to the swopping of a cylinder head, one of which can be chosen on an exchange basis from the Nicholson list. A fact unknown to us before the visit to Northampton was that Les Ryder, whose expertly modded heads find their way onto almost every make of car imaginable, has been 'snapped up' by Bill to work on his heads after years of patient persuasion etc.
(Ryder's head is on 3000 KV — Ed)

After over 1,300 heads, Les has never yet found an unsatisfied customer. His techniques, evolved through years of experience, mean that he can suit a head exactly to a customer's requirements. This means that the head he prepares for a B used on fast motorway trips and country lane chicanery will differ slightly but significantly from the head on a road car used for the occasional sprint or hill-climb. He does, of course, produce heads as near identical as anyone will get for 'off-the-shelf-sales', but to produce a head for a specific purpose, Les likes a talk with the customer to see just what the man wants. This does not necessarily mean that the purpose-modded head will be any more expensive than the one off the shelf, which can be a comforting thought.

Thirty green ones and your own head, so long as it is not too badly gunged or graunched, will supply you with a Stage I modded Nicholson-Ryder head with heavy duty bronze Hidural guides, of which 4 or 5 a week can be turned out at the Northampton garage. Standard 1½ in SUs are quite adequate to throw juice into this one but if you can afford one of the decent inlet manifolds at the same time, the added improvement is not to be sniffed at.

The Stage II and III heads in Bill's range come with 1¾ in. SUs and special manifold and the latter conversion includes special pistons which takes it well out of the scope of this week-end operation. Prices, however, are £80 for the II pack, fitted and tuned, and £114 9s. for the III likewise.

As we've endeavoured to imply before, though, the B is a pretty uncomplicated motor car and we won't insult your intelligence further (ahem) by going into the why's and wherefores. There are two things to watch which may save you lots of trouble later — DO replace every gasket as you go through the job no matter how good they look. No, we are not in the pay of some go-getting gasket factory, we just don't believe in false economy etc. The other thing is to set up the carbs correctly.

SUs being fairly simple devices (we don't think anyone has built electronic, computer-controlled metering devices into them yet) it's easy Once You Know How. It is vital to get both butterflies opening at the same instant, so screw the throttle stops right off and see that both butterflies are completely closed. Adjust the linkage clamp nuts so that both levers are just touching the bottom of the stops. Tighten them up and ensure both butterfles open together. Adjust the fine tuning with the throttle screws and if it's all OK, you've conquered 90 per cent of the difficulties on this job. With 1½s, take the jets right up to the top and then down 12 flats. If you have to move more than 2 flats either way for a decent tickover then either the needles or the jets are wrong.

Another Nicholson tip — some B sensitive types find a very slight flat spot when cruising at about 70 — damn nuisance for us motorway men, so change to the next richest needle and you should be cured. After this head swop, try retarding the ignition 2-3 degrees but remember that no two engines or distributors are alike and use this only as a guide towards finding the optimum setting.

If all this is not sufficient to keep you occupied every weekend until the summer hols, bear in mind this advice on exhausts. The Brabham system, at about 10 gns., is the only one Bill has found which stays together on a B. Ensure your front pipe is not eaten away, hack through it according to the instructions on the packet and the Brabham system fits over it, so you don't loose diameter and there are no clearance problems aft, either.

So, if everything went well, away you go, a happier and quicker B man. Let's hope the machine is conducted with the same skill and verve as Bill's. In 6 years and about 30,000 race miles it has never been bumped or scratched. Not never — (yet anyway!). **DH**

1965 MGB

PRICES

Car for sale at Sheffield at £625
Typical trade advertised price
  for same age and model in
  average condition £630
Total cost of car when new
  including tax £847
Depreciation over 4 years £222
Annual depreciation as proportion
  of cost new .... 6.5 per cent

DATA

Date first registered	23 April 1965
Number of owners	1
Tax expires	31 August 1969
M.O.T. expires	30 April 1970
Fuel consumption	24-30 mpg
Oil consumption	150 mpp
Mileometer reading	38,067

PERFORMANCE CHECK

(Figures in brackets are those of the five-bearing model with overdrive, published 12 February, 1965)

0 to 30 mph	**3.8** sec	(4.0)
0 to 40 mph	**6.1** sec	(6.0)
0 to 50 mph	**10.2** sec	(9.0)
0 to 60 mph	**13.8** sec	(12.9)
0 to 70 mph	**18.8** sec	(17.2)
0 to 80 mph	**25.8** sec	(24.1)
0 to 90 mph	**34.9** sec	(35.6)
Standing ¼ mile	**19.4** sec	(18.9)
In top gear:		
20 to 40 mph	**9.9** sec	(8.6)
30 to 50 mph	**9.3** sec	(8.7)
40 to 60 mph	**9.0** sec	(9.1)
50 to 70 mph	**9.6** sec	(11.1)
60 to 80 mph	**12.5** sec	(13.2)
70 to 90 mph	**16.8** sec	(17.1)
Standing Km	**36.1** sec	(—)

TYRES

Size: 155 SR 14 Pirelli Cinturato on all wheels except spare, Dunlop C41. Approx. cost per replacement cover £7 7s 0d. Depth of original tread 8.5 mm: remaining tread depth. 6 mm (left front), 7 mm (right front), 3 mm (left rear) and 5 mm (right rear). Spare, 2 mm.

TOOLS

Jack and wheel nut mallet in boot. No handbook with car.

CAR FOR SALE AT:

Portland Autos (Sheffield) Ltd., 64-84 West Bar, Sheffield 3. Telephone: Sheffield 21186-7.

NEARLY seven years ago we carried out a used car test on a 1960 MGA 1600 supplied by Portland Autos of Sheffield. Since then a further 95 cars have passed through the series the last of them being, by coincidence, another MG offered for sale by the same firm at exactly the same price of £625. Direct comparison of value is not quite possible because this MGB is twice the age and has covered twice the mileage. But it is still interesting, in these days of depreciated currency, to find that the same sum of money will buy a better car in comparable condition after such a time interval.

As we said in the original Road Test, the MGB is better in every way than the MGA, particular advantages being the improved weather protection and much more spacious body. Although in the original Road Test we obtained better acceleration figures with the B than the A, those for the later test carried out on a 1965 MGB with the new five-main bearing engine (as fitted to this used example) were slightly slower. This four-year-old car is well up to scratch on performance.

There is a lot of oil splash under the back of the engine, and a few drops of oil are left on the ground after the car has stood. Attention here may improve the consumption, as there is no blue smoke to suggest that the engine is burning oil. An oil cooler, an extra at nearly £8 when the car was new, is fitted and helps to keep the pressure well above 60 psi even in sustained fast running. Overdrive was an option, but has

not been added to this example. Without it, the gearing is rather low for high-speed cruising, and discourages sustained speeds much above 80 mph.

The engine sounds very fit, and starts promptly when hot, and equally reliably but after four or five turns on the starter, when cold, and is extremely smooth and quiet. When the car is driven with the hood down, the engine is scarcely perceptible, though the satisfyingly crisp exhaust note is then even more audible. Engine noise level is still low even when the hood is fitted.

The gearbox retains the delightful precision of its short travel change, and although there is some gear whine, particularly in first, it is not much more than we remember from the original road test car. The synchromesh is effective on the three upper gears, and first is easily engaged on the move with a quick double-declutch. It also pays to move the lever towards second gear position for an instant before engaging first, to prevent a crunch of gears. The clutch takes up smoothly, and absorbed full power for standing start acceleration testing.

Very crisp, taut suspension is one of the pleasures of the MGB, and is still unspoilt on this used example, the dampers remaining effective. Two faults on the car as supplied were noticed—stiff steering, due to lack of grease in the kingpins, and slight steering vibration at about 85 mph, which was answered by having the wheels balanced. The steering was improved by greasing, but the offside top bearing is blocked. In spite of this the steering is wonderfully precise, and although the car understeers rather excessively on corners, it holds such a steady, predictable line through a corner that it is a delight to drive fast on a winding road. In a straight line, the car holds exactly to course, almost regardless of cross winds. It is a pity the past owner has not changed the enormous steering wheel for a smaller light alloy one, and the rim of the wheel has cracked badly around the joint of the right spoke.

Brakes are Lockheed discs at the front, drums at rear, with no servo. Firm pedal effort is needed, but the response is reassuring, except in heavy rain when there is a bad delay before the pads bite through the water film. The pull-up handbrake is effective if pulled on hard.

It was a great pleasure to try an MGB again, and it provided a lot of "fun motoring" even when we were caught out with the hood down in a rainstorm on M1. It seems a very genuine car—showing a mileage that would seem correct, and mainly in very sound condition for its age.

CONDITION SUMMARY

Bodywork

The finish in pillar-box red has faded slightly but is still sound and gives a smart appearance to the car. One or two blemishes have been touched up, but the finish looks original. There are some rust patches on each rear quarter where the hood passes over the wing beading, but otherwise the condition is very good. The front and rear aprons have been painted with bitumastic material.

All brightwork and chromium is in good shape and it is only on close inspection that a few shallow rust spots are seen. The interior is very clean and only the extensive creasing of the black leather seats gives away the age. The seats are still comfortable but one now sits even lower than before, suggesting that the cushion has sagged slightly. The rubber floor mats and carpeting over the transmission tunnel and rear luggage space are all in very good shape.

The red pvc hood is about due for replacement. The windows have crazed and yellowed to the extent that it is difficult to see through the mirror what is behind. Some of the clips are also missing so that the hood corners near the doors protrude in the slipstream at speed.

There is quite a lot of rust on the exhaust front pipes but the silencers are good and the general under-body condition is first class, showing little rust and no damage.

This MGB is in very reasonable condition for its age and mileage. Almost everything is working correctly and the bodywork is unspoilt both inside and out although the seats are extensively creased

Equipment

Everything on the car is working satisfactorily except for the heater water valve which is jammed in the "open" position. The running temperature is very low and heater output suffers accordingly.

Accessories

About £70 worth of accessories were added to the car when new and are included in the sale—heater, wire wheels, oil cooler and full-length tonneau cover. There is also a side mirror mounted on the door and Kangol magnet seat belts.

ABOUT THE MGB

Many features of the MGA 1600, such as the front suspension units and disc front brakes were continued in the MGB, which was introduced in September 1962; but the body was entirely new, using monocoque construction, and the B-series engine was stretched from 1,622 to 1,798 cc. A lot of attention was paid in the design to rigidity, and extensive cross-bracing ensured a car which would be rigid even as an open two-seater. The original engine was a three-bearing unit developing 92 bhp (net) at 5,300 rpm on 8.8 to 1 compression.

Many extras were offered including wire wheels, anti-roll bar and an oil cooler, and even such items as twin horns and heater were optional. In January 1963, Laycock overdrive working on 3rd and top became available.

In the following year, October 1964, the MGB appeared at the Motor Show with a revised engine. It retained the same bore and stroke of 80 x 89 mm, but had a 5-bearing crank shaft. This unit continues as the engine for the MGB today, and formed the basis for the engine used in the Austin and later BMC 1800 models.

A new model added to the range for the 1965 Motor Show was the MGB GT—a coupé model with top hinged rear door. □

80,000 MILES IN TWO MG-Bs

FOLLOWING recent correspondence about the Triumph TR range, it may be interesting to relate the experiences of two staff MG-Bs over a period of some 80,000 miles, being a similar, if perhaps more sedate, kind of car.

The first example, FJB 535 C was a black MG-B sports, having the five-bearing crank engine and overdrive fitted. It proved to be incredibly reliable, and during the 45,000 miles it was used by a member of our staff, suffered no major fault whatsoever.

Initially it was supplied with Dunlop C.41 tyres. These produced a pronounced oversteer characteristic in the handling, with resultant rear tyre wear. At 18,000 miles the rear tyres were replaced with G.8s which increased the oversteer. Consequently, at 24,000 miles, the whole set was replaced with Avon Radial tyres. These proved to be absolutely perfect for the car, and made the handling completely vice free. In the dry, it was impossible to cause loss of adhesion under normal hard driving conditions on the road. It would need the freedom of a race circuit to do so. In the wet they gave plenty of warning of impending loss of grip under extremity, but this was so perfectly controllable that the car could be steered almost entirely with the throttle, backing off to induce a trace of oversteer or adding power to provoke understeer. It seemed that Avon Radials suited the "B" like Michelin "X"s suit a "deux cheveaux". One front shock-absorber needed replacing due to a leaking seal at 12,000 miles, and the exhaust system suffered damage due to its lowness and the use of the car following rallies. Two or three welding sessions at various times held this together until 25,000 miles, at which time it was replaced by an excellent custom-made bottom pipe from JanSpeed. This lasted until the car was passed on to another member of the staff at 47,500 miles.

An early improvement had been to replace the standard sealed-beam headlights with Marchal Asymmetric units, which not only had an improved output but could be switched to Continental dipping. At the same time, the original neoprene rubber wiper blades and arms were replaced with Trico wire frames and natural rubber blades. These did not lift at speed and in conjunction with the Trico "add-on" electric washer motor provided much improved windscreen cleaning. Marchal twin-horns replaced the original inaudible and heavy ones.

Some trouble was experienced with front disc roughness, which did not respond to skimming, so the discs were replaced at 15,000 miles. Other expenditure was only the odd bulb, plugs and points, and the dipswitch.

When the car was passed on to a further member of the staff at 47,500 miles the tyres were still in good condition and even now, some 36,000 miles from new, they have about 3 millimetres of tread left all round.

The new owner handed the car to Bill Nicholson for a check-up and rectification as necessary, and this commenced with front suspension overhaul, replacement of all bushes and the dampers. New discs and pads were needed and the rack and pinion needed adjustment. The cylinder head required some new valves and seat grinding. These rectifications seemed reasonable after nearly 50,000 miles of hard use including rally coverage and fast Continental driving.

The original twin 6v. Lucas batteries are still in good order now, despite being five years old. Possibly their position under the rear floor sitting in the cold has helped in this respect, even though this dreadfully inaccessible site tends to let them be forgotten.

The exhaust needed replacement again at 50,000 miles and Brian Muir at Brabham Conversions fitted one of theirs 12,000 miles ago, which shows no sign of deterioration. The appearance of this car was enhanced by the fitting of a new hood by the Car Hood Company at 52,000 miles.

Striking a fallen object burst a tyre and, as was later discovered, also cracked a universal joint, and now at 60,000 miles the 2nd gear synchromesh is rather worn, but the engine is as crisp and powerful as ever. It still shows 60-70 p.s.i. oil pressure and sounds fit for another 40 or 50,000 miles without worry.

FJB 535 C had proved so fine a motor car that its original owner opted for the GT version when the open one was passed on. This was also ordered in black as the other looked so well, a fact which probably contributed to the delivery being six months after the order was placed. Unfortunately, WLT 550 G was not to prove nearly so reliable as its predecessor and a succession of faults began to develop early in its life. The first item to go was the expansion box on the exhaust system. This was a different pattern from the older car and was formed from a cylinder with crimped ends. At 3,500 miles the whole of the underside of this cracked due to resonance and blew out a piece about 4 in. × 3 in. Fortunately, this happened near to a BLMC agent at Machynlleth in 'Wales and was replaced under warranty in a very short time.

Uneven braking then began to make life difficult and it took several visits to the London main depot to eliminate the possible causes of this and discover that the discs were at fault. Subsequently, failure of the rear-wheel brake slave cylinder rubbers, both sides at different times, caused further braking bothers and in one case destroyed the axle oil seal as well. This, of course, necessitated replacement brake liners. The next bother was a blown cylinder-head gasket at 12,000 miles, despite careful checking of nut tightness with the appropriate torque setting on a wrench.

Later the engine developed a subtle rattle at certain revs. This was one of those hard-to-trace but insistent noises that promise ill for the future, and it took a great deal of time and replacement parts at the factory to eliminate this.

Since that time the car has been behaving itself, with the exception of one of the slave cylinder jobs referred to earlier, but the engine still seems rather noisier than that of the original car and produces less confidence in its future behaviour.

WLT 550 G was supplied with Pirelli Cinturatos on its wire wheels and while these provide good handling and reasonable adhesion in the dry, they do not compare so favourably in the wet with the characteristics of the Avons fitted to the open car. Perhaps this is a question of "horses for courses" and the Pirellis would be more suited to an independently-sprung car. Their wear rate seems rather higher than expected, and at 20,000 miles they are almost finished at the rear.

Perhaps WLT 550 G was a "tea-break" car and is not representative of the *marque*. Hopefully, all the early bugs have now been sorted out and it will now live up to the fine example of its predecessor. It is hoped that this is the case, for in GT form the MG-B is a roomy and rapid means of transport and is ideally suited for the sort of long-distance assignments that MOTOR SPORT entails.

Both MG-Bs have provided many enjoyable motoring miles, combining a reasonable standard of comfort with good performance, considering the engine is only 1,800 c.c. Fuel consumption has been at the rate of 28-30 m.p.g. on distance runs, dropping to 23-25 around town. With overdrive gearing at 22 m.p.h. per 1,000 r.p.m., it is comfortable to cruise at 4,000 revs., representing 88 m.p.h., for long spells, with the odd 500-1,000 r.p.m. in hand which can be used to snap out of overdrive to accelerate when needed.—L. A. M.

AUTOTEST

MGB AUTOMATIC
(1,798 c.c.)

AT-A-GLANCE: MG's famous sports two-seater with Borg-Warner three-speed epicyclic automatic box. Smooth transmission. Performance not seriously reduced; good economy for its class. Pleasant town car, still pleasing in country despite firm ride and none-too-convenient cockpit design. Safe, strong and easy to drive.

MANUFACTURER
British Leyland Motor Corporation, Austin-Morris Division, Abingdon, Berks.

PRICES
Basic	£882	0s	0d
Purchase Tax	£271	15s	10d
Seat belts (approx.)	£10	0s	0d
Total (in G.B.)	£1,163	15s	10d

EXTRAS (inc. P.T.)
Automatic transmission*	£104	8s	11d
Folding hood*	£7	16s	8d
Tonneau cover*	£13	1s	1d
Wire wheels*	£32	12s	9d
Radial-ply tyres*	£9	15s	0d
Brake Servo	£10	8s	11d
Hard top	£78	6s	8d

* Fitted to test car

PRICE AS TESTED £1,331 10s 3d

PERFORMANCE SUMMARY
Mean maximum speed	104 mph
Standing start ¼-mile	19.5 sec
0-60 mph	13.6 sec
30-70 mph through gears	13.6 sec
Typical fuel consumption	26 mpg
Miles per tankful	310

EVEN nowadays, when open two-seaters are rarely found without wind-down side windows, weather-tight hoods, bodywork that enfolds driver and passenger and some sort of heater, it seems odd that one can buy a medium-size British sports-car with automatic transmission. Particularly when the model in question is that most traditionally sporting sports car, the eight-year-old MGB. In spite of what, without being unkind, one could describe as the sometimes-reluctant civilizing of the Abingdon idea of the "right" open two-seater, the car is in general surprisingly effective, as it is unique. Open two-seat, two-litre automatics are hardly thick on the ground, and we had a hard job deciding on four not-very-comparative cars for our data pages.

The transmission used is, of course, Borg-Warner's versatile and ubiquitous three-speed epicyclic type 35 box with a torque converter giving up to 2.2-to-1 multiplication. There was no label or plaque on the test car's outside to tell anyone that the little hydraulic people underneath and not the presumably keen sporting flesh-and-blood person at the wheel were making most of the gear-changing decisions (one might suspect that someone was slightly ashamed at the fact—in the main there

Top: External styling touches for the 1970 MGB included a redesigned front grille. The basic shape, however, remained untouched Above: *the new seats proved very comfortable, although less rearward movement means the car is no longer completely comfortable for 6ft 6in drivers* Left: *the instrument panel has been rearranged, but is still far from good ergonomically*

is no need for such feelings). The only evidence in the cockpit is the lack of a clutch pedal and, instead of the normal short gearlever, an even shorter sliding selector lever, with a lift-up tee-handle to guard the reverse and parking lock positions. This moves very pleasantly, being smooth and precise. Position D gives fully automatic changes up and down with kickdown. L2 holds the intermediate gear from 54 mph to its maximum at 79 mph (6,000 rpm); below that speed it will kickdown. L1 holds low ratio from standstill to a maximum of 48 mph.

In this installation, the box is pretty smooth. Even on full throttle, gearchange quality is good—slightly slurred from 1st to 2nd at 38 mph (5,000 rpm), and less so on the next one at the same revs at 62 mph. For best performance, these settings are not ideal. We held both ranges to 41 and 67 mph, a true 5,400 rpm (at which the rev counter indicated 200 rpm higher) for our fastest acceleration runs, the selector having to be "changed up" a little in advance of what the rev counter said because of the distinct lag in response.

The last manual-gearbox MGB test by *Autocar* was in our issue of 12 February 1965. Since then, although the final-drive ratio has remained unaltered, first and second gears are now slightly higher, so performance comparisons between the automatic and that five-year-old car are not entirely applicable to the current range. Nevertheless, the losses inherent in all torque converter automatics do not apparently make such a significant difference as usual. As far as top speed is concerned, there is no difference at all, presumably because of careful re-gearing by the Abingdon development team. The 1965 car, geared at 3.13-to-1 (22.4 mph per 1,000 rpm) in overdrive, pulled 103.5 mph in that ratio at 4,600 rpm. Instead of the current manual model's 3.91 direct top (18 mph per 1,000 rpm, with a 3.20 overdrive giving 22 mph per 1,000 rpm), the automatic uses a 3.7 final drive giving 19 mph per 1,000 rpm. This allows the engine to pull its specified peak power speed of 5,400 rpm at 104 mph mean on the MIRA banking, plus a best on one leg of 106 mph.

In acceleration from a standing start, there is a definite though not unacceptable loss. The torque converter's maximum stall speed is around 2,000 rpm which precludes any wheelspin starts. That shows up in the 0-30 mph time, 4.9 instead of 4.0 sec; it is remarkable that the 10 mph increments all the way to 70 mph are about the same as the 1965 manual car's which makes one wonder whether or not the automatic's claimed 95 bhp is not, in this case, a more healthy team than the earlier car's. For comparison, here are the times in sec from 40 to 90 mph, automatic first: 7.1 (6.0), 10.0 (9.0), 13.6 (12.9), 18.5 (17.2), 26.4 (24.1) and 39.0 (35.6). Over the standing quarter-mile, the automatic at 19.5sec is only 0.6sec slower than that manual car. Leaving the box to its own devices in D instead of over-riding it as explained earlier, the car is ½sec slower to 50 and 60 mph and 2.4sec slower to 90.

Fuel consumption varies between a minimum of around 20 mpg driven hard, to a typical figure for a fast cross .cross-country run of around 26 mpg. Our overall consumption of 25.5 mpg is, surprisingly, appreciably better than the earlier manual car's 22.0 mpg.

The car is perhaps at its best for town traffic on a sunny day, assuming that other people's exhaust fumes don't unduly bother the driver. Even when accelerating hard, there is no undue exhaust and engine noise for the type of car. Driven gently, it is most unobtrusive and gentlemanly; the automatic here comes into its own making one very relaxed with no need

Top: *As long as the side windows are raised, there is good weather protection even with the hood down, as long as the car is kept moving* Above: *the familar-looking engine and its accessories are quite easy to get at* Left: *the boot space is fairly large, but the floor area is cluttered with spare wheel and jack*

ACCELERATION

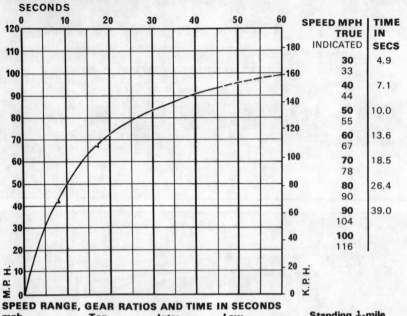

SECONDS

SPEED MPH TRUE INDICATED	TIME IN SECS
30	4.9
33	
40	7.1
44	
50	10.0
55	
60	13.6
67	
70	18.5
78	
80	26.4
90	
90	39.0
104	
100	
116	

SPEED RANGE, GEAR RATIOS AND TIME IN SECONDS

mph	Top (3.7)	Inter (5.36)	Low (8.84)
10-30	—	—	3.7
20-40	—	—	3.7
30-50	—	6.6	—
40-60	—	7.2	—
50-70	—	8.8	—
60-80	14.5	—	—
70-90	19.4	—	—

Standing ¼-mile
19.5 sec 72 mph

Standing kilometre
35.7 sec 88 mph

Test distance
1,414 miles

Mileage recorder
11.2 per cent
over-reading

PERFORMANCE

MAXIMUM SPEEDS

Gear	mph	kph	rpm
Top (mean)	104	167	5,480
(best)	106	171	5,580
Inter	79	127	6,000
Low	48	77	6,000

BRAKES

Retardation measurements made with Bowmonk decelerometer

(from 70 mph in neutral)
Pedal load for 0.5g stops in lb

1	60-55	6	75
2	70-65	7	75-80
3	65-60	8	75-85
4	65	9	75-85
5	65-70	10	75-85

RESPONSE (from 30 mph in neutral)

Load	g	Distance
20lb	0.22	137ft
40lb	0.38	79ft
60lb	0.64	47ft
80lb	0.85	35ft
100lb	0.97	31.0ft
Handbrake	0.36	84ft

Max. Gradient 1 in 3

MOTORWAY CRUISING

Indicated speed at 70 mph . . . . 78 mph
Engine (rpm at 70 mph) . . . . 3,680 rpm
(mean piston speed) . . . 2,150ft/min.
Fuel (mpg at 70 mph) . . . . 27.2 mpg
Passing (50-70 mph) . . . . 8.8 sec

COMPARISONS

MAXIMUM SPEED MPH

Lotus Elan S4 S/E	. . . . (£2,079)	124
Opel GT 1900	. . . . . (£2,057)	115
Triumph GT6 Mk 2	. . . . (£1,210)	107
Ford Capri 2000 GT	. . . (£1,127)	106
MGB automatic	. . . . . (£1,257)	**104**

0-60 MPH, SEC

Lotus Elan S4 S/E	. . . . 7.8
Triumph GT6 Mk 2	. . . . 10.0
Ford Capri 2000 GT	. . . . . . 10.6
Opel GT 1900	. . . . 12.0
MGB automatic	. . . . **13.6**

STANDING ¼-MILE, SEC

Lotus Elan S4 S/E	. . . . 15.9
Triumph GT6 Mk 2	. . . . 17.3
Ford Capri 2000 GT	. . . . . . 18.2
Opel GT 1900	. . . . 18.6
MGB automatic	. . . . **19.5**

OVERALL MPG

Lotus Elan S4 S/E	. . . . 30.0
Opel GT 1900	. . . . 28.7
MGB automatic	. . . . **25.5**
Triumph GT6 Mk 2	. . . . 25.2
Ford Capri 2000 GT	. . . . . . 22.0

N.B. All cars except the MGB have manual transmission

GEARING (with 165—14in. tyres)

Top	. . . . . . 19.0 mph per 1,000 rpm
Inter	. . . . . 13.1 mph per 1,000 rpm
Low	. . . . . . 7.9 mph per 1,000 rpm

TEST CONDITIONS:
Weather: Dry, cloudy. Wind: 3-8 mph. Temperature: 7 deg. C. (45 deg. F). Barometer 29.6 in. hg. Humidity: 60 per cent. Surfaces: dry concrete and asphalt.

WEIGHT:
Kerb weight: 19.2 cwt (2,143 16—973kg) (with oil, water and half-full fuel tank). Distribution, per cent: F, 51.5; R, 48.5. Laden as tested: 23.2 cwt (2,598lb—1,179kg).

TURNING CIRCLES:
Between kerbs L, 33ft 5in.; R, 31 ft 4in. Between walls L, 34ft 8in.; R, 32ft 7in. Steering wheel turns, lock to lock 2.9

Figures taken at 5,600 miles by our own staff at the Motor Industry Research Association proving ground at Nuneaton

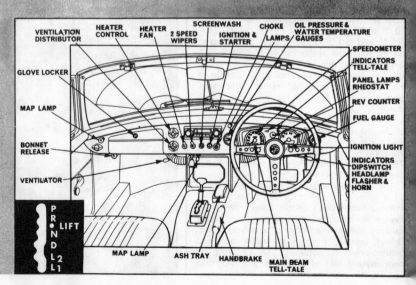

CONSUMPTION

K.P.H.

(graph with axes: K.P.H. 50 60 70 80 90 100 110 120 130 140 150 160 across top; M.P.G. on left 20 30 40 50 60 70; LITRES/100km on right 5 6 7 8 9 10 12 14 16 18 20; MPH 30 40 50 60 70 80 90 100 across bottom)

FUEL

At constant speeds—mpg)

30 mph	41.7
40 mph	39.2
50 mph	35.1
60 mph	31.2
70 mph	27.2
80 mph	22.7
90 mph	19.2
100 mph	14.9

Typical mpg 26 (10.9 litres/100km)
Calculated (DIN) mpg 24.8 (11.4 litres/100km)
Overall mpg 25.5 (11.1 litres/100km)
Grade of fuel
Super Premium, 5-star (min. 100 RM)

OIL

Miles per pint (SAE 10W/40) 400

SPECIFICATION
FRONT ENGINE, REAR-WHEEL DRIVE

ENGINE
Cylinders . . . . 4, in line
Main bearings . . 5
Cooling system . Water, pump, fan and thermostat
Bore 80.0mm (3.16in.)
Stroke . . . 89.0mm (3.50in.)
Displacement . . 1,798cc (109.8 cu.in.)
Valve gear . . Overhead, pushrods and rockers
Compression ratio 8.8 to 1. Min. octane rating 100RM
Carburettors . . 2 SU HS4
Fuel pump . . SU electric
Oil filter . . . Tecalemit full-flow, replaceable element
Max. power . . 95 bhp (net) at 5,400 rpm
Max. torque . . 100 lb.ft (net) at 3,000 rpm
Max. bmep . . 152 psi at 3,100 rpm

TRANSMISSION
Gearbox . . . Borg-Warner 35 3-speed automatic with torque converter
Gear ratios . . . Top 1.0—2.2
Inter 1.45—3.19
Low 2.39—5.25
Reverse 2.09—4.60
Final drive . . Hypoid bevel, ratio 3.7 to 1

CHASSIS and BODY
Construction . . Integral, with steel body

SUSPENSION
Front . . . . Independent, double wishbones, coil springs, lever-type dampers
Rear . . . . Live axle, semi-elliptic leaf springs, lever-type dampers

STEERING
Type . . . . Rack and pinion
Wheel dia. . . . 15.4 in.

BRAKES
Make and type . Lockheed discs front, drums rear
Dimensions . . F 10.75 in.dia.
R 10.0 in.dia. 1.75 in. wide shoes
Swept area . . F 203 sq.in., R 107 sq.in.
Total 310 sq.in. (267 sq.in./ton laden)

WHEELS
Type . . . . . Optional extra, wire-spoked, knock-on fixing, 4.5 in. wide rim. Standard wheels pressed steel Rostyle
Tyres— . . . Dunlop
—type . SP68 radial ply tubed
—size . 165-14 in.

EQUIPMENT
Battery . . . . 2 x 6 volt 58 Ah (total)
Alternator . . Lucas, 16ACR, 34 amp a.c.
Headlamps . . Lucas sealed-beam 90/120 watt (total)
Reversing lamp . 2, standard
Electric fuses . 4
Screen wipers . 2-speed
Screen washer . Manual plunger
Interior heater . Standard, water-valve type
Heated backlight Not available
Safety belts . . Extra
Interior trim . . Pvc seats and headlining
Floor covering . Carpet
Jack . . . . Screw pillar type
Jacking points . One each side under sills
Windscreen . . Laminated
Underbody . . Phosphate treatment under paint

MAINTENANCE
Fuel tank . . 12 Imp. gallons (54.8 litres)
Cooling system . 10 pints (including heater)
Engine sump . 8.5 pints (4.8 litres) SAE 10W/40. Change oil every 6,000 miles. Change filter element every 6,000 miles
Gearbox . . . 14.5 pints SAE Type A. Check oil every 6,000 miles
Final drive . . 2.2 pints SAE 90EP. Check oil every 6,000 miles
Grease . . . 8 points every 3,000 miles
Tyre pressures . F 21; R 24 psi (normal driving)
F 27; R 30 psi (fast driving)
F 21; R 26 psi (full load)
Max. payload . 425 lb (193kg)

PERFORMANCE DATA
Top gear mph per 1,000 rpm 19.0
Mean piston speed at max. power . . . . 3,150 ft/min
Bhp per ton laden 81.9

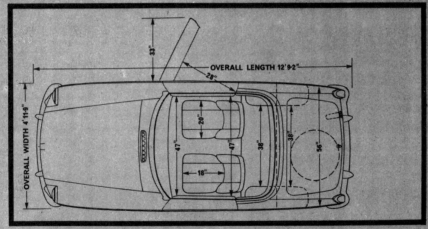

STANDARD GARAGE 16ft x 8ft 6in.

OVERALL LENGTH 12'9·2"
OVERALL WIDTH 4'11·9"

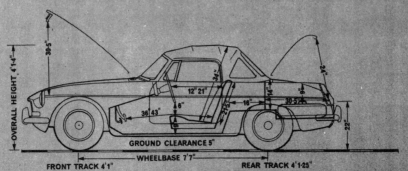

OVERALL HEIGHT 4'1·4"
GROUND CLEARANCE 5"
FRONT TRACK 4'1"
WHEELBASE 7'7"
REAR TRACK 4'1·25"

SCALE 0.3in. to 1ft
Cushions uncompressed

constantly to exercise one's clutch foot and yet always able to move off immediately. One would still like a lighter accelerator pedal effort; its travel is quite long, sensibly ended with an effective stop behind the pedal. An open MGB thus equipped with the hood down is the easy master of traffic driving, thanks to near-total all-round visibility. If fitted, as the test car was, with one of the excellent current press-button-tuning Radiomobile sets, city driving on a pleasant day (assuming you have to drive across such places) is made into something much nearer a pleasure. Even with the hood up visibility is still quite good horizontally.

Thanks to the first and second gear holds, one can impress some of one's own ideas on the transmission in the sort of driving an MG is meant for—proper driving, across country, not just in towns. L2 gives one a useful degree of engine braking, selection of second being a little slow but not excessively jerky from the high end of the ratio's range. When cruising at 20 to 25, the transmission heterodynes quite badly. Again, somewhat surprisingly, in spite of the slight slowing of in what is not by contemporary international standards a very great performer, the automatic 'B is remarkably satisfying on the open road.

That is due to a combination of virtues which in the main vanquish some vices of old-fashioned design or tardy development. Steering is certainly heavy, unnecessarily so to judge by several competitors. As in a good Vintage car, you do not notice this on the move fairly fast; but at low speeds and when parking, the MGB designer's adherence to an extreme

amount of castor angle (9 deg) becomes rather a nuisance. It may be retorted that the car's extremely good straight-line stability—which is undeniably valuable on long journeys—and also the quick self-centring are products of this steering geometry. Going by other good-handling front-engine rear-wheel-drive cars of more up-to-date design, there are other ways of achieving the same result. Nevertheless, the MGB steers basically very well indeed—completely positively, with little slop, an average lock, and lots of that valuable thing, "feel".

In handling, the car is very well-mannered. It has no treachery in its character, Grip, wet or dry, on Dunlop SP68 radial-ply tyres is excellent. Basically an understeerer, led gently but fast into a tightening corner it will continue to understeer until it has scrubbed off the excess speed. "Thrown", it will kick its tail out in an easily controllable way thanks to the high geared steering. Roll is not excessive, and one soon finds oneself placing it nicely on corners.

Brakes are rather heavy but effective. Our 70 mph fade test showed only slight deterioration; heavier use produced further increase in pedal loads but still within reasonable bounds. The hand brake held easily on 1-in-3, from which re-starts are easy.

The ride is pretty firm and you notice most bumps, though it takes a big one to make it bump-skid on a corner. The MGB's many well-wishers would still like to see the car endowed with the good independently sprung rear-end that it clearly deserves—and needs. A quite extraordinary virtue, and one which one does not usually look for in this sort of car, is the very low level of road-noise. There is very little bump-thump and hardly any tune-roar. The former may be due to the fact that one is not, as in a saloon, sitting inside a steel sounding-box; none the less this is remarkable.

On the whole the driving position is

everything it should be. Shorter drivers would be glad of a steering column adjustable for length; for them the 15.4in. dia. steering wheel is too close and the scuttle a little high. One certainly sits very much *in* the car, which adds a feeling of security to the overall impression of strength. Unlike in previous 'Bs, our tallest testers found that there was just enough rearward seat movement for their length of leg; previously there has always been more than our one 6ft 2in. driver wanted. The seats are exceedingly comfortable; only a rally type seat would hold one better sideways. On a 450-mile 12-hour "day-return" trip to the hills of Wales from Surrey, neither occupant could complain of any back aches or other discomfort.

The hood is very snug and effectively weatherproof when in use, though anyone who crammed him- or herself crosswise into the space behind the seats would find a draught round his neck. Wind noise is below average for such cars. Our principal objections to both the "optional" hood fitted to the test car and the standard hood are, most important, the time it takes even a practised owner to erect or furl it, and also the the most questionable sharpness and prominence of several of the hood irons, which are uncomfortably near one's head. Take your MGB across France and hit one of the finer specimens of *chaussee deformee* at speed and you will feel what we mean. Like nearly all other British sports-car makers short of Jaguar, MG should take a lesson in simple hood design from Alfa Romeo.

With the hood down, the 'B takes on its most pleasant form. Provided that you can keep moving at a minimum of 40 mph, no rain or snow will touch you—it all goes over the top or round the side, even with the side windows down, by some happy quirk of aerodynamics. Only at or around maximum speed does one's head receive any buffeting. The on-off water-valve heater is not very controllable but in the wintry weather of the test period successfully kept one's lower half warm with the top down; a good coat or anorak and a scarf looks after the rest of you, even when it is freezing.

Controls are mainly quite acceptable. The "gearchange" is easy to reach and the reasonably comprehensive instrumentation is readily visible. So far as the speedometer and mileometer on the test car were concerned, that was almost a pity, as both were more than 10 per cent optimistic; we would suspect that an incorrect type was fitted to that particular car, as such error is not at all typical nowadays. Instrument and switch layout is pleasingly simple, almost crude, which may not worry some owners, but we would like to see some improvement here—not restyling, or a loss of the basically functional appearance, but much better "ergonomics" in the same effect if not style of the Mk 2 Triumph 2000, and some reasonable stowage space.

Summing up the MGB automatic, one can say that it is a much better motor car than we expected, though there are several points where it falls down. From the transmission viewpoint, there is little that needs doing, and the car performs quite satisfactorily. Because we have not tested an MGB for such a relatively long time, there are features about this prettiest of sports car which we feel are worth criticizing. We would not want to see the looks of the car greatly altered, and would not envy anybody who was asked to improve on it in that respect. But lighter steering, better (all-independent but still geometrically sound) suspension, improved cockpit controls and hood would give the MGB another well-deserved eight years of international success. □

Standard wheels are of the Rostyle sculptured type, the wire-spoked ones on the test car costing £33 extra

MEET AN OLD FRIEND

*The MGB, in spite of
its exterior updating,
takes one back
to when it all began*

Soft summer breezes, deserted country lanes, and a real honest to goodness sports car . . . enthusiasts come out of the woodwork when the weather turns nice and roadsters appear like magic. What better way to enjoy a day of open air motoring on the back roads than driving the latest version of the car that started the popular swing to the sports car way back when . . . the MG!

In the late 1940s the MG TC arrived in America, and the budding cult of sports car nuts latched onto the odd little car that was largely responsible for the turn to sporty images in the automotive market. In many ways one had to be a complete buff to enjoy a T series MG. The TC, in particular,

came complete with a horse cart type ride, cramped cockpit and luggage space, somewhat less than ideal weather protection, and a whole lot of spirit. A primitive car to be sure, but the T series MGs made a whole generation of people aware that driving a sports car could be real fun.

When folks discovered that a car could be used for purposes other than basic transportation, the foreign makes grew in number and popularity in the U.S. The pre-war design of the MG lost ground, and the MGA was born in the mid-fifties. The enclosed body style, actual trunk, and relatively decent weather protection on the A, plus a low price tag put the MG back on the list of the top sellers in the enthusiast market. To this day there are many who swear that an MGA is the easiest driving sports car ever built, and the most forgiving vehicle ever placed on four wheels. But the march of progress eventually comes, even to the British auto makers, and by 1962 the MGB appeared. Hailed by the faithful as a sacrilegious departure from tradition, the B easily held its place as one of the fine, conven-

tional sports roadsters of the times. The GT, a hardtop, more expensive version soon arrived to keep the roadster company.

The original MGB had most of the delights of the earlier cars, and few of their disadvantages. For instance it was the first MG roadster with wind-up windows, but it retained the fine handling qualities of the early models. Over the years of the model run the U.S. federal regs have taken their toll of some of the nicer touches of the MG appointments. Still the MGB is quite a good example of that particular breed of vehicle known as a sports car.

Despite its somewhat dated design, the MGB would make a good answer to the question of ''What is a sports car?'' A sports car, by definition, is myriad things. We like to think that any car which is a pleasure to drive under all types of road conditions could qualify as a sports car. We don't subscribe to the theory that one must be uncomfortable and battered by the elements in a sports car. Neither do we feel that the addition of more horsepower, extra stripes and instru-

MGB steering wheel is sporty and well positioned. The instruments are well placed and legible. Check the old time map light in the center of the dash.

Pedals are well spaced by British standards, but gas pedal is still bare metal. Rubber insert and floor mat spare the carpeting from heavy wear.

ments makes a sports car out of a mundane sedan. Basically, a sports car is a machine that encourages one to get in and drive just for the sheer pleasure of driving, and a machine that makes daily driving chores more fun than drudgery. In our opinion the MGB is a fun car, never meant to haul the entire family, freight the household goods, and the like, but designed as a sporting machine for the pure enjoyment of driving.

What's Under the Hood

The Mark II designation for the MGB denotes a few styling changes, but the drive train remains the same. In fact, the only major changes since introduction happened early in the game. In late 1964 the five bearing crank became standard on the engine, and synchromesh first gear was added a couple of years later. The engine in the tried and true, four-cylinder unit, fed by twin SU HS 4 carburetors and an electric fuel pump, an MG standard since the T series. The engine is the final version of the venerable BMC B series block used in the MGA. It started life at 1489 cc, then went to 1622 cc, still in the MGA series cars. Currently the 80 mm bore and 89 mm stroke give a total engine displacement of 1798 cubic centimeters (109.8 cubic inches). The overhead valve engine is rated at 92 horsepower at 5200 rpm with a torque figure of 110 at 3000 rpm. Although the compression ratio is listed at 8.8 to 1, the B requires premium fuel in most areas. The U.S. cars come with an oil cooler, fitted just behind the water radiator, as standard equipment. The engine and all its accessories fit nicely in the bay, and access for both major

and minor work is quite good with most of the vital areas well on top and easily reached.

The familiar, all synchro four-speed transmission is standard equipment. There is an optional overdrive that operates on third and fourth gear. In either case the final drive ratio is 3.91 to 1. Our test car had just the plain four-speed with the traditional sport throw gear stick and well spaced ratios. The engine revs freely through the gears to peak power and the warning orange line of 5500 rpm; 6000 rpm is the redline, but power drops off before that figure is reached. The standard clutch is eight-inch diameter and very positive in action.

The MGB is now ''a bit long in the tooth'' as the British say, and the suspension is particularly dated. At the front the independent suspension incorporates parallel wishbones, coil springs and hydraulic lever arm shocks. At the rear the semi-elliptic leaf springs and the lever arm shocks, along with the live axle emphasize the need for some modernization of the underpinnings. The front brakes are Lockheed discs of 10.75-inch diameter, and 10-inch diameter drums are on the rear wheels. There is no power assist for the brakes and none is needed. The rack and pinion steering unit works easily without assist also, and the large diameter steering wheel, over 15 inches, is a help here, especially at low speeds.

Like all British cars the MGB has a 12-volt electrical system, and finally an alternator has replaced the Lucas generator both cursed and praised by owners over the years.

Road wheels are the 14-inch standard disc type, but most MGBs come

with the optional wire wheels. For the U.S. the time-honored ''do-undo'' ears on the center hub of the wire wheel are long gone down the safety standard tube, and a ''safe'' center hub adorns the export cars. Still the wire wheels on the test car do much to enhance the good looks of the MGB. Since the option is only about eighty bucks extra, it is well worth the money for the cosmetic value.

Styling and Appointments

Style is a much maligned word today, particularly when applied to the automobile. The motoring enthusiast generally believes that style is the application of form following function, and he is willing to put up with some inconveniences in style and comfort to gain better overall performance. A true sports car should be a delight to drive and also a pleasure to the eye. The MGB is not sleekly modern and aerodynamic in looks, but the style is classic, good looking, and functional. The car certainly does not look out of step with the times, although the base design is approaching the ten year mark.

Basically unchanged since introduction, the unit body MGB has acquired all the proper reflector lights on the sides, which are fitted for the export market only. A small British

Three windshield wipers seem superfluous, but law is law.

The trunk is barely adequate and the spare plus tool kit have little covering. Soft luggage can be stowed in the nooks and crannies, but area behind the seat is better for normal bags.

added to the seat backs in a tasteful manner, and they are unusual in that they seem to fit the average size person and mate to his head position. The seats have been changed and all for the better. They are as comfortable as any bucket, and far better than seats in most popular sports cars. Seat adjustment is quite good with fully reclining mechanism for the seat backs; all but the tallest drivers will find a proper spot for comfort in driving. The average size person sits well inside the car rather than on it and the door reaches over the shoulder for most. The cozy fit and the comfort of the seats give a feeling of security, plus they offer good leg support. The MGB can be driven all

Leyland badge has been placed on the flanks just forward of the doors, and the MG nose badge has been moved back to the grill, although the raised spot on the hood remains, no doubt to accommodate the hood latch. Export models have rubber inserts on all bumper over riders, and for our market the rear bumper is split to allow proper placing of the rear license plate.

In order to meet the local regs the export MGB has no less than three windwhield wipers fitted and it does look like too much mechanism for such a small surface. It is the BMC solution to the rules calling for a cleaning of a certain percentage of area of the windshield, and it does lend a cluttered look to the car.. Still the basic lines are clean and simple. The B has a purposeful look and gives the impression of being smaller than it is in actuality. Our test car was equipped with the optional wire wheels, mentioned earlier, and also the Dunlop SP 66 tube type radial tires. The radials are really worth the small extra cost, since they have better longevity than the standard tires, look better, and compliment the car's fine handling qualities. Aesthetically we think the wire wheels are a must also, because they give the final touch of "sports car" to the MGB's appearance.

Inside the cockpit things have changed a good deal since 1962. Gone is the glove box, gone are the toggle switches, and gone is the centrally located key slot. The pas-

senger side of the dash is heavily padded and blank. The instrument panel has been updated to meet the crash padding regs, but it hardly seems an improvement. The three spoked steering wheel has shrunk by an inch in diameter and acquired a leatherish rim cover and sportier spokes. The steering column has grown bulbous with the locking mechanism and the impact absorption bits and pieces. Too the new MGB had the mandatory buzzer warning for key-in-slot when the driver's door is open. Bless the British, they have found the most annoying sounding buzzer that the ROAD TEST staff has ever encountered. This would undoubtedly be the first bit of hardware yanked by the tinkering owner.

The handy, short throw gear lever is still in the same spot on the tunnel, which seems ideal as always. The hand brake lever rides in the age old position between the tunnel and the passenger seat, and the ashtray is parked forward of the gear lever within easy reach of both occupants. The mandatory headrests have been

day long without one suffering discomfort of fatigue.

Instrument placement is quite the same although extra and rather unattractive padding has been added to the dash. Directly in front of the driver is the rectangular oil pressure gauge, which, even after many years, still strikes an oddly dissonant note tucked in among all the round dials and knobs. To the right is the large and legible speedometer with a resettable tripmenter, and further right is the water temperature gauge. On the left is the matching tachometer, redlined at six grand, and the fuel gauge. Warning lights complete the instrumentation, and the heater/fresh air controls are mounted just below the main panel.

The familiar octagon still adorns the center of the handsome steering wheel, but this is not the horn button. The horn works from the button on the end of the light dimmer switch to the right of the steering column; turn indicators operate from a matching stick on the left. Over in the middle of the dash is the slot for a radio, the brake warning light button and

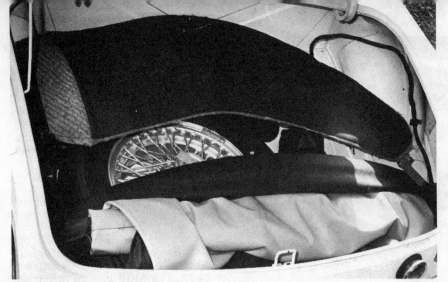

With the top down, top and struts consume most of the usuable space in the trunk.

cigarette lighter. A bit of whimsey above the radio is the ancient style map light . . . the same bit of hardware, probably the same part number, that has been fitted to BMC cars for many years.

New to us is the stowage slot suitable for maps on the side panel by the passenger's right leg. It will hold a few pieces of paper, but anything small will slide to the bottom; one must have a fairly small hand to retrieve items from this, the only in-cockpit storage space. Nicely padded sunvisors stay put well even with the top down. The windup windows are expected these days, but they were quite a departure for MG back in 1962. Small wing windows are a pleasure to have, and make life easier in bad weather.

Leg room is decent in the MG with the pedals well spaced for a British sports car. Somewhat old-fashioned is the lack of rubber covering for the accelerator pedal, but this and other touches held over from the early Anglo Saxon designs are part of the charm of an MG.

The MGB has a trunk, but don't plan on carrying much real luggage. The spare wheel takes up a goodly portion of the available space, and should the top be down on the car, the struts and vinyl just about fill the trunk. There is good storage space behind the seats, enough so that two people could travel with something between minimal and reasonable baggage provided it was carefully packaged.

The roadster top is something else again. It is incredibly archaic in design and absolutely ridiculous for the 1970s. It does provide good weather protection and fits well when erected. There is little wind noise at speed either. But . . . when one wants to

remove the top the fun begins. One person can do the job as easy as two, but it takes longer. First you must unhook and unsnap the vinyl top, then painstakingly roll it up in the prescribed fashion. Next the whole thing is supposed to slip into the odd shaped bag supplied . . . we never made it. The next step is unhooking the struts, which by the way, ride dangerously close to the head when the top is up. Finally the struts are removed, folded, and put into another case and the whole mess goes into the trunk. The tonneau cover is stored in another bag, so it comes out and goes on the car in classic style by use of rear hooks and lift-a-dot fasteners. On the test car we found it impossible to close the extra cost tonneau to the attachment points on the dash—it just wouldn't make it over the headrests. We doubt it ever would, no matter how much stretching and tugging was done with the aid of water and hot sunlight. Earlier MGBs had a top that folded down in one piece behind the seats, and we can't figure why the manufacturer back peddled to this ungainly arrangement. It is the one really sour note on the otherwise neat little sports car.

On the Road

Take the MGB out on the road and the petty annoyances of its aging design fade instantly. "Safety Fast" is an old MG slogan, and the B is a good paragon of the phrase. It has the superb roadholding and forgiving handling of the earlier cars that wore the octagon, and it does everything with the fine manners of a real thoroughbred. The rack and pinion steering is fairly light and responsive, and becomes lighter and more positive as speed increases. Straight line stability at speed is excellent, and on the winding roads the steering is all one could ask for with no noticeable slop, quick self-centering, and plenty

of that indefinable "feel." The B with its standard front engine/rear drive through a live axle is basically an understeering car. It keeps the understeer under most road conditions, but the tail can be kicked out easily in hard cornering. If one drives with gay abandon, the B will save all but the most inept driver from disaster. There is power enough for throttle steer, and if one is over exuberant in a tight corner, a flick of the wheel and some reduction in throttle will straighten out the car's line of travel.

The front disc brakes provide plenty of "whoa" to match the "go," and repeated hard use in the mountains brought out little evidence of fade. Pedal pressure is firm, but not heavy. The hand brake works surprisingly well holding the over a ton car easily on a husky hill.

Ride is firm in the British tradition, but not at all objectionable, plus the car is quiet. One can feel the bumps but it takes a big one to upset the MG's stability. If the car was to be described in one word, it would be called "sure-footed." The MG inspires confidence and makes one and all feel like a real hero. For years, from the T-series MG to the fabulous Minis, the cars built at Abingdon seem to share the characteristic of a sure-footed stance on any road that makes one feel he is just a bit better driver than the rank and file.

Power comes on smoothly through the gears; with over 90 horsepower after desmogging, the B engine is peppy and quite responsive. The all synchro gearbox is a pleasure to use with ratios well chosen for overall performance. Cars like this are not designed for blistering speeds in the quarter mile, but on the highway the performance is well up to the demands of the wildest of California traffic. The B does a zero to 60 (entering a freeway) in just 12.9 seconds; for passing it will go from 40 to 60 in seven seconds, and less if one downshifts to third gear. The car will cruise all day well above legal speeds, and when the road is long it will exceed 100 miles per hour.

While sports cars in general are not noted for fuel economy, the smaller engined cars can be surprising. Driven hard with heavy use of the gears on mountain roads, the B delivers well over twenty miles per gallon. Steady cruise on the interstate will increase the average by three or more mpg, giving an effective driving range of some 250 miles per tank. Oil consumption on the test car was not measurable in the 900 miles of driving.

A.

Hood must be propped open

B.

Heater and defroster motor

C.

Brake fluid reservoir

D.

Twin SU-carburetors

E.

Sealed cooling system

F.

Oil filler cap

G.

Dip stick

Four cylinder, in-line engine is a BMC staple as are the twin SU carbs. Engine access for maintenance is excellent; oil cooler plumbing is visible in front of the water radiator.

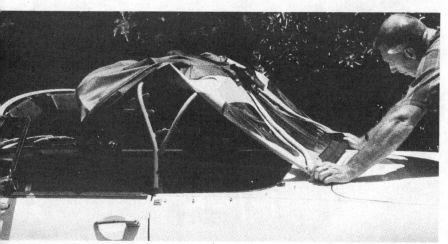

Dismantling the top is an exercise in frustration. Proper folding allows easy storage in theory, but the staff never managed to get the job done right. Struts are separate and must be stowed also.

Summary

The MGB is a pleasant car to own, and great fun to drive. It is certainly not the most sophisticated sports car around, but neither is it the most primitive available today. It could be termed everyman's sports car. The low price tag of just over three grand keeps the MG within reach of most budgets, and the forgiving and delightful handling make it a fun machine on any road. It is good looking to our eyes, and the style is more timeless than faddish. The comfort and convenience is well above stand-ard, with the exception of the top and trunk. It is small, but more than adequate for two people of generous stature. The real sports car buff does not require many convenience factors anyhow, and the biggest carps we have would not bother the average buyer.

The MGB has good performance, fine brakes and handling, a history of reliability, and it is easily maintained. It will deliver many hours of pure motoring enjoyment to its owner. The B is very much an MG in the purest sense of the name. It has just enough little quirks and left over hardware to make one certain that the frugal British are still saving patterns and dies from earlier cars. It makes us realize that some of the old hands must still be in residence at Abingdon building MGs. And that is a strangely comforting thought in today's chaotic world. □

MGB
Data In Brief

DIMENSIONS

Overall length (in.)	153
Wheelbase (in.)	91
Height (in.)	49.4
Width (in.)	59.9
Tread (front in.)	49.25
Tread (rear in.)	49.25
Fuel tank capacity (gal.)	12.0
Luggage capacity (cu. ft.)	3.0 (usable)
Turning diameter (ft.)	32

ENGINE

Type	4 cylinder, in-line, water-cooled OHV
Displacement (cu. in.)	109.8
Horsepower (at 5400 rpm)	92
Torque (lb./ft. at 3000 rpm)	110

WEIGHT, TIRES, BRAKES

Weight (as tested. lb.)	2305
Tires	155 SR 14 Dunl፡ radial
Brakes, front	፡isc
Brakes, rear	

SUSPENSION

Front	Independer፡ coil sprin፡ ፡hocks
Rear	Live axle ፡prings, ፡n shocks

PERFORMAN፡

Zero-60 mph ፡	12.9
40-60 mph (sec.)	7.0

MG-123 TROUBLE-FREE

Except for a couple of minor troubles, our test MG is showing up well and is providing SCW staff with some enjoyable motoring.

MG 123 has now notched up more than 6000 miles, all virtually trouble free. While the engine is still a little stiff it's singing sweetly as a bird. It will probably need at least another 2000 miles before it frees for operation to full potential. We have put up the miles in varying conditions — from Interstate trips to stop-start Sydney peak-hour traffic — and so far the car hasn't made a murmur of protest.

We've had our minor troubles: two flat tyres; a broken throttle cable right in the middle of the 5 pm rush; a broken overdrive switch . . . and the wind got under the aluminium bonnet while propped open for oil and water check. The broken overdrive switch probably broke through over-enthusiastic use.

We found third gear and overdrive ideal for city traffic, especially in Sydney where there are two types of drivers—the quick and the dead. By using overdrive instead of top gear in traffic we found we could switch in instant power for passing manoeuvres. The overdrive when switched out immediately adds 1000 rpm to the engine speed and the car is virtually accelerating before the throttle is brought in. It's well worth the extra money to have it fitted.

Originally, we ran figures on the car with only 3000 miles up, but it was still very stiff and they were not a true indication of the car's performance.

Through the gears, first runs out at 35 mph and 6000 rpm; second at 50 mph; third at 75 mph; and top, 100 mph. Using overdrive, third will run to 95 mph and 6000 rpm, while we saw 115 mph on the speedo before we ran out of road using overdrive on top. Over the quarter, the best time we recorded was 18.1 sec, but with a few more miles and some fine tuning we should see a figure in the high 17s.

A word of warning. Make sure the gas station attendant correctly slots the bonnet prop. If not, a windy day could see your bonnet take wings. This happened in Melbourne, 500 miles from home. A gust of wind caught the incorrectly-propped bonnet and we watched horrified as it

MG 123 is living the proper life of a sports car . . . and with the right kind of passenger. The engine is now freeing up and the performance improving.

A Mini boot strap was screwed to the side of the bonnet and the mudguard to stop the aluminium bonnet flying over the windscreen when propped up in windy conditions.

bent itself over the top of the windscreen. It was a Sunday and the long trip back to Sydney ahead. Some inexpert panel beating got the bonnet to close—and there it solidly stuck. The engine co-operated: no oil, water or de-lousing needed.

In Sydney, British Leyland fitted a new bonnet and the boot strap from a Mini screwed to the lid and the side of the engine bay to stop it happening again. As a safety measure—and a financial one, as well—we recommend this to all B owners. The Mini boot strap can be picked up at any BLMC dealer and is inexpensive insurance when compared with the price of an aluminium bonnet.

The headlights are adequate for normal touring on country roads but we found they ran out in excess of 70 mph. Rather than hang extra QIs off the front and spoil the look of the car, we decided to fit a pair of Cibie Biodes in place place of the normal headlights. These fit into the existing holes in the guards and wire up to the sealed beam connected. On low beam, the Biode works as a normal headlight but high beam brings in the QI. This is a separate light mounted inside the normal headlight. The fitting of these is a little tricky as the dip switch has to be bridged to stop the normal headlight going out when the QI is switched on by the high beam switch. We'll explain the fitting of these in the next issue.

Meanwhile MG 123 is serving its masters well.

\#

MG 123 PERFORMANCE AT 6000 MILES		
SPEEDS IN GEARS:		
First		35 mph at 6000 rpm
Second		50 mph at 6000 rpm
Third		75 mph at 6000 rpm
Top		100 mph at 6000 rpm
O/D: Third 95 mph at 6000 rpm, top 115 mph		
Third (overdrive)		95 mph at 6000 rpm
Top		115 mph (approx) at 5500 rpm

ACCELERATION THROUGH GEARS:			
0-30	3.4 sec	0-60	12.5 sec
0-40	6.0 sec	0-70	17.0 sec
0-50	8.9 sec	0-80	24.1 sec

ACCELERATION IN THIRD GEAR:			
30-50	3.3 sec	50-70	7.0 sec
40-60	3.5 sec		
Standing quarter mile			18.1 sec

MOTORING PLUS

Federalized MGB

A good deal of Motoring Plus is devoted to sports cars and performance. This week is no exception: we deal with sports cars and with performance, the subject being a "Federalized" MGB, an open tourer with overdrive, soon to be shipped to the States and bought under the Personal Export scheme by a reader, Mr Sean Walmsley, who was kind enough to lend it to us for test. But this time the theme is loss of performance rather than improvement, for this export version of the MGB, a 1971 model, was considerably slower than the home market car we tested in December 1969. The emission control equipment should have little effect on maximum power, so our borrowed car must have been below par, even though it was carefully checked by British Leyland. At the same time we considered the car to be much

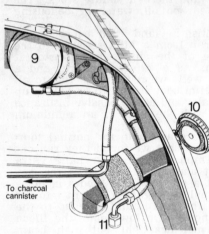

To charcoal cannister

9, 10, 11

improved by the numerous detail modifications to switchgear, controls and so on.

The key component in the emission system (see diagram) is a positive displacement vane-type pump which squirts air into the exhaust ports so that any unburnt gases can complete their combustion in the manifold. It incorporates a relief valve to limit its output at high rpm and is protected by a non-return valve in its output line so that exhaust gases cannot blow back into it. The outlet side of the pump is also connected to the *inlet* manifold via a gulp valve to consume the slug of neat petrol that evaporates when the throttle is suddenly closed after a period of high-output running. The gulp valve is sensitive to very low manifold pressure which triggers a diaphragm incorporating an air bleed to release the valve slowly and ensure response only to transient conditions.

The remaining pipes and canisters which festoon the engine form part of the interconnected evaporative loss and crankcase breathing systems. Evaporative loss reduction begins at the fuel tank which is fitted with a sealed filler cap and an internal compartment into which fuel can expand when ambient temperatures are high. Apart from a small bleed at the top, this compartment is air-locked, and so is not filled when fuel is added to the tank. Fuel vapour escapes through a vent pipe to a canister of charcoal in the engine compartment which is called an *ad*sorbtion canister because the vapour is *ad*sorbed on to the surface of the carbon granules, not *ab*sorbed into them. To prevent liquid fuel from reaching the canister there is a separation tank in the fuel line which is mounted in the boot above the main tank.

Vapour from the carburetter float chambers is passed through a further set of pipes to the charcoal canister which is purged or cleansed of the condensed vapour within it by the crankcase breathing system. External air

is admitted to the bottom of the canister and drawn through into the engine at the rocker box and out of it from the crankcase through an oil separator to the inlet manifold.

So much for the visible accoutrements of emission control. The system also uses special emission carburetters equipped with throttle dampers to give smooth deceleration and with limit valves in their butterflies which open on the overrun to admit more fuel and air to make the mixture combustible.

Another feature of the system is its "software". Sections of the owner's handbook are marked with a symbol in the form of an eye looking at a cloud of gases streaming from an exhaust pipe, and there are warnings that the maintenance checks and adjustments described in these sections should only be entrusted "to your approved pollution control service station".

Such stations are a rarity in Britain where emission control equipment is a mystery to the average British garage, and Mr Walmsley suspected that the engine had been badly tuned at the car's 3000 mile service. Accordingly, he had it checked over—both from the performance and from the pollution point of view—at the British Leyland, MG Division, Air Pollution Control Centre at Abingdon. Here some adjustment of ignition timing was found necessary, after which the car was said to be up to scratch in every respect and put through the full Federal test which it passed with flying colours:

	Test Result	Limits
Carbon monoxide	7.23	23.00 gm/mile
Unburnt hydrocarbons	1.20	2.20 gm/mile
Oxides of nitrogen	2.10	4.00 gm/mile

Emission control equipment is designed to work on the idling, overrun and part-throttle running phases of driving, and should have little or no effect on maximum power or full throttle acceleration and hence on our performance tests all of which involve these last

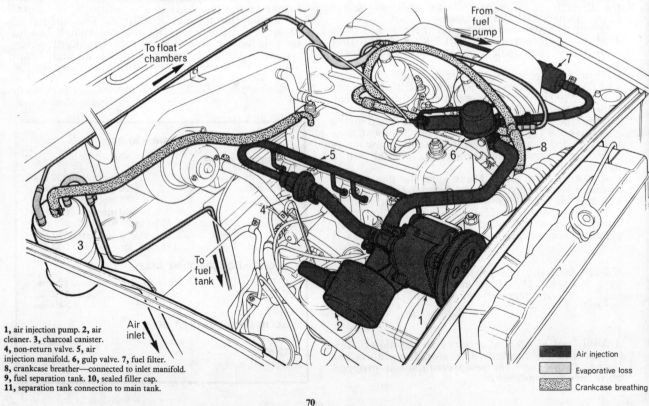

To float chambers

From fuel pump

7

To fuel tank

Air inlet

5, 6, 8, 4, 3, 2, 1

1, air injection pump. 2, air cleaner. 3, charcoal canister. 4, non-return valve. 5, air injection manifold. 6, gulp valve. 7, fuel filter. 8, crankcase breather—connected to inlet manifold. 9, fuel separation tank. 10, sealed filler cap. 11, separation tank connection to main tank.

■ Air injection
□ Evaporative loss
▨ Crankcase breathing

Externally, US versions of the MGB are distinguished by triple wipers and warning lights on the car's flanks. All cars now have a new kind of hood which is easier to erect than before

two conditions. The detoxed version of the MGB unit (for 1971) has the same camshaft overlap, compression ratio, and size of carburetter as its less fastidious UK brother. A little power is absorbed by the air injection pump, however, and maximum power is decreased slightly from 95 (net) bhp at 5400 rpm to 92 bhp at the same speed.

But our borrowed car went considerably slower than should be the case with this small reduction in output, the maximum speed being 98.9 mph, for example, instead of the 105 mph attained by our road test tourer. Out of consideration for the clutch of this privately owned car we did no standing-start acceleration tests, but found all the top and third gear

acceleration times to be down on those of the standard car. The fuel consumption was a little better at low speeds, and a little worse at high speeds, while the touring fuel consumption (computed from a lower speed) was almost identical. But the reduced efficiency imposed by the emission equipment during overrun and idling made the overall fuel consumption poorer at 21.9 mpg than the 23.7 mpg of the standard car.

Apart from dual-circuit brakes, this export version of the MGB is mechanically identical to the home market model, having the same 3.91:1 final drive ratio. Externally it is distinguished mainly by triple wipers, and warning lights on its flanks—orange at the front, red at the rear—which go on with the headlamps. Like all the latest cars it is fitted with a new-style hood which is easy to erect and lower.

Inside there are numerous minor changes which go with the left hand drive layout. The seats are of a different type, incorporating built-in headrests, and give a little less legroom, though it is possible to heel and toe—something which cannot be done easily in the standard car. We were surprised to see several sharp projections, such as the heater vents, in this region of the car, which looked capable of inflicting leg injuries in an accident. The standard headlamps are very poor and we were infuriated by the warning buzzer which operates when a door is open and the ignition key left in place.

We liked the revised facia layout, except perhaps for the rectangular oil pressure gauge squeezed in between the speedometer and rev counter. The minor control layout is much better than standard, with a central horn push on the wheel and a pair of stalks to control the various services. The left hand one takes care of dipping, flashing and indicating, while the right hand one controls the washers (push in), the two-speed wipers (up and down), and the overdrive (backwards and forwards) —this is the first time we have encountered an overdrive stalk shared for other functions, but we found it easy to use in practice. All these are things we would like to see on cars sold in Britain. ∎

1, courtesy light switch. 2, brake fluid warning light and test switch. 3, lights master switch. 4, fuel gauge. 5, heater volume control. 6, rev-counter. 7, oil pressure gauge. 8, speedometer. 9, heater distribution control. 10, temperature gauge. 11, choke. 12, panel lights. 13, heater fan switch. 14, interior light. 15, warning buzzer switch. 16, lights/indicator stalk. 17, horn button. 18, ignition/steering lock. 19, wash-wipe/overdrive stalk. 20, hazard warning switch. 21, hazard warning tell-tale. 22, cigar lighter. 23, ashtray. 24, spare switches. 25, radio.

	Federal MGB	British Market MGB
Maximum speed		
Lap	98.9 mph	105.0 mph
Best ¼ Mile	101.1	108.3
In Top		
20-40 mph	11.2 sec	9.1 sec
30-50	10.0	8.8
40-60	9.6	8.6
50-70	11.5	9.9
60-80	14.9	11.3
70-90	21.3	13.9
In Third		
10-30 mph	7.6 sec	6.6 sec
20-40	6.9	6.1
30-50	6.5	5.9
40-60	7.5	6.1
50-70	9.2	7.2
Fuel consumption		
Steady		
30 mph	41.0 mpg	39.0 mpg
40	39.0	36.0
50	36.3	33.0
60	32.6	30.0
70	28.8	27.0
80	24.5	25.0
90	21.0	21.8
Overall	21.9	23.7
Touring	29.4	29.2

Supertune
Magnum MGB

Its makers would call this a "tweak." Whatever the word,
it's worth from 50 to 80% more power and costs $20! / By John Christy

In one sense, supertuning an MGB might seem to be a form of superfluity since the makers are willing and able to supply a whole list of bits and pieces to make it go quicker than originally intended. They even have a section in the standard owner's manual that lists some of these good things. There is only one hitch in that in this age of ecological awareness a good part of the equipment might not be compatible with the edicts of the Environmental Protective Agency. It's also expensive. If you want to go racing, that's one thing but if you want to use the car for what its makers intended — putting some fun in your day-to-day driving and commuting life — that's another. You obey the gospel as laid down by the smog lictors or one of these days they'll make you park it.

Fortunately, as those of you who have been with us for the past year are aware, there is another way to have a quicker car than your neighbor and still stay legal. In a word — supertuning.

Since the later MGB, from about '68 onward, has been given what used to be known as a Stage II tune to make up for the added emission equipment, we wondered a bit just how much good the procedure would do. In other words was what was sauce for the Japanese, German and Italian geese be equally tasty for the English gander or would it be a case of one man's meat being another's poison? We needn't have worried. The development of the kit was a bit more complicated than normal due partially to the fact that the metering needles in the S.U. HS-4 carburetors are totally different from those in the earlier H-4 and HD-4 carburetors but the results were spectacularly worth the effort — from 80 percent gain at the low end to a 50 percent gain at the top! The particular MGB in question was not new; it was a demonstrator '72 unit with a

little over 9,000 miles on the meter and so was fairly representative of your average, basic MG with something between six months and a year on the street.

The MGB, despite its miniscule 92 Federalized horsepower, is a gutty little beast that acquits itself well at stoplights and in passing situations. Part of this, perhaps most of it, is due to the fact that it has 110 lbs.-ft. of torque at a relatively low engine speed of 3000 rpm. As a consequence we felt that it would probably put out a fairly respectable amount of power at the rear wheels in comparison with other engines of similar size we had dynotuned before. Wrong. The pattern was, if anything, a little under some of the newer cars with similar displacements and almost an exact duplicate of most of the rest. It started out with 12 horses at 2000 rpm delivered to the ground and edged its

Supertune

way slowly up to 34 at 5000 above which point number two plug went away. With the plug working it peaked at 5300 with a touch under 36 horsepower.

The diagnostic pattern was what we have come to expect in almost every case with emission-tuned engines. It is obvious that the various manufacturers have little faith in the average buyer's ability to keep an engine in proper operating condition and so build themselves a fairly fat cushion in the emissions department. Also, since every single import must now undergo an emissions check at the port of entry, they make sure each one will pass. In this case the air/fuel ratio check showed that it was running dead lean, almost to the point of being stoichiometric (the theoretical point of total combustion with CO_2 and water being the only by-products). This was also born out by the plug condition. These were N9Y Champions, normally considered a fairly cold range, but they were on the point of being fried and one, as mentioned, did have a high-speed breakdown.

The ignition pattern was also as expected in that while the total amount of mechanical advance was good at 33° it rose too slowly and, in fact, was still rising at over 4000 rpm. The vacuum advance was, for a change, spot-on with no whip or need for limitation. The emissions readings were well below the requirements, especially in the case of carbon monoxide (CO) which was less than half of the amount allowed.

The distributor was pulled which on the MGB is no mean feat since it is buried way down in the bowels of the engine compartment and held by a form of clip that must have been built by the same fellow who designed the Darby handcuff. The one blessing is that the distributor has a slot drive so that you don't have to go messing about trying to make sure the proper gear teeth are meshed when installing it. To be fair it does install far more easily than it is removed. Usually when a distributor is modified to produce a faster curve, only one spring, normally the secondary, needs to be changed. In this case both of them had to be replaced by special lighter units since even the original primary spring by itself was too stiff. The resulting curve brought full advance in at a point between 3200 and 3300 rpm with a resultant quickening of all the other points on the curve as well. It took four different sets of springs to find the right curve but now the combination is known, they'll wind up in the kit.

Next came the carburetors. For the past few years these have been the HS-4 model S.U. which is similar in most ways to the earlier H and HD types known sund loved (or cursed) by genera-

Above: Carburetion on the MGB since 1968 has been the HS series, in this case HS-4, replacing the older H-4. Metering needles, pistons and carburetor bases differ but action is the same. Below: The first operation on the ignition is to remove the breaker plate. With the plate off, the advance springs are exposed. Both of these were replaced before a proper curve was found.

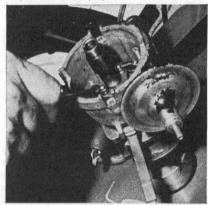

Below: To those familiar with the S.U., H and HD series, the difference between the new HS needle and piston is easily seen. The seat in the piston is larger and needle is equipped with a flexible base and a tension spring. We haven't been able to determine if there is as wide a selection of these new needles as there was in the earlier fixed-seat versions.

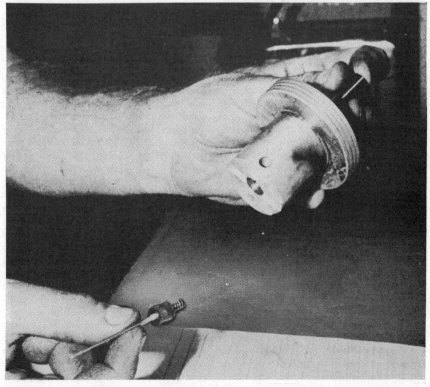

Supertune

tions of owners of British cars. However the HS (for smog?) series differs in two significant details from the older types. First, the old gland nut that raised or lowered the jet for leaning or richening is gone. In its place is a tricky recessed screw that is so placed that the average tinkerer won't bother to try to fool with it. This is no giant problem because with a certain amount of effort and expertise you can still make adjustments though not the extent allowed in the past. The real bummer is that they have changed the design of the metering needle that is pulled upward out of the jet according to the demands of the engine. The old needle sat solidly in a socket in the bottom of the piston that both raises it and provides a variable venturi action that makes the S.U. carburetor the versatile instrument that it is. The new one has a two-part base and sits flexibly in a much larger hole in the bottom of the piston. Over the years so many of the older needles were developed for different demands that you could tailor just about any air/fuel ratio curve you wanted at an infinity of throttle openings by just playing around with a handful of variously contoured needles. Failing that you could take a lean needle and recontour it to suit yourself. With the new one you can't casually chuck it in a jeweler's lathe and carve away too easily and there aren't that many different ones around either.

However, we did the best we could under the circumstances. We won't detail the process because it was a bit shade-tree and should not be followed unless you have a dyno and an air/fuel meter for a guide. We left the needles lean at the idle and low-cruise portions in the interest of ecology and worked mainly on the power and wide-open areas, a touch here and a bit there, going on and off the dyno for fuel checks for a major part of one afternoon. We finally got a combination that produced the right fuel curve and still produced an idle CO reading of only 2.5%, a reading that actually dropped under load. The HC reading was lowered, if you can believe that, from the low stock reading to a nice, clean 450 parts per million which isn't all that much higher than the air you breathe around the average garage.

This one proved to be one of those supertunes that you can feel instantly in the seat of the pants. Where the MGB had been typically spritely and quick at stoplights, it now moved out with a strong surge that belied the small displacement and power rating. Except for the odd muscle car or Corvette, it jumped off ahead at stoplights without any particular effort. Where the new-

Above and right: On the final runs on the dynamometer the power was not only raised but the meters showed an HC cleanup (left gauge) and a legal CO reading under load.

MGB DYNOTUNE

RPM	HP Stock	HP Tuned
2000	12	22
2500	17	26
3000	21	32
3500	26	36
4000	31	45
4500	32	48
5000	34	51
5250	36	53
5500	NA	50

Note: Figures represent rear wheel horsepower as observed on the Geraghty Dynamometer. They are not absolutes and represent comparison data only.

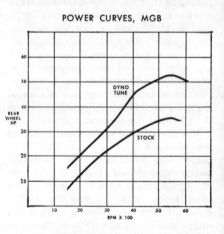

POWER CURVES, MGB

found urge really showed up, however, was on hills and in mid-range passing situations. Hills that previously had required second gear to make with reserve power could now be taken in third gear and quick passes could be made either with one downshift or none at all depending on the situation. Due to the limitations of the stock camshaft in any dynotune situation there cannot be much improvement beyond the stock peak engine speed — in other words there are seldom any extra revs added although on occasion there is enough extra efficiency so that there is useable power beyond the point of peak. So it was with the MGB which now snapped right up to the redline where it previously let you know it was getting reluctant when the tachometer hit the yellow zone. Except for the lack of extra revs the feeling was distinctly similar to that produced by the racing "prodifica-

tions" of a couple of years ago though naturally a bit milder. The nice part about this is that while the prodifications took money and time, this procedure with a $20 kit can be done in one afternoon or one day if the directions in the kit are followed *to the letter*. By the time you read this, such a kit will be on the market. For those who came in on this series late the address is Geraghty Dyno-Tuned Products, 4062 Verdugo Road, Los Angeles, CA. 90065. At first the kits will be for MGBs of the later, smog-tuned specification but very shortly they will be available for all MGBs with either the HS series carburetors or the earlier H-4 series with fixed needles. It should be noted that in every case the year of manufacture, type of carburetor and distributor number should be supplied when inquiring. We can assure you that the results are worth the effort of doing it right. /MT

74

THE MGB has proved that an impeccable pedigree is a prime essential for a successful sports car, and that technical innovation, though desirable, is not a necessity for success in the field of the sporting car.

The design is depressingly conventional in nearly all respects from the pushrod 4-cylinder engine to the semi-elliptic rear springs and live rear axle, but it shows the successful way in which lessons can be learned from a predecessor, and how modern techniques, when applied to a tried idea, can produce an acceptable contemporary result. The MGB owes a great deal to the previous MGA, sharing the same engine, but in increased capacity form, the same suspension layout and components, and substantially the same interior layout. The most important difference between the two designs is in the method of construction, as the MGB has a unitary construction body unit, as opposed to a separate chassis, as seen on the MGA. The weight penalty of the unitary construction is the main reason for the use of a 1,798 c.c. version of the B-series BMC engine, and although the MGB was one of the first British sports cars to employ this method of construction, the initial sturdy design was good enough to allow well over 300,000 MGBs to be sold since the introduction in September 1962.

During the long and distinguished life of the MGB, the design has remained basically unchanged, and the revisions that have taken place have been of detail only, and the most important of these are detailed in the accompanying table.

When the MGB was first introduced, the B-series engine had three main bearings, and the resultant avoidance of frictional losses meant that these versions were slightly faster than the later five main bearing engines. However, the later engine is considerably smoother, and is capable of higher sustained revs, and is probably the more desirable unit. It is important to remember that both British Leyland and other companies retailing exchange units can only exchange like-for-like, and do not provide five-bearing engines in exchange for three-bearing.

In service, it would be fair to say that the British Leyland B-series engines give remarkable longevity, and the three-bearing engine is good for up to 70,000 miles, only requiring valve and cylinder head attention in the interim. The life of the five-bearing engine is even better, and 100,000 miles can be expected before attention to the bores and crankshaft will be required. All the dealers to whom we spoke were full of praise for the excellent reliability record of the car, and there are clearly few faults of mechanical design.

The most important area for close attention when buying secondhand is the bodywork, as this more than anything affects the price to be paid. The MGB demonstrates better than most cars how important it is to avoid the build-up of mud inside wheel arches, as most of the rust problems with the car stem from the action of mud in the arches. The other bad areas are inside the sills, of which more later.

The guide to approximate "Asking Price" given in the data panel is unavoidably general where examples over four years of age are concerned. By their very nature, sports-cars can be expected to have had a pretty hard life. All-too-often they are bought with very nearly the last penny by people who ought to know how to look after them but in fact, do not. The MGB has a very wide appeal, as it is easy to drive, has very sure-footed handling and in absolute terms, it is not that fast. Therefore, the condition that a used example is in after four or five years depends to a marked extent on the degree of conscientiousness with which it has been serviced and maintained generally. We were interested to hear in our enquiries into the model, that the average length of ownership is less than 18 months, a figure that is more typical of a saloon car than a sports-car. It is likely, therefore, that an older example will have had a number of owners, and that the standard of maintenance will have suffered as a result. It is advisable, in the light of this, to look for an example with as few owners as possible, consistent with the other

Above: Dateless elegance with just a hint of muscle gives tremendous appeal to the open and coupé models (Below)

yardsticks of overall condition such as mileage, complete service record and good visual appearance.

What to look for

All B-series engines sound "tappety", as the tappet clearances are meant to be wide. A noisy top end is therefore not a worry, unless it is very bad. There is little incidence of timing-chain stretch, but care should be taken to be certain to differentiate between excessive "thrash" from the timing chain and the other noisy goings-on at the top of the engine. The usual checks should be applied for big-end and small-end knocking, but in fairness, there is, again, little incidence of these problems.

The engines are generally oil-tight, and one should suspect any car on which there is an excess of oil in the engine bay. The cause may be relatively simple, but it is as well to bear in mind that some eight hours are needed by a garage with all the proper equipment to take the engine out and refit the unit.

This figure of eight hours should be remembered when considering any replacement job involving the engine or the gearbox, as the gearbox cannot be removed without first removing the engine. If the engine unit and gearbox are removed together, the front of the car must be set some 8in. above the normal height on axle stands, as the length of the combined engine and gearbox requires clearance below for the gearbox tailshaft. In order to clear the steering column, it is a good idea to remove the oil filter, as it is this unit that gets in the way.

Before the introduction of the all-synchromesh gearbox in 1967 on the Mk II model, the 2nd gear synchromesh was weak, especially when changing down from 3rd to 2nd gear. If you are taken for a demonstration run by a dealer or a private seller, watch out for a double-declutch when changing down into 2nd. The quoted time to strip and overhaul a gearbox, replacing 2nd gear synchromesh is $5\frac{1}{2}$ hours, so even at today's inflated servicing costs, this would make a considerable saving over an exchange unit at £44.

While back axles do not cause much trouble in service, they are assembled in manufacture with generous tolerances. This may result in a degree of backlash, which will make itself evident as a distinct "clonk" when the drive is taken up, and another one if the car is reversed. It is important to establish whether worn universal joints are contributing, or indeed, causing the backlash. With the car on a lift, there should be no play in the UJs and no signs that the centre spider is moving in the yokes. If there is any wear, the UJs are simply and cheaply changed, and it will then be possible to establish the seriousness of the back-axle play.

Wear in the hubs is unlikely to be worse than average and the normal checks should be made with each wheel individually supported.

ERX 498C

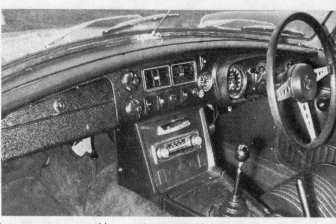

Left: The interior of the original MGB shows the leather upholstery, long gearlever and sprung-spoked steering wheel
Right: In contrast, the Series III car has the shorter gearlever, identifying the all-synchromesh gearbox, facia level ventilation and a neat centre console incorporating a glove locker and the ashtray.

Front suspension wear is limited to the bottom trunnion, and the kingpins. Either of these two will show up on the road if the car is put into neutral at less than 10 mph, and the brakes are lightly applied. If there is a "clonk", and then another one when the car is reversed, then both the trunnion and the kingpin should be checked.

The steering ball-joints do not wear any faster on the MGB than on other cars with a similar system and the M.o.T. test should therefore ensure that the joints are given at least annual attention. The only other item of steering equipment to look at is the steering column top bush which is prone to wear. This can be checked by trying to move the steering wheel vertically, when there should be no loose movement.

There are no Achilles' heels where the hydraulic brakes are concerned, and the only

aspect of the braking that may cause any trouble is the handbrake. Even on a new car, the handbrake is not very good, and on a used example, the brake may have difficulty in meeting the requirements of the M.o.T. test. It is essential that the cable is freed off fully, and that the handbrake compensators are not jammed. Provided that these items are in order and that the shoes themselves are in good condition and free from grease, the handbrake should be all right, although it is best to consider it as a parking brake only.

That about covers the mechanical and suspension items that should be looked at carefully, so we can move on to the crucial rust problem that is almost certain to be affecting examples over four years old.

There are three areas on the MGB that may be badly affected by rust and each of these result from the design of the car. The most

serious problem is with the sills, and more importantly, the side members contained within the sills. Water and mud are able to get into box formed by the outer sill panel and the side members through the lower join between the two. Once this area is well saturated, rust begin to attack the sill panel from the inside, and the outer and lower faces of the side members. The first signs of the dreaded disease will appear on the outsides of the sill panels which should really be replaced, as any other action will only put off the inevitable day. It is essential to look very carefully at the condition of the side members when the sills are off, as eventually these can be so eaten away that the structural rigidity is affected, and to plate them sucessfully to restore it could well cost a three-figure sum.

The best general advice that one can give is to avoid any car that is showing bad signs

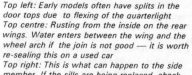

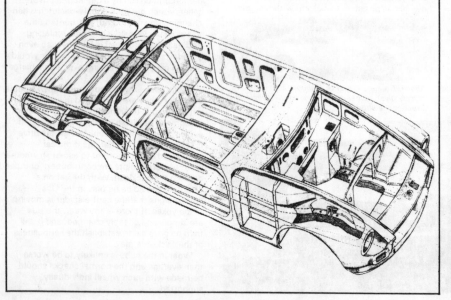

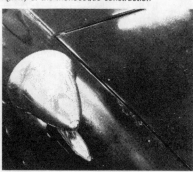

Top left: Early models often have splits in the door tops due to flexing of the quarterlight
Top centre: Rusting from the inside on the rear wings. Water enters between the wing and the wheel arch if the join is not good — it is worth re-sealing this on a used car
Top right: This is what can happen to the side member. If the sills are being replaced, check these

Left: The offending mud-trap at the back of the front wheel arch can be clearly seen. Mud trapped here can lead to the condition seen in the picture below. The cutaway shows the immense rigidity of the monocoque construction

USED CAR CHOICE MGB . . .

Above: Regular lubrication of the front suspension will help to reduce wear. The lever arm dampers are easily replaced. When checking for front suspension wear, support each side in turn by jacking beneath the coil spring lower support

of rusting in this area, as it is highly likely that the problem is not confined to the sills alone, and could be very serious indeed. If one's budget forces one to look at cars over five years old then do be careful, and remember that if the rust situation is bad here, then any action taken will only prolong the car's life and cannot insure it. The other two areas of rust can be recognized easily, and are not as serious as the sill problem.

Beneath the two front wings, there are bad mud traps at the back of the wheel arches where the wing joins the box member that reinforces the top of the engine bay and the windscreen. Mud collects in the area below the wing top, and its action eventually results in signs of rust showing on the top surface of the wing itself, about 14 in. forward of the windscreen and an inch or so in from the edge of the bonnet. This action is avoided if this area is washed out regularly with a hose, and this is advisable on new or used cars alike.

The last area that should be looked at carefully is on the rear wings. If the join between the inner wheel arch and the rear wing itself is not good, then rust will start inside the space between the two panels. This will show first as paint bubbles about an inch in from the edge of the wheel arch. If the damage appears on the extreme edge of the wheel arch, this is less serious and more easily dealt with, as the action is external rather than within the body itself which is the case in the former example.

Where to buy and how much to pay

As with most sport-cars, there are a number of reputable dealers who specialize to some extent on the MGB. Because they know the bad points both mechanical and structural, they are unlikely to buy-in any examples that are too far gone. It is pretty safe to say, therefore, that the examples that they have for sale are in sound shape. Similarly, the excellent British Leyland Gauntlet Guarantee for 6 months will ensure that the car was up to scratch when it was offered for sale by a BLMH dealer.

On older cars, however, the buyer will be

Above: One of the changes on 1969 cars was the adoption of the recessed grille seen here

left much more on his own to decide on the condition of the car. If there is a warranty on offer on a used example from a dealer, the usual warnings that it should be in writing and preferably to cover parts and labour, apply.

The general rule over how much to pay, is that it is sensible to pay a little over the odds for a particularly low mileage or one- or two-owner car, as the MGB can be kept in good condition if it is maintained properly, and if the owner is aware of the few shortcomings of the design.

Since the model has been in production for over 10 years, there has been time for various specialists to have a good look at the car and to be able to provide a good service as a result. It is possible for instance to buy new hoods from several companies as well as from a British Leyland dealer, and reconditioned engines, gearboxes etc. are available at reasonable prices from a number of sources.

With the reservation over the slight difficulties over the removal of the engine, it is true to say that the typical "no-nonsense" MG design means that the car is easy to maintain and should give a few problems to the home do-it-yourself man.

As with most British cars, the best value-for-money is a two to three-year-old example with lower than average mileage, which can be kept for a further two years and sold then — before the rot sets in. In this way, someone else suffers the original depreciation and you have the car for the best years of its life.

In the compiling of this guide to the MGB we have been given considerable assistance from both S. H. Richardson of Slough, and also University Motors, to both of these our thanks are due. In the case of Richardsons, as they are about the only dismantlers of MGBs, we were grateful to be able to see beneath the skin of some older examples to be able to appreciate the damage that can be taking place on outwardly reasonable examples. □

Significant data

Mean maximum speed (mph)	3 brg Sports 103	5 brg Sports 104	MGB GT 102	Auto Sports 104
Acceleration (sec)				
0-30	4.1	4.0	3.8	4.9
0-40	6.2	6.0	6.1	7.1
0-50	8.5	9.0	8.7	10.0
0-60	12.2	12.9	13.0	13.6
0-70	16.5	17.2	17.8	18.5
0-80	22.9	24.1	25.4	26.4
0-90	32.6	35.6	36.9	39.0
Standing ¼-mile (sec)	18.7	18.9	18.5	19.5
Top Gear (sec)				
20-40	11.4	8.6	11.2	—
20-40	11.4	8.6	11.2	—
30-50	9.7	8.7	10.1	6.6 (Inter)
40-60	8.7	9.1	9.6	7.2 (Inter)
50-70	10.4	11.1	10.8	8.8 (Inter)
60-80	12.0	13.2	13.7	14.5 (Top)
70-90	15.7	17.1	19.0	19.4 (Top)
Typical fuel consumption	26	27	24	26
Dimensions				
Length			12ft 9.2 in.	
Width			5ft 0 in.	
Height			4ft 1.4 in.	
Kerb weight (cwt)	18.5	19.0	21.2	19.2
Date of original Road Test	21/9/62	12/2/65	1/7/71	16/4/70

MGB Sports and GT

Model introduced (in open form) in July 1962. 1,798 c.c. 3-main bearing engine. Heater, anti-roll bar, oil cooler and folding hood optional. Price incl. P.T. £950.

1963 changes: strengthened hand brake lever, rear springs modified. Glass fibre optional hardtop available. Laycock overdrive optional.

1964 changes: closed circuit crankcase breather. 5-main bearing crankshaft and oil cooler standard. Electric tachometer.

1965 changes: 12 gal. fuel tank. Sealed propeller shaft (no grease points). MGB GT introduced with opening rear door, at £1,013.

1966 changes: front anti-roll bar standard on Sports and GT.

1967 changes: reversing lamps standard on Sports and GT. Mk II version of Sports and GT introduced with all-synchromesh gearbox, alternator. Door trims and seats revised. Automatic optional extra.

1969 changes: plated radiator grille replaced by matt black vertical grille, with MG emblem in centre. Leather rim steering wheel with perforated spokes. Reclining front seats optional.

1970 changes: ventilation improved, interior courtesy lights, self-locking boot and bonnet stays. Steering lock.

1971 changes: Mk III version of Sports and GT introduced with centre console between seats, rocker switches, facia-level ventilation from grilles in facia centre. Armrest between front seats. Collapsible steering column. Nylon seat inserts on GT.

1972 changes: new grille reverting to original chromed surround, but with latticed centre sections. Padded armrests replace doorpulls. Full nylon seat coverings on GT.

Chassis Identification

Sports (3-bearing):	GHN3 101 onwards
Sports (5-bearing):	GHN3 48766 onwards
GT coupé:	GHD3 71933 onwards
Sports Mk II:	GHN4 138801 onwards
GT coupé MK II:	GHD4 139824 onwards
Sports Mk II: 1969 revisions	GHN5 187170 onwards
GT coupé Mk II: 1969 revisions	GHD5 187841 onwards
Sports Mk III:	GHN5 258001 onwards
GT coupé Mk III:	GHD5 258004 onwards

Approx. selling price range	Normal mileage models available	
	Sports	GT
£150-£250	1962; 1963	
£250-£350	1964	
£350-£450	1965	
£450-£550	1966	1965
£550-£650	1967; 1968	1966; 1967
£650-£750	1969	1968
£750-£850	1970	1968
£850-£950	1970	1969
£950-£1050	1971	1970
£1050-£1150	1972	1971
£1150-£1400		1972

Details of item to be renewed or work to be done	Labour	Spares
Short engine (exchange, £30.00 Deposit pending return of old unit)	£26.40	£71.25
Gearbox (exchange)	£26.40	£44.00
Clutch (Plate, pressure plate and carbon bush)	£28.05	£13.60
Starter ring gear	£36.30	£2.20
Both propshaft UJs	£5.80	£5.50
Exhaust system	£3.30	£14.50
King Pins (both sides)	£14.85	£8.00
Shock absorber (exchange)	£2.45	£10.00
Front wing — Sports	£30.00	£23.00
— GT	£25.00	£23.00
Sills — both sides	£30.00	£10.00
Door		£23.50
Hood		£38.45

1975 MGB:
Maintaining the Breed

BY JIM WILLIAMS

• Some devotees of MG folklore have claimed that MG's fiftieth anniversary should have been celebrated at least two years ago. But seeing as how "Old Number One," Cecil Kimber's first sports model MG wasn't built until 1925, British Leyland has decided that 1975 is to be the jubilee year. Whatever the case, the MGs have been around a very long time and, like the strange circle of stones on Salisbury Plain, there are those who find mystical significance in the octagon-shaped badge of "Morris Garages." Thus it seems fitting that some of the most confusing and circuitous developments in MG history should take place with this model year.

Only the MGB roadster and the Midget will be sent to the U.S. in '75. The popular MGB/GT isn't coming because it's *too heavy*. No, it isn't

because British Leyland was planning on air-mailing the gold-medallion birthday cars to the States this year, although BL creates the impression that licking stamps and stuffing MGB/GTs into postboxes might not have been much more difficult than making them meet federal emissions requirements.

When a car is certified for emissions, it is "driven" on a chassis dynamometer with a built-in inertia set to match the weight of the car. Obviously, the higher the inertia setting, the harder an engine must work, and it logically follows that emissions will also be higher. Mechanically, the GT and roadster were identical but there was a difference in weight—and even though it was less than 150 pounds, it was enough to mean that no MGB/GTs would make it. A sad fact, and one that also gives a pretty

good indication of the roadster's margin of victory.

Assuming that the scales of justice are fair, the engineers at Abingdon apparently decided that the most expedient step toward better emissions was to make the car as light as possible. So they unbolted the front anti-sway bar and made it an option; the oil radiator also disappeared, as did one carburetor. On the left side of the venerable MG engine there is now only *one* carburetor and it's not even a SU. It's a 1.75-inch Zenith-Stromberg. For sure, the primary consideration for this switch was improved emissions in the normal sense (i.e. a cleaner-running engine, not a lighter car) and it apparently works very well. Except for California, 1975 MGBs meet emissions standards with no catalytic converter. The single carb also brings an MG first, an automatic choke, and though you'd never guess it from the husky exhaust note, a loss of almost 15 horsepower.

On paper, 15 hp figures to be about a 19-percent drop in power from last year. But surprisingly, the new MGB doesn't feel all that anemic under general tear-around-town driving. There's still torque to spin the tires away from a stop and chirp them in second if you are ungentlemanly with the clutch. Where the B really loses out, however, is on the top end—90 mph is it.

Thanks to other modifications inspired by federal standards, the '75 MGB reflects further changes in character. Even with the new "soft" nose and tail, the B's bumpers didn't comply satisfactorily with bumper regulations because they were still too low. On the short term, BL reckoned the only thing to do was make the car taller—jack it up about an inch and a half on its suspension. Visually, the added height is not *that* noticeable, but driving is quite another matter. There's been an appreciable gain in suspension travel which reduces the chances of bottoming. So rather than riding like a buckboard, the new B's ride is fairly compliant for a traditional sports car. The softness of the suspension and the raised center of gravity does encourage a fair amount of unsporty body roll. Still, the car will weave and bob through corners like a giant-slalom ski racer after a few hot buttered rums. On the skidpad the cornering capability of the new B is only 0.69 G—about the same as the average American-built sedan.

One of the biggest complaints about recent MGBs has been the amount of right-foot effort required to make them stop. On the new B, however, the power-assisted disc/drum brakes work almost perfectly. Pedal pressure and control are good, and since the bias is slightly toward the front, stops are straight and true. Stopping distances are only slightly better than average, due largely to the poor adhesion available from the standard 165SR-14 fabric-cord radials.

Another area where the B shines is interior space. There's plenty of leg room and shoulder room for two adults. The instruments and fittings bear an honesty and functionality in the best MG

tradition—there's no fake wood and the covering on the large steering wheel is actually stitched, not molded. The top folds easily, and when it's up it's not a bad umbrella. Wind-noise is minimal for a convertible. The relatively high interior noise levels (82 dBA at 70 mph) are attributed to its straining engine.

In general, the new MGB is a pleasant car. The fact that the speedometer needle will never see the last quarter of

the 120-mph counter is its only real detraction. It is the lowest-priced "full-size" sports car available in the U.S., and it is 100-percent MG. And to a lot of people, that still says *sports car*. In 50 years, MG has produced a vast variety of models and even a fanatic like Syd Beer will admit that they all weren't perfect. But you can be sure that in years to come the '75 MGB will find a special place in MG lore. •

Largely because of the means employed by British Leyland to comply with federal standards, the latest MGB represents a considerable break with sports car traditions.

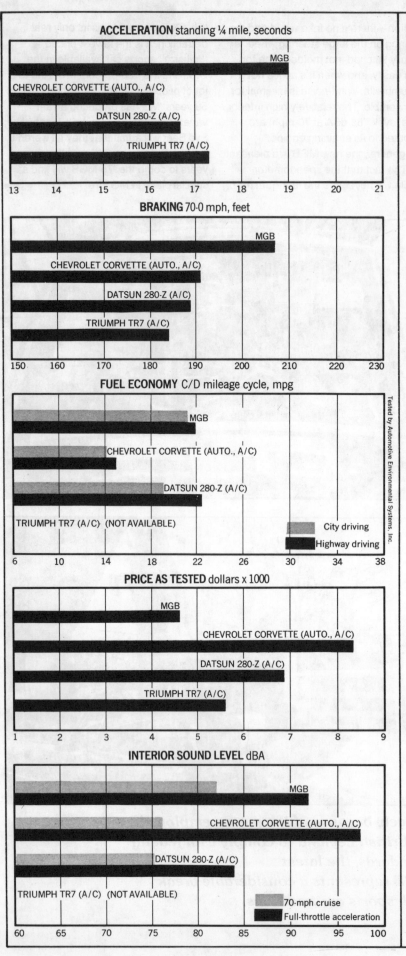

ACCELERATION standing ¼ mile, seconds

- MGB
- CHEVROLET CORVETTE (AUTO., A/C)
- DATSUN 280-Z (A/C)
- TRIUMPH TR7 (A/C)

BRAKING 70-0 mph, feet

- MGB
- CHEVROLET CORVETTE (AUTO., A/C)
- DATSUN 280-Z (A/C)
- TRIUMPH TR7 (A/C)

FUEL ECONOMY C/D mileage cycle, mpg

- MGB
- CHEVROLET CORVETTE (AUTO., A/C)
- DATSUN 280-Z (A/C)
- TRIUMPH TR7 (A/C) (NOT AVAILABLE)

City driving / Highway driving

PRICE AS TESTED dollars x 1000

- MGB
- CHEVROLET CORVETTE (AUTO., A/C)
- DATSUN 280-Z (A/C)
- TRIUMPH TR7 (A/C)

INTERIOR SOUND LEVEL dBA

- MGB
- CHEVROLET CORVETTE (AUTO., A/C)
- DATSUN 280-Z (A/C)
- TRIUMPH TR7 (A/C) (NOT AVAILABLE)

70-mph cruise / Full-throttle acceleration

Tested by Automotive Environmental Systems, Inc.

MGB

Importer: British Leyland Motors Inc.
600 Willow Tree Road
Leonia, New Jersey 07605

Vehicle type: front-engine, rear-wheel-drive, 2 passenger convertible

Price as tested: $4620.45
(Manufacturer's suggested retail price, including all options listed below, dealer preparation and delivery charges, does not include state and local taxes, license or freight charges)

Options on test car: base MGB, $4350.00; AM/FM radio, $132.50; trim rings, $37.95; dealer prep, $100.00

ENGINE
Type: 4-in-line, water-cooled, cast iron block and head, 5 main bearings
Bore x stroke . . . . 3.16x3.50 in, 80.3x88.9mm
Displacement . . . . 109.8 cu in, 1800cc
Compression ratio . . . . 8.1 to one
Carburetion . . . . 1x1-bbl Zenith Stromberg
Valve gear . . . . pushrod-operated overhead valves, solid lifters
Power (SAE net) . . . . 62.9 bhp @ 5000 rpm
Torque (SAE net) . . . . 86.7 lbs-ft @ 2500 rpm
Specific power output . . . . 0.57 bhp/cu in, 34.9 bhp/liter
Max. recommended engine speed . . . . 6000 rpm

DRIVE TRAIN
Transmission . . . . 4-speed, all-synchro
Final drive ratio . . . . 3.91 to one

Gear	Ratio	Mph/1000 rpm	Max. test speed
I	3.33	5.4	32 mph (6000 rpm)
II	2.17	8.3	50 mph (6000 rpm)
III	1.38	13.0	65 mph (5000 rpm)
IV	1.00	18.0	85 mph (4700 rpm)

DIMENSIONS AND CAPACITIES
Wheelbase . . . . 91.1 in
Track, F/R . . . . 49.0/49.2 in
Length . . . . 158.2 in
Width . . . . 59.9 in
Height . . . . 50.9 in
Curb weight . . . . 2340 lbs
Weight distribution, F/R . . . . 50.9/49.1 %
Battery capacity . . . . 12 volts, 66 amp-hr
Fuel capacity . . . . 14.0 gal
Oil capacity . . . . 3.6 qts
Water capacity . . . . 6.0 qts

SUSPENSION
F: . . . . ind., unequal-length control arms, coil springs
R: . . . . rigid axle, semi-elliptic leaf springs

STEERING
Type . . . . rack and pinion
Turns lock-to-lock 2.9
Turning circle curb-to-curb . . . . 32.0 ft

BRAKES
F: . . . . 10.8-in solid disc, power assisted
R: . . . . 10.0x1.7-in cast iron drum, power assisted

WHEELS AND TIRES
Wheel size 5.5x14-in
Wheel type . . . . stamped steel, 4-bolt
Tire make and size . . . . Pirelli Cinturato CA67, 165SR-14
Tire type . . . . fabric cord, radial ply, tubeless
Test inflation pressures, F/R . . . . 27/32 psi
Tire load rating . . . . 1200 lbs per tire @ 36 psi

PERFORMANCE

Zero to	Seconds
30 mph	3.7
40 mph	6.0
50 mph	9.2
60 mph	13.7
70 mph	18.9
80 mph	33.5

Standing ¼-mile . . . . 19.0 sec @ 70.7 mph
Top speed (observed) . . . . 90 mph
70-0 mph . . . . 207 ft (0.79 G)
Fuel economy, C/D mileage cycle . . . . . . 21.5 mpg, urban driving
22.0 mpg, highway driving

MGB

An old favourite with a new nose. Tolerable performance. Increased ride height increases roll and takes the edge off handling. Rather heavy steering. Superb gearchange. Ride unchanged. Good economy. Still enjoyable but needs improvement

The 1½in. increase in ride height (achieved by packing the front cross-member and putting more camber in the back half-elliptics) seriously increases roll, and makes the car roll-oversteer too readily, and therefore somewhat twitchy even under public road conditions. Thanks to quite high-geared steering and a not too rapid transition to this condition (below), slides like this (on a closed track) are not unpleasant and can be corrected fairly easily

THE MGB, Britain's most successful sports car, has now been with us for nearly 13 years. Of late, there have been only detail changes, the most obvious of which is the very cleverly blended "soft-front" 5 mph bumpers, re-action-moulded by Messrs Marleyfoam Ltd. out of Bayflex 90 polyurethane, and the 1½in. increase in ride height, adopted to meet American bumper height dictates. There are other smaller changes, though few notable which might have re-moved some of the 'B's long-criticized defects. At the an-nouncement of British Ley-land's new contender for the American market, the TR7, we gathered that the MGB's exist-ence was not threatened – a good thing, since the MG name still carries more successful and deep-seated sporting associa-tions than the less laurel-win-ning one of Triumph, which is one reason for continuing it – and that it was, in the words of a British Leyland executive, ex-pected "to soldier on as it is" – not such a good thing, except that it gave us a reason for Road Testing the 'B once again, to see how it measures up against the rest of the market today.

Performance

Little has changed under this heading, except that in spite of the 1cwt increase in weight over the last open overdrive MGB tested (12 February 1965), the car is usefully faster in both acceleration and maximum speed. It has been suggested that this may be explained partly by the fact that the latest test car is on radial-ply tyres where the 1965 car was on cross-plies. From a standing start, and in spite of a rising wind, the car reached 50 mph in 8·2sec where its identically geared predeces-sor took 9sec, 60 mph came up in 12·1 (formerly 12·9), the quarter-mile in 18·3 (18·9) and 80 in 22·7 (24·1). In overdrive the maximum speed was 105 mph mean (103½ before), with a best leg of 111 on the MIRA banking. In direct top the car will rev well beyond the peak power speed at its 104 mph mean, and just over-rev at its 109 mph best. With the hood and side windows down the car has more drag, the maximum in direct top dropping by 3 mph.

Starting is never any problem, only a small amount of rich mix-ture being needed for a short while. The tickover when warm is, as before, lumpy but reliable

at an indicated 700 rpm. Another MGB characteristic that continues is the flickering of the oil pressure gauge needle on tickover. As suggested later on, there is no difficulty making maximum use of the B-series engine's famous economy, which is made easy to achieve by the excellent flexibility. The engine has a crisp feel to it, though it shows its touring an-cestry in the effects of the rela-tively heavy flywheel; it cannot be described as the most excit-ing or eager of performers.

The gearchange is one of the most characteristic and indi-vidual features of the MGB. After the majority of conven-tionally laid-out modern saloons one might criticize it mildly for the very slightly greater effort required. There is also the choice of ratios, a more important defect to the press-on driver, who will resent the somewhat low second gear; even revving the engine to its 6,000 rpm maxi-mum only achieves 50 mph in that gear, followed by the same quite large drop in revs on the change to third. The engine is not a peaky one, however, and what power there is spreads itself well enough to cover the

 **MGB**

gap. Returning to the gearchange itself, its behaviour is on the whole most pleasing. There is no slop whatsoever, the movement across the gate is much narrower than most, and coupled with the general preci-sion of the fore-and-aft movements, it has more of a machine tool feel to it, solid and strong, than a motor car one. The quite large diameter gearchange knob helps too, fitting the hand well. Like a machine tool, it sometimes baulks a little, on selecting first or reverse from rest – but synchromesh is adequate without interfering too much. Pleasingly, you have only to press the lever against a sideways spring guard for reverse, which is always easier than a lift-up or push-down guard. Overdrive engagement is better made with the smoothing help of the clutch.

By today's standards the clutch pedal effort is pleasantly reduced to only 25lb. Both engine and transmission coped well with the 1-in-3 restart, and the handbrake proved very effective.

Comparisons

MAXIMUM SPEED MPH
Alfa Romeo 2000GTV....(£2,999) 120
Triumph TR6 PI.........(£2,366) 119
MGB.................(£2,133) 105
Opel Manta Rallye......(£2,040) 105
Ford Capri II 1600GT......(£2,087) 104

0-60 MPH, SEC
Triumph TR6...................8.2
Alfa Romeo 2000GTV...........9.2
Ford Capri II 1600GT.........11.4
MGB........................12.1
Opel Manta Rallye............12.2

STANDING ¼-MILE, SEC
Triumph TR6..................16.3
Alfa Romeo 2000GTV...........16.4
Ford Capri II 1600GT.........18.2
Opel Manta Rallye............18.2
MGB........................18.3

OVERALL MPG
Ford Capri II 1600GT.........27.4
MGB........................26.1
Opel Manta Rallye............25.3
Alfa Romeo 2000GTV...........21.1
Triumph TR6..................19.8

Performance

ACCELERATION

True speed mph	Time in Secs	Car Speedo mph
30	3.5	31
40	5.5	41
50	8.2	51
60	12.1	62
70	16.5	72
80	22.7	82
90	34.5	92
100	—	102
110	—	112

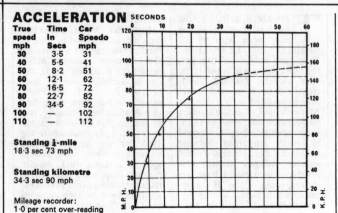

Standing ¼-mile
18.3 sec 73 mph

Standing kilometre
34.3 sec 90 mph

Mileage recorder:
1.0 per cent over-reading

GEAR RATIOS AND TIME IN SEC

mph	O.D. Top (3.205)	Top (3.909)	O.D. 3rd (4.425)	3rd (5.40)	2nd (8.47)
10-30	—	—	—	7.4	4.2
20-40	—	10.8	8.5	6.2	4.0
30-50	14.2	9.5	8.3	6.1	4.6
40-60	13.4	9.3	8.3	6.9	—
50-70	14.0	10.9	9.3	7.9	—
60-80	17.7	12.6	—	—	—
70-90	25.8	17.0	—	—	—

GEARING
(with 165SR–14in. tyres)
O.D.Top..21.83 mph per 1,000 rpm
Top......17.9 mph per 1,000 rpm
O.D. 3rd..15.81 mph per 1,000 rpm
3rd ......12.96 mph per 1,000 rpm
2nd ...... 8.26 mph per 1,000 rpm
1st ...... 5.2 mph per 1,000 rpm

MAXIMUM SPEEDS

Gear	mph	kph	rpm
O.D. Top (mean)	105	169	4,750
(best)	111	179	5,100
Top (mean)	104	167	5,800
(best)	109	175	6,100
O.D. 3rd	95	153	6,000
3rd	78	125	6,000
2nd	50	80	6,000
1st	31	50	6,000

BRAKES
FADE (from 70 mph in neutral)
Pedal load for 0.5g stops in lb

1	30	6	30–35
2	35	7	30–35
3	30–35	8	30–35
4	30–35	9	30–35
5	30–35	10	30–35

RESPONSE (from 30 mph in neutral)

Load	g	Distance
20lb	0.25	120ft
40lb	0.65	46ft
60lb	0.95	31.7ft
Handbrake	0.35	86ft
Max Gradient	1 in 3	

CLUTCH
Pedal 25lb and 5½in.

Consumption

FUEL
(At constant speed – mpg)

	Direct Top	O.D. Top
30 mph	42.6	46.5
40 mph	40.8	46.0
50 mph	37.0	43.0
60 mph	32.5	38.8
70 mph	29.2	32.2
80 mph	23.7	26.8
90 mph	19.6	22.3
100 mph	16.8	18.8

Typical mph 28 (10.1 litres/100km)
Calculated (DIN) mpg 29.3
(9.6 litres/100km)
Overall mpg 26.1 (10.8 litres/100km)
Grade of fuel Premium, 4-star
(min 97RM)

OIL
Consumption (SAE 20/50) 500 mpp

TEST CONDITIONS:
Weather: Dry, overcast
Wind: 15–25 mph
Temperature: 3 deg C (37 deg F)
Barometer: 29.8in. Hg
Humidity: 90 per cent
Surface: Dry concrete and asphalt
Test distance 1,247 miles

Figures taken at 6,300 miles by our own staff at the Motor Industry Research Association proving ground at Nuneaton.

Dimensions

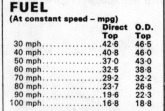

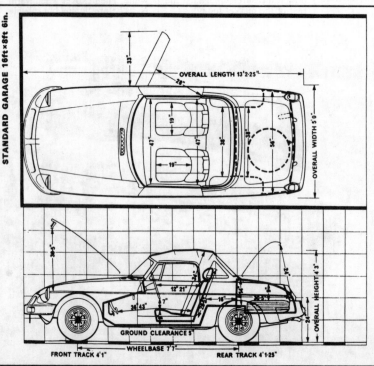

TURNING CIRCLES:
Between kerbs
L, 34ft 2in. ; R, 35ft 4in.
Between walls
L, 33ft 11in. ; R, 35ft 1in.
Steering wheel turns, lock to lock 2.9

WEIGHT:
Kerb weight 20.4cwt (2,289lb–1,039kg) (with oil, water and half full fuel tank)
Distribution, per cent
F, 50; R, 50
Laden as tested: 23.25cwt (2,604lb–1,182kg)

Noise

The MGB remains an inoffensive sports car with its exhaust noise, which as a result of slight changes to meet ECE requirements is rather quieter than before, lacking that characteristic hollow note that previous examples have made accelerating through certain revs. Like all convertibles, it is rather noisier inside when the hood is up. There is less than average bump-thump from the suspension, and what there is does not make itself conspicuous amid the usual sports car noises of engine and wind. Listening to the wireless in the test car at 70 mph was just possible, but only just; in town, which is the only place where the right-minded MGB driver will want a wireless, it can be heard easily, of course, though whilst on the subject we feel from bitter experience of slashed hoods that all car radios (and cassette players) should be made so that they can be unplugged from the dashboard and taken away when the car is left parked in town, especially in soft-topped cars.

Engine noise stems from the customary sources, and is not too much, though now that British Leyland have such extensive experience of electric fans, we would welcome the replacing of the normal belt-driven fan on the car, since it produces a surprising amount of whine as the revs rise. As before, one is unduly conscious of the wiper mechanism, which is too noisy. Noise levels drop as far as the MG's crew are con-

Specification

MGB

FRONT ENGINE, REAR-WHEEL DRIVE

ENGINE
Cylinders	4, in line
Main bearings	5
Cooling system	Water; pump, fan and thermostat
Bore	80·26mm (3·16in.)
Stroke	89·0mm (3·50in.)
Displacement	1,798 c.c. (109·7 cu. in.)
Valve gear	Overhead; pushrods and rockers
Compression ratio	9·0 to 1. Min octane rating: 97RM
Carburettors	Twin horizontal SU HIF4
Fuel pump	SU electric
Oil filter	Full flow, renewable cartridge
Max power	84 bhp (DIN) at 5,250 rpm
Max torque	102 lb. ft. (DIN) at 2,500 rpm

TRANSMISSION
Clutch	Single dry plate, diaphragm spring
Gearbox	Four-speed, all synchromesh, with overdrive
Gear ratios	Top 1·0 O.D. top 0·82
	Third 1·382 O.D. third 1·133
	Second 2·167
	First 3·036
	Reverse 3·095
Final drive	Hypoid bevel, 3·909-to-1
Mph at 1,000 rpm in top gear	17·9 mph (21·83 mph in overdrive)

CHASSIS and BODY
Construction	Integral, with steel body

SUSPENSION
Front	Independent; coil springs, wishbones using lever-type hydraulic damper as upper arm
Rear	Live axle; half-elliptic leaf spring, lever-type hydraulic dampers

STEERING
Type	Rack and pinion
Wheel dia	15½in.

BRAKES
Make and type	Lockheed disc front, drums rear, with servo
Dimensions	F 10¾in. dia
	R 10in. dia, 1·75in. wide shoes
Swept area	F 209·2 sq. in., R 106 sq. in.
	Total 315·2 sq. in. (269 sq. in./ton laden)

WHEELS
Type	Pressed steel Rostyle disc 5in. wide rim
Tyres – make	Pirelli on test car
– type	Cinturato radial ply tubeless
– size	165SR–14in.

EQUIPMENT
Battery	12 Volt 66 Ah.
Alternator	Lucas 45-amp a.c.
Headlamps	Tungsten sealed beam, 150/100 watt (total)
Reversing lamp	Standard

Electric fuses	6 (including 2 line fuses)
Screen wipers	Two speed, self parking
Screen washer	Standard, electric
Interior heater	Standard, water valve
Safety belts	Standard, static type
Interior trim	Pvc seats
Floor covering	Rubber mats plus carpeted tunnel
Jack	Screw pillar
Jacking points	One each side
Windscreen	Laminated
Underbody protection	Phosphate treatment before painting

MAINTENANCE
Fuel tank	12 Imp gallons (54 litres)
Cooling system	10 pints (inc heater)
Engine sump	6 pints (3·4 litres) SAE 20/50. Change oil every 6,000 miles. Change filter every 6,000 miles
Gearbox and Overdrive	5+1 pints. SAE 20/50. Change every 24,000 miles (overdrive only)
Final drive	1½ pints. SAE 90EP. No change
Grease	8 points every 6,000 miles
Valve clearance	Inlet and exhaust 0·013 or 0·015in. (hot or cold respectively)
Contact breaker	0·015in. gap
Ignition timing	6deg BTDC (static) 14deg BTDC (stroboscopic at 600 rpm)
Spark plug	Type: Champion N9Y. Gap 0·025in.
Tyre pressures	F 21 ; R 24 psi (normal driving) F 27 ; R 30 psi (high speed) F 21 ; R 26 psi (full load)
Max payload	424lb (192kg)

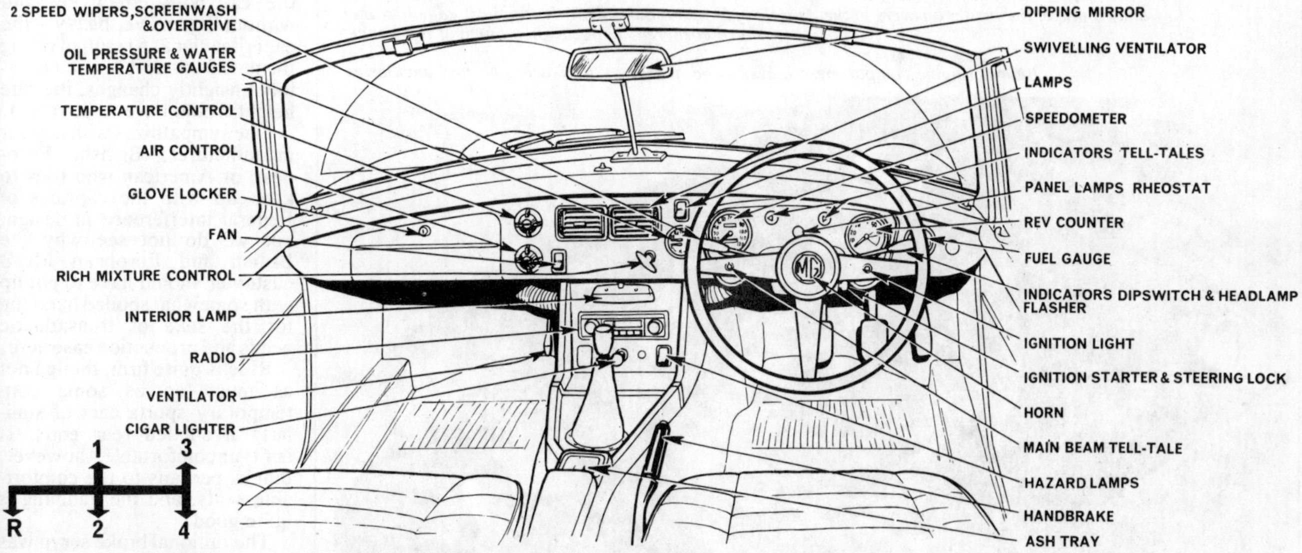

Dashboard and controls diagram labels:

Left side: 2 SPEED WIPERS, SCREENWASH & OVERDRIVE; OIL PRESSURE & WATER TEMPERATURE GAUGES; TEMPERATURE CONTROL; AIR CONTROL; GLOVE LOCKER; FAN; RICH MIXTURE CONTROL; INTERIOR LAMP; RADIO; VENTILATOR; CIGAR LIGHTER

Right side: DIPPING MIRROR; SWIVELLING VENTILATOR; LAMPS; SPEEDOMETER; INDICATORS TELL-TALES; PANEL LAMPS RHEOSTAT; REV COUNTER; FUEL GAUGE; INDICATORS DIPSWITCH & HEADLAMP FLASHER; IGNITION LIGHT; IGNITION STARTER & STEERING LOCK; HORN; MAIN BEAM TELL-TALE; HAZARD LAMPS; HANDBRAKE; ASH TRAY

Gear diagram:
```
1   3
R   2   4
```

Servicing

	3,000 miles	6,000 miles	12,000 miles
Time Allowed (hours)	1·20	3·12	3·55
Cost at £4.30 per hour	£5.16	£13.42	£12.60
Engine oil	—	£1.62	£1.62
Oil Filter	—	£0.85	£0.85
Air Filter	—	£1.25	£1.25
Contact Breaker Points	—	—	£1.52
Sparking Plugs	—	—	£1.48
Total Cost:	£5.16	£17.14	£19.32

Routine Replacements:	Time hours	Labour	Spares	TOTAL
Brake Pads – Front (2 wheels)	1·00	£4.30	£4.26	£8.56
Brake Shoes – Rear (2 wheels)	1·58	£6.79	£5.49	£12.28
Exhaust System	1·00	£4.30	£24.00	£28.30
Clutch (centre+driven plate)	8·58	£36.89	£13.59	£50.48
Dampers – Front (pair)	1·75	£7.53	£18.67	£26.20
Dampers – Rear (pair)	1·25	£5.38	£25.58	£30.96
Replace Half Shaft	2·42	£10.41	£11.50	£21.91
Replace Alternator	1·16	£4.99	£10.45	£15.44
Replace Starter	1·08	£4.64	£22.00	£26.64

cerned when the top is down, which is another reason why the car is at its best used open.

Economy

Overdrive is an option even more worth having these days, for obvious reasons. With fuel the price it is at present, and assuming at least a 10 per cent saving in consumption, it would pay for itself (£102) in 37,000 miles. It is a genuine overdrive: the car is only slightly under-geared in top, and a higher final drive is not offered if overdrive is not specified. On a long run, especially on motorways, the gains from using overdrive are impressive – over 10 per cent more economy at a steady 70 mph and 14 per cent at 90 mph. The flexibility of the B-series engine extends the usefulness of overdrive well down into the town speed range, where even at 30 mph there is a 9 per cent gain. Most owners should do better than our overall 26·1 mpg, returning anything between this figure as a bottom limit and up to over 30 mpg with gentle driving. Oil consumption is tolerable, at 500 miles per pint. As a matter of interest we carried out some steady speed consumption tests with the hood down; the increased aerodynamic losses were betrayed by a 4 per cent deterioration in the direct top figure at 30

Above: The polyurethane front bumper and grille surround (produced by Marleyfoam Ltd. for British Leyland) is one of the neater answers to the American 5-mph requirement. Its topmost edge is rather sharp cornered, noticed when opening the bonnet

Below: Engine compartment leaves good access to the power unit and ancillaries

mph, 5·1 per cent at 50 mph, 10·9 per cent at 70 mph and 13·3 per cent at 90.

Handling, ride and brakes

It is in the handling of the MGB that the biggest changes are to be found. Because of the extra ride height the car rolls quite a lot more than before, with a consequent and at first slightly alarming noticeable increase in roll oversteer, to the extent that we would suspect a detectable loss in overall road-holding. It is not entirely spoiled, since the basic stability that was always such a splendid feature of the car is still there, but with any marked movement of the steering wheel there is now a twitchy response.

The steering itself remains on the heavy side, having the still extraordinarily large amount of castor to overcome (7deg – a normal maximum today is around 3deg, and usually a lot less), but it still gives superb feel of what the road surface is like, and self-centres properly. Gearing is on the high side as it should be in a sports car, needing barely 3 turns for a 33ft turning circle. Unlike the MGB V8 GT, where because of stiffer rear springs the transition to oversteer is a sharp lurch, the MGB is not too abrupt, in spite of its now more skittish tail.

It is a fact to be proud of, that 80 per cent of all MGBs made are exported to the United States. American regulations dictated the development of the absorbent front. Crash loading demanded that if the new front was to be attached to the rest of the car both effectively and without expensive, heavy – the car is heavier as a result of fitting the new front as it is – and possibly unsightly changes, the ride height would have to be raised.

One sympathizes with any car manufacturer, British, European or American who tries to keep up with the caprices of Federal interference in design, but we do not see why the British and European MGB customer should have to put up with somewhat spoiled handling for the sake of transatlantic needs and production ease here.

Ride is quite firm, though not as much so as some contemporary sports cars of similarly live-axled rear ends. It isn't uncomfortable, however, thanks perhaps to the comfortable seats, and the damping is quite good.

The optional brake servo was fitted to the test car, making much lighter work of the good braking response. Over 1g was available with care, for only 55lb pedal effort. Fade resistance was good as before.

Controls and comfort

On the whole, it is even more comfortable to drive an MGB than before. There is still the large amount of legroom available to suit most sizes of driver,

so that one can travel unusually long distances without fatigue. The pedals could be improved with better-placed throttle and brake pedals, to make heel and toe changes less awkward; there is a convenient place to leave the left foot when not using the clutch.

One does not foul the steering wheel with one's thighs, nor is it too far away from one. The stalks on each side of the column deserve high praise now, because not only has the two-speed wiper and electric washer switch now left the facia and been arranged via the left-hand stalk switch, but it also controls the overdrive, which used to be done by a less convenient toggle switch on the dash. Also British Leyland have not for once adopted the unnecessarily clumsy, ill-shaped Marina stalks with their unwanted sharp corners, but instead used a simple, smooth, black plastic knob which is more in keeping with the car's unpretentiously functional character.

One old-fashioned feature which disappeared from the MGB for a while, then returned, and which we warmly applaud, especially as it is not yet found in other BLMC cars, is the horn switch, which is the large boss in the middle of the steering wheel. Pleasing wind tone horns are fitted.

Nothing has been done about the curious old water-valve heater. Turn on the twist knob which is intended to deal with temperature, and one has a choice of either quite usefully hot or cold – there is virtually no variation possible. Distribution is a matter of flaps and a lever under the dash. The centre cold air vents work well when the hood is up, but are starved if,

Above: Neat cockpit is functionally laid out, with no pretensions and plenty of room even for large drivers. Below: Black-crackle-finished dashboard has changed little apart from the ineffective cold-air vents. Unfortunate experiences in other cars with soft tops or sunshine roofs has taught that radios (an extra here) need to be quickly detachable, so that they need not be left in an unattended car

Boot has just adequate room for two people's luggage, provided that they use squashy baggage

as is essential, the single-speed blower is used to boost heater flow. We understand that facia layout and heater controls are to be improved shortly however. It is surprising how good the sealing of the hood is, preventing draughts on chilly days; we were impressed with the car's weather-tightness during the first day of the test, which was very rainy.

Folding the hood down is still not the quickest of jobs – one would be glad if MG took a good look at the hood arrangements on one of the 'B's Italian equivalents, the Alfa Romeo 2000 Spider, where hood operation has been reduced to something appreciably simpler. In the open condition the car is at its best, by a long way. Visibility isn't bad in the hood-up state by small convertible standards, but there are blind spots on the quarters, and because one's eye-level is not far below the underneath of the header rail, one has a somewhat curtailed view out of anything high. All that goes, of course, with the hood down, when the gain in all-round view puts one on a par with the cyclist in traffic, without his vulnerability. Buffeting at speed is not seriously present, even with the wind-up side windows down.

Boot space is limited; the experienced MGB owner who wishes to tour has suitably squashy baggage, which will make the most of the space left by the spare wheel and tool bag. There is still that irritating locker in front of the passenger, which can only be opened with the key, which you either leave in the lock assuming that there's never going to be an accident which will bring anyone within its reach, or else you leave it on your ignition key ring, which is less than convenient. The space behind the partly reclinable seats is useful for a lot of purposes, though it is not secure from the gaze of the thief.

Conclusion

Summing up, it is obvious that the MGB more than ever needs some redesign. We feel that it would be bad sales policy for British Leyland either to drop the MGB in any of its markets since the MG name is still better known to the enthusiast, or simply let the car continue unimproved, since it is already far behind some of its international competitors. A new 'B is needed now, more than ever before, an open car of modern design, especially in suspension and performance, and preferably with a better convertible arrangement than the old-fashioned fabric hood. At the same time, one does not envy the body designer who has to follow such a pleasant-looking sports car, which is still, in spite of its failings, many of the things that a sports car should be. □

MANUFACTURER:
MG Car Division, British Leyland Motor Corporation, Abingdon-on-Thames, Berkshire

PRICES			
Basic	£1,823.00	Number plates	£7.50
Special Car Tax	£151.92	**Total on the Road (exc**	
VAT	£157.99	**insurance)**	**£2,195.41**
Total (in GB)	**£2,132.91**		
Seat Belts	Standard	Insurance	Group 6
Licence	£25.00		
Delivery charge (London)	£30.00	**TOTAL AS TESTED ON**	
		THE ROAD	**£2,195.41**

MGB Roadster

The MGB roadster and its forebears are some of the cars that originally shaped the meaning and definition of the term sports car in the United States after World War II. In fact, the MG cars and their British cousins have supplied a lot of the language and comparative bases involved in sports car ownership and competition, and helped to bring the term "teabag and tennis shoe set" into sharp focus. However, the current version of the MGB roadster is sadly lacking in many traditional sports car areas, even though it does very well in others.

The problem with the MGB seems to stem from its advanced age. No major changes have been made in the package since 1962 and a great many are needed. There have been adjustments to the U.S. federalization process, not the least of which are its new ride height—an inch-and-a-half taller—and its anemic 1798cc engine. The overhead-cam powerplant is now fitted with a single zenith carburetor with a 1½-inch throttle bore, as opposed to the twin SU setup which was always considered an integral part of MGB's rugged charm. The carburetor and other engine systems had to be changed to conform to U.S. emissions regulations, to the point where now there is only a taste more than 60 horsepower on tap. There is enough torque to move the car along, but both the MG Midget and the Triumph Spitfire 1500 will out-run the MGB in a quarter-mile and in

0-60 times as well. The single-carb engine runs out of steam altogether at about 4500 rpm.

The ride height modification was made in lieu of having to construct a whole new bumper system to conform to U.S. car bumper height. MG simply raised the whole car off its wheels, resulting in a fairly soft ride with a lot more roll in the body, which MG owners have been used to. Tests show that the MGB will now only generate cornering forces on the order of .68 g on a 200-foot circle, which is about the average for American sedans and well below sporty driving levels.

The MGB is one of your basic cars, with decent seats and storage, acceptable instrumentation, quick steering and solid shifting, to go along with its relatively soft ride. Two of the car's best features are the option list (wire wheels, two different sound systems, luggage rack) and paint availability (seven colors, allowing the owner to differentiate his MGB, pretty well, from all the rest).

But in the final analysis, the car has been on the market occupying its niche, far too long without significant modernization, its enviable SCCA competition record nothwithstanding. Surely suspension, engine, and braking upgrades will increase the price of the car, but it will then be closer to being on an even footing with the competition, which gets fiercer as the MGB gets older. [MT]

Honey B

Compared to more modern JRT sports cars — not to mention contemporary machinery made elsewhere — the MGB is something of an anachronism. Yet after 17 years and half a million sales it looks set to become a classic in its own time

"A PHILOSOPHICAL combination of VW Beetle and Morgan," is how motoring historian Graham Robson summarises the MGB in his book* — an apparently unapt and unflattering summarisation at first glance, for how can a sports car be likened to the utilitarian Beetle, or the clean modern lines of the B be equated to the vintage styling of the Morgan?

Robson intended no slur on the MGB however, and on further consideration you begin to see what the man is getting at: the ubiquitous Beetle is synonymous with reliability and durability; the faithful B's credentials are well founded on that score: the Beetle was a long-running sales success; the B is approaching its 17th birthday still selling strongly, the world's most popular open sports car. And like the Morgan the MGB has, albeit in a more modern form, an honest simplicity of styling (at any rate in its pre-rubber-bumper form) that will never date; moreover, it was as many as 10 years ago that a *Motor* road test described the B as "vintage but competitive".

Though time and changing standards have thrown the MGB's vintage aspects into ever sharper relief — reinforced by the knowledge that its 1800 cc pushrod engine's basic design dates back to 1947, and its basic front suspension is derived from that of the 1947 MG YA saloon, which in fact was a pre-war design

— the significance of the MGB when it was introduced in 1962 was quite the opposite.

By the early 'sixties, sales of the B's successful predecessor, the MGA, were wilting. Some sales were undoubtedly being lost to the A's new Midget stablemate, but there was also the fact that although its performance and road manners were still competitive, rivals like the Sunbeam Alpine and Triumph TR4 were introducing a new element of comfort and civility to the sports car market that showed up the A as a stark, cramped, noisy bone-shaker of a car.

Thus the emphasis with the MGB was to retain the driver appeal of the A while raising standards of comfort and accommodation to more modern and competitive levels. The basic mechanical layout and components remained as before, but the all-new structure was, for the first time on an MG roadster (discounting the Austin-Healey-based Midget), a monocoque — and an immensely strong and rigid one too. The A's front suspension and delightful rack and pinion steering were carried over, the whole assembly mounted on a detachable crossmember. For the rear, various kinds

of coil-spring suspension were tri[ed] but in the end cost-effectiven[ess] determined that the live rear a[xle] continued to be sprung and loca[ted] by simple leaf springs. But [the] springing was much softer than [on] the A—in spite of a slight increase[d] weight which led MG to up-size [the] A's 1622 cc engine to 1798 cc, th[us] turning a potential slight loss of p[er]formance into a useful gain.

Since those early days, de[sign] development has been continuo[us] but essentially the MGB of today [is] the same car that *Motor* summaris[ed] in its first 1962 road test as [a] "delightful modern sports car wit[h] marked bias towards the 'grand to[ur]ing' character ... a pleasure [to] drive". Thus began the career of [the] world's best-loved sports car.

For 1965 the MGB engine receiv[ed] the 5-bearing bottom end introduc[ed] with the 1800 B-series variant fit[ted] to the new Austin 1800 saloon, a[nd] in a *Motor* re-test we concluded t[hat] the B was — in spite of a margi[nal] performance loss possibly cau[sed] by the extra bearings' additio[nal] internal friction — "a contempor[ary] mixture of grand tourer with sp[orts] car lines and the ability to cru[ise] effortlessly around the 100 m[ph]

88

Motor's original 1962 test car displays its simple but elegant lines. Early cars had a choice of folding (as here) or completely detachable hoods

If anything the GT version, introduced for the 1966 model year, is even prettier; note the handsome, and much lamented, all-chrome grille

The MGC, introduced in late 1967, was distinguished by a bonnet bulge needed to clear its 2.9 litre 'six', and by 15 in instead of 14 in wheels

Enthusiasts decried the new grille introduced with the 1969 model year, but the acceleration of that year's roadster test car was the best yet

HOW THEY PERFORMED: 1962-1973

	MGB 1798cc	MGB o/d 1798cc	MGB GT o/d 1798cc	MGB o/d 1798cc	MGB GT o/d 1798cc	MGB o/d 1798cc	MGC o/d 2912cc	MGB GT V8 o/d 3528cc
MAXIMUM SPEED, mph								
Mean	108.1	106.5	107	105.0	107.6	106.2	118.2	125.3
Best 1/4 mile	111.8	107.2	—	108.3	—	109.7	123.8	127.9
ACCELERATION, Sec								
	3.7	4.7	4.0	3.6	3.6	3.7	3.6	2.9
	5.8	7.1	6.0	5.7	5.6	5.5	5.1	4.3
	8.5	9.0	8.8	7.8	8.2	8.0	7.6	5.9
	12.1	12.6	13.2	11.0	11.6	11.5	10.0	7.7
	16.3	16.1	17.9	14.9	15.9	15.8	13.7	10.5
	22.5	21.2	23.8	19.8	21.4	21.8	17.7	13.0
	32.9	30.9	35.8	27.5	30.2	29.8	22.6	17.3
	—	—	—	39.2	46.3	—	30.1	23.4
Standing 1/4 mile	18.7	18.8	19.5	18.2	18.2	18.5	17.6	15.8
DIRECT TOP, Sec								
	8.9	9.4	11.0	9.1	9.2	9.9	10.3	6.4
	8.9	9.0	9.8	8.8	8.8	9.3	9.4	6.2
	8.9	9.2	10.5	8.6	8.9	9.1	10.8	6.2
	10.0	9.3	12.5	9.9	10.5	10.5	11.7	6.3
	13.2	10.8	14.6	11.3	12.7	12.4	11.9	6.6
	17.4	14.8	20.0	13.9	16.1	15.5	12.5	7.6
	—	—	—	21.0	—	—	14.6	9.8
FUEL CONSUMPTION								
Overall mpg	23.0	21.3	20.9	23.7	27.4	23.5	19.3	19.8
Touring mpg	28.0	30.1	29.2	29.2	33.0	29.0	25.6	25.7
Test date	24.10.62	9.1.65	19.2.66	27.12.69	31.10.70	22.1.72	4.11.67	25.8.73

The grille situation improved somewhat with the 1973 model year; that was the MGB at its best, before US regulations spoiled the styling

Perhaps the most desirable of all was the pre-rubber-bumper V8; we liked our road test car's "astonishing controllability and responsiveness"

October 1974 saw the arrival of the US-inspired black urethane bumpers

MGBs appeared with honour at Le Mans in the early 60s; first in class and one of only 12 finishers in 1963, first British car home in 1964; and in 1965 the car above was 1st in class, 11th overall, of only 14 finishers

mark''. It was still legal in those halcyon days!

Late 1965 saw the introduction of the pretty MGB GT coupé, with notable mechanical differences confined to the fitting of a front anti-roll bar, and a Salisbury type rear axle, both subsequently standardised on the tourer in November 1966 and July 1967 respectively. The GT's rear seats were strictly for small children only, but the luggage capacity and versatility were usefully improved while, as we said in our 1966 road test, "this increase in carrying capacity (was) achieved without any lessening in virility or sacrifice of the traditional MG virtues . . . astonishingly smooth and flexible engine". At the same time, though, certain long-standing failings like the gearbox's unsynchronised first gear and the large gap between 2nd and 3rd, or the fact that the heater was an extra-cost option, were beginning to become all the more irksome.

MG listened to at least some of the complaints, for by the time of our next test, of a tourer in 1969, the gearbox had gained first-gear synchro and slightly better ratios (with the introduction of the MkII in 1967), the heater was now standard, and there was an automatic option (also 1967). 1969 changes included better (reclining) seats, minor facia changes, Rostyle wheels and a new black plastic open grille that upset many purists who abhorred the passing of the traditional chrome design. It still wasn't possible to heel and toe and we still criticised some of the minor controls, but the acceleration was better than ever and we concluded that the MGB was "still a fast and satisfactory sports car".

Changes for 1971 included an improved heater, automatic stays for bonnet and boot lids and a redesigned hood for the tourer; we tested the GT, however, and found it "a very agreeable means of transport (with) very few rivals" and titled it Establishment Sports Car, but we noted that with advancing age the B's ride, in particular, was beginning to feel more dated as were some aspects of its interior layout.

Some of the latter were improved with the 1972 Mk III, which also gained face-level fresh-air ventilation, and in our tourer road test of that year we observed that "while it doesn't set the highest or latest standards of performance or cornering power, it is the kind of car that people buy because it is reliable, good value for money, and fun to own . . . we still like the well-mannered B".

That was our last formal road test of a standard B, but there have been many changes since then, not all of them, perhaps, for the better. For 1973 there were various trim and equipment changes; during the course of 1974/1975 a brake servo, overdrive and radial ply tyres were standardised, the automatic option was withdrawn, one 12-volt replaced the previous two 6-volt batteries, and, along with the US market, all others also got the raised ride-height suspension (to meet American bumper-height regulations) and massive rubber energy-absorbing bumpers, beloved of touch-parkers but loathed by the purists. Finally, for 1977, the facia and all thereon

were revised, a new pedal layout finally allowed easy "heel-and-toe" gearchanges, the engine cooling fan went electric, the overdrive switch was incorporated in the gear lever, and there were chassis revisions including lower-geared steering and anti-roll bars at both ends.

At the time of writing that is how it still stands, but there are two important (though regrettably short-lived) chapters in the B's biography that I have not yet covered. 1967-1969 were the years of the MGC, in which form the MG was offered with a seven-bearing development of the Austin-Healey 3000's 2912cc six-cylinder engine, with torsion bar front suspension (necessary to make room for the engine) and lower-geared steering (to keep steering effort within bounds in view of the heavier engine). It was not destined for success; the performance, in particular the top gear acceleration at low speeds, wasn't all that it should have been, and the combination of the steering's greater effort and lower gearing detracted from it as a pleasurable driving machine. Production was discontinued after fewer than 10,000 had been built, but now the C has somewhat of a cult following among those who can ignore its lack of sporting qualities, and appreciate instead its excellent refinement and loping, effortless and stable high speed cruising capabilities.

The MGB GT V8 though, was more deserving of success. Introduced in mid-'73, it was an MGB GT (no tourer was offered) with the GM-derived, Rover-developed 3.5-litre all-alloy V8 that made it rapid, refined and reasonably economical transport; yet, ironically in view of the engine's origin, the V8 was never Federalised so it could be sold on the US market, and indeed the car was never offered with left-hand-drive at all. Thus it was only sold on the home market where it was quite well received by the Press. But, although announced mid-1973, the car did not go seriously on sale until 1974, by which time the fuel crisis was biting hard and cars with large V8 engines were hardly at a premium. It was expensive, too, and although just over 1000 were built in 1974, sales petered out thereafter and by the time it was axed at the end of '76, fewer than 3000 had been built.

But while these bigger-engined variants have fallen by the wayside, the basic four-pot soldiers on, still winning friends with its easy-going manners and reliability, though neither the handling nor the performance have benefited from the changes to meet American bumper-height and European emissions requirements. With the B-series engine now having been replaced in all its other applications by the new ohc O-series engine, it can only be a matter of time before the same unit is fitted to the B (in twin-carb/2 litre/110 bhp form?), possibly mated to the Rover/Jaguar/Triumph 5-speed gearbox. Whatever happens, though, enthusiasts can rest assured that the MGB still figures in BL's forward plans for some years to come.

*The MGA, MGB, and MGC: A Collector's Guide by Graham Robson. Motor Racing Publications

MGB

We complain. British Leyland makes money. Time stands still.

AGING IS AN important (and inevitable) process in the scheme of things, especially with regard to fine cheeses, wines and people. In the arena of automotive design, however, aging can be a negative concept. Some car designs do age quite well and become classics, but others don't—the MGB seems to fall somewhere in between. This most modern (!) MG model is now nearly 17 years old and no successor is looming on the horizon. In fact, as British Leyland is pleased to note, MGB sales continue to run at healthy levels each year, so as long as the demand is constant, why spend the money to redesign or create a new model?

Well, that makes good business sense, but it's less than satisfactory for the enthusiast who would like to see an up-to-date sports car once again sporting the MG octagon, a marque badge that dates back to 1923, when it stood for Morris Garages.

The MGB was a nearly completely new car design when it went into production in June 1962, taking over from the MGA. The traditional MG ladder-type frame gave way to monocoque construction and while the inline, overhead-valve, 4-cylinder engine was basically a carryover from previous models, it was given an increased cylinder bore to bump displacement up from 1622 cc to 1798, where it remains to this day. While its driveability is reasonably good, aside from a reluctance to start when cold in our mild southern California climate, emission controls and a change in 1975 from two carburetors to one have reduced the engine's output from 94 SAE gross bhp (approximately 83 SAE net bhp) at 5500 rpm in 1962 to a current figure of 62.5 SAE net bhp at 4600 (the compression ratio is now 8.0:1 versus the original 8.8:1). Torque is currently 88 lb-ft at 2500 rpm compared to 107 at 3500 at the time of the B's introduction. Straight-line acceleration is not what it used to be, of course, but British Leyland recently made a helpful revision to the cooling system, replacing the engine-driven fan with a pair of electrically controlled ones, that has restored a small measure of the car's earlier performance. Our latest test revealed a 0–60 mph time of 13.9 seconds and the run through the standing-start quarter mile was accomplished in 19.8 sec at 69.0 mph. These figures are considerably better than those recorded in our last test of the MGB (June 1976); but a portion of the difference results from use of our new computer test equipment, which is operated by the driver alone and thus dispenses with the weight of an observer.

The engine is coupled to a 4-speed, fully synchronized manual

This instrument panel is the third design used in the MGB since its introduction in 1962. The controls have been modernized along the way too.

gearbox that is crisp and precise in the best MG tradition. Our test model had the optional ($250) hydraulically actuated (via an electric switch on the top of the gearshift knob) overdrive, which has a ratio of 0.82:1. At or well above the present maximum speed limit in the U.S., cruising in 4th gear is pleasant and easy; the overdrive makes it just that much more so. The overdrive can be used with 3rd gear too, giving the driver increased flexibility in selecting ratios for various driving conditions, as when driving in the 25/45-mph range on city thoroughfares.

On the road, the MGB's handling characteristics are not those for which the car was once justifiably admired. The suspension design has remained fundamentally unchanged, comprised of unequal-length A-arms and coil springs at the front and a live axle on leaf springs at the rear. Admittedly not modern, this is not a hopeless layout; but MG chose to meet U.S. bumper-height requirements (new in 1974) by jacking the car up some 1.5 in. on the suspension! The result is a car that looks odd despite the handsome treatment of the bumpers themselves, defying the traditional notion that sports cars are low-slung, and one which does not progress through corners the way it should. On constant-radius turns, such as our skidpad, the MGB tends to leap rather than drive around the circle, and on the road there is more body roll than most drivers find comfortable combined with a feeling of awkwardness through medium to slow bends. Those who remember driving older MGBs can only lament what has become of a formerly good-handling sports roadster.

In matters of ride and noise, the MGB never was a comfortable or quiet car; sports cars were not expected to be in the days when it was conceived. But for those unfamiliar with the tradition it may need repeating here: Rattles, squeaks and gobs of wind noise are part and parcel of its character and must be accepted as such. Roadsters like this were always at their best with the top down; in this form all such unpleasantries are minimized.

The interior appointments have been downgraded and upgraded over the B's lifespan; today the car is livable for most drivers and passengers, though devoid of the leather seat facings it once had. We had some disagreement among our staff concerning the seats, with one group describing them as comfortable and pleasant while others felt there was considerable room for improvement, including one person who said he felt as though his lower back had been abandoned entirely.

Other criticisms centered around the seatbelts, whose guides were not firmly attached, allowing the belts to become easily tangled; and the handbrake lever, which is located between the

Seatbelt reels and their covers proved problematical on the test car.

seats and frequently smacks occupants on the elbow as they enter or exit the car. The ventilation system is traditional British, i.e., lots of heat from the heater but precious little fresh air for cooling.

Well, that's why the top is convertible, right? Which leads us to the hassle involved in putting up or lowering the top. To a man and woman, every staffer who accomplished the feat came back with mixed feelings: pride at having done it, wonder as to why it has to be so complex. It requires an untoward amount of fiddling and pulling and even a little cursing to achieve the desired result.

Despite our criticisms of the MGB, it can be an entertaining sports car to drive if one keeps in mind its limitations. The rack-and-pinion steering is just right, for instance, with the proper balance of feedback and effort. Unfortunately, the brakes are only fair; stopping distances are rather lengthy and the brakes have a tendency to lock up more than we like. But a sunny day, an amiable companion and a winding country lane stretching before you can restore a lot of your enthusiasm for sports-car driving. The MGB still fits this scenario quite well. Despite its faults and limitations, and because of its virtues, many thousands of people keep driving and enjoying motoring as it used to be. ⓜ

PRICE

List price, all POE	$5995
Price as tested	$6590

GENERAL

Curb weight, lb	2335
Weight distribution (with driver), front/rear, %	52/48
Wheelbase, in.	91.1
Track, front/rear	49.0/49.2
Length	158.2
Width	59.9
Height	51.0
Fuel capacity, U.S. gal.	13.0

CHASSIS & BODY

Body/frame	unit steel
Brake system	10.8-in. discs front, 10.0 x 1.7-in. drums rear; vacuum assisted
Wheels	styled steel, 13 x 4½J
Tires	Dunlop SP68, 165SR-14
Steering type	rack & pinion
Turns, lock-to-lock	2.9
Suspension, front/rear: unequal-length A-arms, coil springs, lever shocks, anti-roll bar/live axle on leaf springs, lever shocks	

ENGINE & DRIVETRAIN

Type	ohv inline 4
Bore x stroke, mm	80.3 x 89.0
Displacement, cc/cu in.	1798/110
Compression ratio	8.0:1
Bhp @ rpm, net	62.5 @ 4600
Torque @ rpm, lb-ft	88 @ 2500
Fuel requirement	unleaded, 91-oct
Transmission	4-sp manual
Gear ratios: 4th OD (0.82)	3.21:1
4th (1.00)	3.91:1
3rd OD (1.13)	4.42:1
3rd (1.38)	5.40:1
2nd (2.17)	8.48:1
1st (3.44)	13.45:1
Final drive ratio	3.91:1

CALCULATED DATA

Lb/bhp (test weight)	40.1
Mph/1000 rpm (4th gear)	18.4
Engine revs/mi (60 mph)	3260
R&T steering index	0.93
Brake swept area, sq in./ton	248

ROAD TEST RESULTS

ACCELERATION

Time to distance, sec:	
0–100 ft	3.8
0–500 ft	10.6
0–1320 ft (¼ mi)	19.8
Speed at end of ¼ mi, mph	69.0
Time to speed, sec:	
0–30 mph	4.0
0–50 mph	9.4
0–60 mph	13.9
0–70 mph	20.5
0–80 mph	31.7

SPEEDS IN GEARS

4th gear (5000 rpm)	93
3rd (5500)	74
2nd (5500)	49
1st (5500)	32

FUEL ECONOMY

Normal driving, mpg	18.5

BRAKES

Minimum stopping distances, ft:	
From 60 mph	177
From 80 mph	320
Control in panic stop	fair
Pedal effort for 0.5g stop, lb	25
Fade: percent increase in pedal effort to maintain 0.5g deceleration in 6 stops from 60 mph	60
Overall brake rating	fair

HANDLING

Speed on 100-ft radius, mph	32.5
Lateral acceleration, g	0.698
Speed thru 700-ft slalom, mph	53.0

INTERIOR NOISE

All noise readings in dBA:	
Constant 30 mph	70
50 mph	75
70 mph	85

SPEEDOMETER ERROR

30 mph indicated is actually	32.5
60 mph	61.0
70 mph	70.5

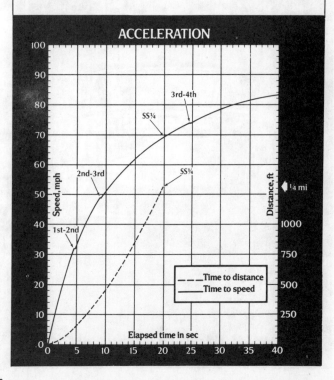

The MG Legacy
"Shed a Little Tear With Me..."

Photo Story by Walt Woron

DRIVING SOUTH from San Jose (Calif.) through picturesque Los Gatos with its diverse shops, through rolling countryside spotted with sprawling ranches and lush growth, a short climb over an 1800-ft rise separating the hot inland from the cool Pacific, down a two-lane road snaking its way through towering trees to quaint Soquel (founded in 1852), then past miles of artichoke fields cooled by ocean breezes to Monterey-by-the-Bay, I came to the slow realization that I wasn't just doing this to avoid clogged freeways and main highways; I was yearning for the MGB I was driving to remind me of what I'd been sorely missing all these years. I wanted it to transport me to yesteryear, to help me revisit my youth, to give me reason to cry over the demise of a marque that did as much as any other car to introduce (reintroduce?) the sport of driving to this country.

Try as I might, instead of recalling the fun of driving my first sports car—a '49 MG-TC—all the visions that flashed through my mind, like the two-dimensional photos whirring through an old nickelodeon, centered on the *defaults*. How times have changed, I mused. Modern-day *sedans* handle and perform not only better than that old TC that I loved so much, but the latest B I was now driving as well.

You push the B into a corner with some trepidation; you're concerned how it'll respond and if you'll get through safely with that anemic engine up front. And no wonder.

For one, the B's suspension system is archaic, consisting of wishbones and coils up front, a tube axle with semi-elliptics and lever-type shocks out back. Even the Toyota Tercel can outhandle the B. The steering, though, is quick, as it has been on every model MG I can remember, even including the Magnette sedan of the '50s.

The tiny (110ci/1798cc) ohv four, with a compression ratio of 8:1, puts out so few horses (67) that Jaguar Rover Triumph Inc. wisely excludes it from their brochures. The absolute best I got through the gears to 60 mph was a miserably slow 15.8 secs. That's no better than a Chevette Scooter and just 0.2 sec quicker than a Rabbit Diesel. But, its small displacement has the advantage of great fuel economy. On the 500-mile trip from San Francisco to Monterey to Sacramento and back to SF, the B averaged over 28 mpg.

The short throws of the transmission reminded me of the first impressions I got from the TC—that that's how a quadrant *should* be set up. It's just average in smoothness.

The driving position is not at all bad. The seat-to-wheel position is slightly offset and there isn't as much legroom as I like for my 5ft 11in frame, which caused me to drive with a bent right leg, making for tiring drives over long distances. The optional thick-rimmed wheel is much better than the skinny wheel the TC had.

The seats are more comfortable than the TC—wider and thicker. The B is also certainly appointed plusher, with more instruments and controls—with air conditioning even being optional. The multi-choice radio systems are decidedly of finer quality than was available back then. But, in those days they used real leather and not vinyl, as durable as it may be.

The ride is somewhat less choppy than I remember it being in the TC, which with its thin tires mounted on high 19-in wire spoke wheels gave the original "buckboard ride" sports car of that era were known for. Even so, on seemingly flat freeway surfaces, the B humps and bumps and jostles and vibrates. No matter what kind of road you're on, the body shakes and trembles, and the suspension transmits the surface both through the seat and the vibrating steering wheel—as it always has.

Though the B has rollup windows, where the TC merely had side curtains you put on yourself, there's still windnoise, but it's snugger. The engine also buzzes noticeably, with the four with 4-speed winding a fairly high 3400 rpm at 60 mph. It really needs the optional 5th/overdrive.

The top still goes down, of course, and that's fun—as what convertible isn't? And though I don't know if I'd want to do it today, in the days of the old TC you could fold the windshield flat (forward) and drive *right into* the wind, your eyes tearing, your face squeezed into a grimace by the sting, and imagining you were Tazio Nuvolari.

With the top down, the MGB becomes a whole new experience. Is it just imagination, or does it run better? Go faster? Even handle more precisely? All psychological, of course.

And, you're in sensurround. It's exhilarating and refreshing to sense the movement of fence posts flashing by. To be encased in a constantly moving tunnel of majestic trees covering the roadway. A feeling you're never aware of in a closed car. Roads that could be boring become avenues of escape. Country lanes take on even more beauty. Even freeways become tolerable.

But, is the MGB a sports car? Sadly, no. And in that might be part of the reason it's no longer with us. It's just a nice, small, economical convertible. For what it might have been—and what it should have been—I must shed a tear.

Radical only for its unitary construction and modern shape, the MGB was well-received upon its introduction in 1962. This version is equipped with optional wire wheels and whitewalls

To B or not to B?

The MGB — one of the best-loved of British sports cars and certainly the biggest selling — is now rated as an excellent classic buy. Mark Hughes and Mike Walsh chart the B's progress through 18 years of production, and advise on the pleasures and pitfalls of buying one

Today, just over three years after the last MGB rolled off the Abingdon production lines, Britain's best-selling sports car has an enigmatic character. Motoring snobs and those with memories too short to remember its early years love to knock the MGB, forgetting the fact that it was universally acclaimed upon its introduction to the world at the Earls Court Motor Show of 1962, and that for the first 10 years or so of its life it was far from the anachronism which it later became.

But for the rubber-bumpered horrors unveiled in 1974, and the MGB's long drawn out pensionable age until 1980, the car's memorial would be a happier one. The 'B' – a fresh, swinging sports car which belonged well and truly to the sixties – never deserved to be dragged, kicking and screaming, all through the seventies, ending its days after 18 years a shadow of the fine figure of 1962. Since its reputation has suffered with the undignified treatment meted out to it by British Leyland's corporate bulk and American-inspired safety regulations, let's go back to the beginning to restore the gloss to its image – a gloss, of course, which thousands of die-hard MG enthusiasts know all about.

The fledgling MGB had a hard act to follow. MG had gone from strength to strength with the MGA, that model having clocked up 100,000 units shortly before it was superceded, making it thus far the most successful sports car ever, from MG or anyone else. It was fast, handled well and was relatively inexpensive, but thoughts at Abingdon were turning towards the need, as they saw it, to make a sports car which was rather easier to live with.

Their new car would have more lithe styling, offer more in the way of creature comforts, and add up to a more practical proposition. At the same time, in anticipation of even higher sales, the new car's production would have to be simplified, notably by adopting the unitary construction so far unseen on any British sports cars apart from the Austin-Healey Sprite and Sunbeam Alpine. Combining body and chassis as one unit was intended to carry a weight advantage, for the MGA's separate chassis, though strong, was heavy – in fact, due to complexity, the 'B' turned out to be heavier.

Project name EX 205

Chief Engineer Sydney Enever began work on the new project, coded EX205, in 1959, borrowing his basic body shape from the sleek EX181 record car of '57. Despite toying at first with independent suspension all round, Enever soon opted for the proven MGA layout of ifs by coil springs and wishbones with lever arm dampers, and a live rear axle with semi-elliptic leaf springs. The familiar ohv

B-Series engine was chosen in favour of the twin overhead cam unit of the hotter MGA, but bored o to raise capacity by nearly 200cc to 1798cc, ar power from the 86bhp of the last MGA to 94bh Apart from siamesing the bore castings and beefir up the main bearings, there were few substanti changes to the unit, cylinder head gear and twin S carburation remaining the same. Transmission w unchanged with the exception of a higher back ax ratio.

In many ways, then, the recipe was as before, b monocoque construction allowed much more eco omical use of space, with more passenger ar luggage room within a 3ins shorter wheelbase. S good was the packaging that there was even spa under the bonnet – intentionally! – for a straight-s engine at some time in the future . . .

Having begun MGB production in June 196 Abingdon was in a position to offer immedia delivery upon the car's launch at the Motor Show few months later, and, indeed, more than 4500 ha been produced by the end of the year. Pricing w competitive at a whisker under £950 inclusive taxes, undercutting logical rivals like the Triump TR4 and Sunbeam Alpine. As those early sal figures show, response was immediately favourab from both public and press.

'The MGB is an important model,' enthus *Autocar,* 'because it completes the BMC's trend aw from the traditional British sports car with a sepa ate chassis frame. It is a forward step, too, in th the car is faster, and yet more docile a comfortable.'

Motor noticed it too when it wrote: 'Those who now the MGA will realise what a different car the MGB is as soon as they discover how easy it is to get nto.' Deeper doors, wider and more comfortable seats, wind-down windows, smart facia and a neater hood design all added up to the idea of a sports car that was easier to live with – though a heater was still n option, together with those desirable wire wheels. All the performance and handling of the MGA, it was hoped, would be found in a less austere, boneshaking package.

The only criticism of this 'civilized' MG to creep n anywhere was that the ride had become perhaps too soft, but no one reported any detriment to the handling. Writing for *Autosport*, the late John olster summed it up: 'Though the ride is soft for a ritish sports car it is still appreciably firmer than at of a typical saloon. There is some roll during ard cornering but this is not excessive, and does t obtrude during normal road driving . . . the eneral impression is that the roadholding has not en allowed to suffer in obtaining a flat and mfortable ride.'

The MGB's performance, found all road testers at e time, was improved over the MGA in every spect. It accelerated more quickly, reaching mph in 7.6secs and 60mph in 11.4secs, while aximum speed was close to the 110mph mark. Yet ese figures – more than respectable for the time – re achieved by a relatively straight-forward four-linder which impressed for both its smooth run-ng and flexibility. It could pull strongly from less an 20mph in top gear, yet was less fussy towards e 6000rpm red line than the MGA's smaller unit.

ctive in competition

At a time when BMC were active in competition, e MGB soon enjoyed its own successes despite ing overshadowed by the Mini Cooper's rallying ploits, which would eventually include four wins the Monte Carlo Rally. MGBs made occasional lying forays, but their activities were more promi-nt in motor racing, particularly long distance nts. The first major race, the 1963 Sebring 12 urs, saw an inauspicious debut when two cars tered privately but prepared by the Abingdon npetitions department suffered oil surge and ran ir main bearings. At Le Mans that year, however, ingle car with an extended, streamlined nose npleted the 24 hours in the hands of Paddy pkirk and Alan Hutcheson, finishing 12th overall d winning its class despite spending an hour and a f in the Mulsanne Corner sand.

he object of the exercise – to prove the car's iability – had been met, and the success of simply ishing this gruelling event would be repeated in following two years. Hopkirk and Andrew dges finished 19th in 1964, but failed to pick up class win even though their average speed of 9mph (how frustratingly close to the 'magic' !) was much higher – the *Motor* Trophy for the hest placed British car was, however, handsome npensation. The final MGB appearance in 1965 another finish – 11th overall and second in class. MGB driven by the Morley brothers won the GT egory on the 1964 Monte, but that achievement ed against Hopkirk's first outright win for BMC. Competition successes undoubtedly helped to ld the MGB's reputation, but sales were immedi-y on the increase in any case, thanks to the ple, practical virtues of a car which proved to e a much wider appeal than the MGA. Pro-ction in the first full year (1963) exceeded the vious record year for the MGA (1959), and tinued to rise in '64, '65 and '66, thanks in part overwhelming demand from the United States. beam and Triumph were worried particularly by export success, but had good reason to be nkful that so far the 'B' was available only in -top Tourer form. A detachable hard-top was n offered as an option, as was Laycock overdrive n the beginning of 1963, while the specialist npanies quickly jumped in with their own hard-offerings in a number of styles of varying taste.

he first real landmark in the MGB story came years after launch in 1964 when the engine was

Sliced down the middle, this display GT exposes overhead valve gear, five main bearing crank and transmission line

Speedwell's design was one of many hard-tops available

Neat dashboard and spoked steering wheel of an early 'B'

Hopkirk/Hedges averaged 99.9mph at Le Mans in '64 . . .

revised to take a five bearing crankshaft instead of three. Power output went up by 1bhp to 95bhp, but, if anything, the engine was slightly less free revving though smoother lower down the rev band. Since replacement engines have all been of the later spec, it would be rare now to find a three bearing engine. The previously optional oil cooler also became standard.

Autocar noticed the difference under the bonnet: 'Over the most used rev range – 1500 to 4500rpm – the improved crankshaft support is immediately apparent to anyone who remembers the earlier model, and even when revving the engine in neutral before driving off, one notices that what little harshness there was previously has gone.'

After two years of record sales, the MGB GT's appearance in October 1965 was perfectly timed to stimulate another sector of the sports car market just as demand for the roadster tailed off slightly. John

SPECIFICATION

Engine	In-line 'four'
Construction	Iron block and head
Main bearings	Five bearings (3 pre-Sep '64)
Capacity	1798cc
Bore × stroke	80.26 × 88.9mm
Valves	Pushrod ohv
Compression	8.8:1
Power	95bhp (net) @ 5250rpm
Torque	110lb.ft @ 3000rpm
Transmission	Four speed manual (optional overdrive)
Top gear	18.2mph per 1000rpm 21.9mph per 1000rpm (o/d)
Final drive	3.91:1 ratio
Brakes	Disc/drums
Suspension F.	Ind by coils, wishbones, lever arm dampers
Suspension R.	Live axle, semi-elliptics, lever arm dampers
Steering	Rack and pinion
Body	Monocoque, all steel
Tyres	165 × 14

DIMENSIONS

Length	12ft 9.3ins
Width	4ft 11.7ins
Height	4ft ¼in
Weight (unladen)	2030lb

PERFORMANCE

Maximum speed	103mph
0-60mph	11.4secs
Standing ¼ mile	18.7secs
Fuel con.	24mpg

Thornley, MG's General Manager, had always wanted to build 'a poor man's Aston Martin', and so was proud to reveal a closed coupé version of the 'B'. Still strictly a two seater, the MGB GT was an eminently practical sports car which would appeal to those namby-pamby mortals unwilling to buy a car without a lid.

An extra 220lbs weight impaired acceleration slightly, but the better shape gave a slightly higher top speed, and stiffer suspension and a weightier tail improved the already exemplary handling manners. By the end of 1966, a third of production was of the GT model, and, thanks to this elegant – almost exotic – model, another record year was achieved. The GT's introduction also saw a new Salisbury-type rear axle, which was quickly used on the Tourer as well. Since significant bodyshell modification was necessary to accommodate this bigger axle, early Tourers cannot be fitted with the later axle.

There was sufficient modification to the MGB for the 1967 Motor Show for the revised car to be christened the MkII, though there were no external changes. The real difference was the adoption of an all-synchromesh gearbox, and, for the first time, automatic transmission was available as an option. An alternator replaced the old dynamo.

Two trends which ultimately played a part in killing the MG name were rearing their heads during the late sixties. In the United States, Ralph Nader was getting worked up about the danger of the motor car, his endeavours resulting in the Safety Act of 1966 which required all manufacturers to meet 22 safety requirements. This was serious for MG, as a great deal of Abingdon's resources had to be diverted from producing cars into the task of designing new components. America's Clean Air Act, which set down stringent air pollution regulations, gave the engineers further headaches.

Meanwhile, politics back at home were helping to bang a few more nails into MG's coffin, for BMC took over Jaguar in 1967 to form a new body called British Motor Holdings, and a year later Leyland moved in on BMH, absorbing MG under an umbrella which also embraced arch rivals Standard-Triumph. There were no concrete changes at the time, but it marked the beginning of the insidious process by which MG's identity was slowly strangled as BL's sports car future became Triumph orientated.

Mechanical changes from here on were virtually nil and so the MGB went into that prolonged retirement for which the critics ultimately hammered it. In 1969, though, when a range of cosmetic changes were introduced, the MGB still had a fresh, modern shape and was more than a match for the opposition. *Motor*, in a road test of the MkII, were surprised by its youth: 'We expected to find this ageing design, first introduced in 1962, to be completely outclassed by subsequent progress... we are happy to report that our expectations were, for all the important things, largely unfounded. The MGB is still a fast and satisfactory sports car.'

The changes for the 1969 Motor Show spruced up the appearance of the MGB. Gone was the familiar vertical slatted, chromium radiator grille, and in its place a recessed matt black example. Rostyle wheels replaced the original steel rims but wire wheels remained an option, and British Leyland badges – *Mon Dieu!* – appeared on the flanks. Further detail changes came two years later, but the feeling now was that improvements in trim were beginning to be a disguise for the fact that the car was becoming long in the tooth.

Motor again, in 1972: 'It's a best seller with no pretensions: while it doesn't set the highest or latest standards of performance, or cornering power, it is the kind of car that people buy because it is reliable, good value for money and fun to own.'

Theo Page's splendid cutaway takes you under the surface of a roadster. Clearly visible are coil springs and discs at front, leaf springs and drums at rear, and those troublesome box section sills

But the regression really took hold in 1975, when Abingdon – far from autonomous by now – shocked both MG enthusiasts and lesser motoring mortals by announcing that henceforth the ghastly American spec MGB would have to be sold in Britain in the interests of economical production. This, as is well known, meant ugly black polyurethane mouldings at front and rear and – the really dumb step! – a ride height increase of 1½ ins to bring the headlamps up to the specified level. Why couldn't the British market have been spared the ungainly sight of an MGB on stilts, for we were not forced to accept the federal engine spec of single Zenith-Stromberg carburettors (instead of the twin SUs which had been with the MGB since its launch)? Body strengthening and extra weight also meant that the MGB was slower than on its launch.

The motoring press by now were keeping their MGB enthusiasm well in check, *Autocar* saying in 1975 that it was 'already far behind some of its international competitors.' The magazine went on to detail the real shortcomings: 'It is in the handling of the MGB that the biggest changes are to be found. Because of the extra ride height the car rolls quite a lot more than before, with a consequent and at first slightly alarming noticeable increase in roll oversteer, to the extent that we would suspect a detectable loss in overall roadholding.'

Reaction in the United States was no less scathing, even though *all* the cars available there had suffered changes for the sake of the law. *Car & Driver* were clearly disappointed when it stated: 'Largely because of the means employed by British Leyland to comply with federal standards, the latest MGB represents a considerable break with sports car traditions.'

As the BL heirarchy went forward with their rationalisation plans, it became clear that sports car production, such as there was thought to be a place for it in the future, would be under the Triumph banner, and that the MG name would finish when the 'B' and the Midget finally perished in 1980 (only to re-emerge for the prestige Metro in '82).

Production history

Over its 18 year life, an incredible number of MGBs were produced. Exact production figures are difficult to deduce, but it seems that the eventual total was not far short of half a million, making the evergreen 'B' the best selling British sports car of all time. To be more precise, around 454,000 were built, and just over two-thirds of those – a staggering 300,000 plus

– went to the United States. Of the grand total, j over a quarter were GTs.

Chassis numbering began in July 1962 with 1 and the first specification change came a year la when the folding hood became standard equipm from chassis 19586 – previously this had been optional alternative to the do-it-yourself vari which had to be stowed in the boot. Two years a launch the five bearing engine came along (4876 together with standardized oil cooler and electro rev counter. A few months later, in March 19 fuel range was increased by raising tank capac from 10 to 12 gallons (56743), while in October that year the elegant GT was unveiled. This began with chassis number 71933, prefixed by letters GHD instead of the GHN of the Tourer stands for MG, H for the engine type, N for Tourer body, D for the GT body). The Tou gained a standard front anti-roll bar from 108039

The changes become very confusing in 1967, year of the Mk11's appearance in October. Ear that year, the Salisbury-type axle introduced on GT was standardized for the Tourer (129287), reversing lamps became standard (Tourer, 1004 GT, 016928). The Mk11, of course, saw the M receive the all-synchromesh gearbox of the MGC alternator in place of a dynamo, and negative ea electrics (Tourer, 138801; GT, 139824).

The first external styling changes came two ye later, in late 1969, from chassis 187211. A reces black radiator grille, Rostyle wheels, reclining se minor facia changes and British Leyland badging the wings began the trend towards much m frequent detail re-designs in an attempt to keep MGB superficially with the times.

A year later, in August 1970, more fiddling ca in the shape of a better heater, interior cour light, a Michelotti-designed hood mechanism, automatic boot and bonnet stays to replace th infuriating manual props (219000). A year pas and – yes, you've guessed – more improveme (258001). The changes were all within the ca including a revised facia with different switchg and auxiliary instruments, fresh air vents at level, brush nylon seats and a centre console.

August 1972 saw the next annual, American-s update, with more external changes (294251) more elegant black grille with chrome surro made this arguably the most attractive M variant, while minor differences included rut faced over-riders, yet another type of stee wheel, a cigarette lighter, standard radial tyres

ated rear window (on the GT), and a tonneau
ver for the Tourer.
A year went by, and then came the next revisions.
zard warning flashers and standard brake servo
the British market were this time the order of the
y, while the automatic transmission option was
eted (328101).
And then in 1974 came the bombshell, and the
GB ceased to be a car which could be taken
iously (from chassis 360301 on). No enthusiast
ntemplating buying a classic MGB will choose a
ber bumpered car, unless it has been through the
orious conversion to look like a proper MGB
in.

yers spot check

e would imagine that buying a 'B' is a relatively
ple operation, bearing in mind the practical
ign of the car. But (ignoring the later 'cow
cher' series) remember that even the youngest
me bumper variant is now 10-years-old and
sooner or later require mechanical and struc-
l renovation. Due to the car's innate ruggedness
reliability, owners too easily abuse and poorly
ntain their cars.
he most difficult car to buy is that in the
-price range. An MGB for £1000 can easily
ire as much work as an MoT failure costing
to nothing. And remember, too, there is no
rtage of 'B's on the market, so take time and care
n buying.
he body is the most crucial area to any prospec-
buyer – the mechanics in general are relatively
le and inexpensive to rectify. The sills undoubt-
need critical attention, particularly the side
nbers hidden underneath, which will affect the
ctural rigidity of the body when badly corroded.
late and successfully restore this area will now
in excess of £200 per side and replacement of
the outer sill cover is a short-term measure, at
, which disguises the condition of the core.
ays ask to see bills for any restoration work. It is
cult to check specifically the condition of these
ons but any rust on the outer sill will probably
n the inside is far worse.
lso check that front and rear wing channels on
ill are clear, as they are too easily covered when
has been applied. The sill can also be checked
the inside by peeling back the mat at the very
t of the footwell. It is far less expensive to
hase a car with new sill sections than to renew
at a later date.
he overall condition of the rest of the
ocoque will provide an indication as to rusting
e internal core. Other tell-tale signs are rust
ling along the bulkhead seam from the bonnet
e windscreen (probably indicating corrosion of
nner front box section) and between the rear
l arches and the chrome trim. Replacement
l arch sections can save minor damage but
y deteriorated examples could require complete
replacement, necessitating extensive cutting
of metal followed by expensive welding. The
wings are bolted on but replacement requires
n removal – a very awkward task.
ors, particularly on the tourer, will split below
uarterlight due to bad alignment and it is worth
king for rot around the base. Also check under
arpets (especially with the roadster) on both the
nger's and driver's sides for floorpan decay.
r crucial areas are jacking points, rear corners
e boot floor, and seat belt mountings, where
sed rusting could mean MoT failure.
the mechanical side the MGB is no real
em but certain points are worth remembering.
work that is needed on the gearbox will require
g out the engine so check the condition of the
h thoroughly. The early gearboxes (pre-1967)
veak synchro on second so noisy changes from
to second are a sign of wear. On the later
s noisy first and reverse gears and chattering
are indications of bad condition.
e choice of overdrive is a matter of preference.
eel that even with the adjusted ratios on
verdrive cars the engine cries out for a fifth
However, it is one less item to go wrong and

The MG Owners Club tends towards more social events

The MG Car Club organises close, competitive racing

The SEC was a limited edition post-production 'B'

on the market non-overdrive cars are marginally
cheaper. Overdrive faults are often caused by bad
servicing; a dirty filter or faulty solenoid are the
main problems.
The suspension is relatively trouble-free and in
general easily maintained. At the front, the rubber
bushes of the wishbone arms are very exposed and
perish badly. Many cars have been converted to the
stronger V8 bushes. The dampers are easily replaceable while kingpins can be checked by jacking up
the car and testing for play. At the rear, the
leaf springs can become tired and broken and the
best pointer to suspension condition is the handling
at speed. Worn dampers and springs cause the car to
wallow when cornering hard. The handbrake is the
worst aspect of the braking system but it is always
worth checking for corroded pipes and scored discs
at the front. A noisy back axle, particularly clonking
on acceleration, generally means worn UJs and it is
worth checking for propshaft play.
The MGB has two six volt batteries situated either
side of the propshaft underneath the rear seat shelf
for optimum weight distribution! The condition of
the battery supports is worth noting but when test
driving a car it is advisable to leave the cover off to
check for back axle noise.
The engine is generally good news, being synonymous with reliability. All B-series engines were
designed with very wide tappet clearances and a
noisy top end is quite usual. Be suspicious of excessive oil leaks as the engines are generally very oil
tight, while normal checks on compression and oil
burning are obvious; in general engines run on the
warm side. It is worth remembering that a replacement Gold Seal unit can be bought for the relatively
low cost of £360. Cars with the three-bearing crank
are the most difficult to keep running, especially in
terms of availability of major components.
With the roadster careful inspection of hood and
tonneau is advisable as these are costly to replace.
Wire wheels certainly improve the car's looks and
value but should be checked carefully, particularly

the splines at the rear. Essentially, buy either the
very best example you can afford or a genuine
rebuild project.

Rivals when new

Due to the MGB's over long production run, it has
competed against almost every mass produced
sports car of the last two decades. Priced at a very
competitive £949 when launched in 1962, its most
direct competition on the home market was the
Sunbeam Alpine. *Small Car* magazine concluded
in a back-to-back test that the Alpine won on
comfort, ride and silence, but ultimately the 'B' was
chosen for sheer charisma and fun per mile.
The Alfa Duetto Spyder and Triumph TR4 were
far more expensive, better equipped, and with
greater performance. The Fiat 1500 and 124
Spyders proved tough competition 'across the
pond', but felt the challenge too great on the home
market, where few right-hand drive cars were
available. The Triumph Spitfire lacked masculine
appeal and the competition pedigree of MG, never
achieving favour with the die-hard sports car fan.
By the seventies the MGB fared poorly in group
tests – 'capable but undistinguished' was a common
label. Mid-engined competition – in particular the
Fiat X1/9 – merely emphasised the dated concept of
the 'B'.
The competition was a little tougher for the GT.
The original design was a novelty and was soon
imitated in the form of the Triumph GT6 and Ford
Capri, which were in general more refined solutions
to the fastback design. The new generation of
sporting saloon cars with superior performance and
comfort – the Alfa Romeo GTV and Ford Mexico
are examples – had definite effects on sales during
the seventies.
It was the enthusiast's loyalty to the Octagon that
Leyland so desperately exploited during the
seventies which sadly stretched the 'B' far beyond its
competitive life.

Clubs, specialists and books

MGB enthusiasts have a choice of joining two
specialist clubs, the MG Owners Club and the MG
Car Club. Whichever you join depends on the type
of owner you are. The MGCC is descended from the
original factory supported club, but has only
recently acknowledged the average MGB owner/
enthusiast. It has excellent racing connections, and
produces a club magazine covering all MGs with a
strong emphasis on pre-war cars. The club caters for
the type who proudly owns an MGB but dreams of
driving a K3 Magnette in the Mille Miglia. The
club's race meetings, particularly the May Silverstone extravaganza, are excellent days out.
The MG Owners Club was born out of the Car
Club's disinterest in 'modern' MGs. The club offers
a glossy monthly magazine (now with full colour)
specifically aimed at the MGB/Midget owner, plus an
annual year book, special offers on spares and tools,
and an important 'recommended' suppliers system.
The club's very competitive insurance scheme alone
makes membership worthwhile. Some people criti-
cise the Club for its professionalism and mourn the
early days when every member knew each other
(national meets are now much more impersonal)
but such is the problem of a very successful club.
The MGB owner is better catered for by
specialists and spares outlets than most modern
cars. Several firms are dominant, due more to their
efficiency and personal advice than to exploitation of
the market. The Sprite and Midget, B, C and V8
Centre at 22-28 Manor Road, Richmond, Surrey,
TW9 1YB (01-948 6464) offers an unrivalled spares
service. Other recommended suppliers are MGB
Spares and Services, Beech Hill Garage, Beech Hill,
Reading, Berks (0734 884774); Romney Shield, 25
Rutherford Close, Leigh on Sea, Essex (0702
529070); Southern MG Centre, Unit 6C, Redkilm
Close, Horsham (0403 55266); Barry Stafford,
113-115 Stockport Road, Cheadle Hulme,
Stockport, Cheshire (061 480 6402).
Many specialists sell spares and have full work-
shop and restoration facilities. Highly respected are
Brown and Gammons, 18 High Street, Baldock,

Herts (0462 893914); Motobuild Ltd, 128 High Street, Hounslow, Middlesex (01-570 5342); Motorspeed MG Specialists, Unit 10, Newcroft, Tangmere, Chichester, W. Sussex (0243 781765); Ron Hopkinson MGB/C/V8 Parts Centre, 1102 London Road, Alveston, Derby (0332 756056); John Hewitt, 82 High Street, Knott Mi-l, Manchester (061 236 5110).

Tony Brier, 62 Far End Lane, Honley, Huddersfield, W. Yorks (0484 664669); Peter Wood, Portway Road, Twyford, Bucks (029 673 310); and LV Engineering, 11/12 West Hampstead Mews, London NW6 3BB (01-624 5488) are noted specialists in mechanical work. There are many other firms, but these listed were regarded highly in a survey carried out among enthusiast members of the MG Owners Club.

Perhaps the most essential book for the prospective buyer is *MGB, C and V8 – A complete guide to repair and restoration* by Lindsay Porter. Don't be put off by the title, because the most valuable section of the book is the extensive buying guide which includes a costing code for maintenance and restoration work. The rest of this tome provides a good companion to your workshop manual.

Haynes's *Super Profile: MGB* by the same author is a good general introduction to the type which again includes basic buying tips.

More historical accounts of MGB development are *The MGA, MGB, MGC* by Graham Robson and the slightly weightier *MG: the A, B, and C* by Chris Harvey. Wilson McComb's *MGB* is a more personal story from the inside, as he spent 10 years running the PR department at Abingdon, and includes many amusing anecdotes from his own MGB experiences.

Reprints of original road tests feature in the two Brooklands Books volumes, *MGB 1962-1970* and *MGB 1970-1980*, which include useful features on buying and tuning 'B's.

Prices

Top line MGBs, like the car featured on our front cover, which have had the full restoration treatment by a respected specialist, can sell for over £3000. But this is probably only applicable for a pre-1969 car, with fully restored leather seats, complete and original detailing, and concours standard finish.

This is not the type of car most prospective MGB buyers would consider. A much sounder proposition for everyday motoring is the 'B' around the £2000 mark, generally the last of the chrome bumper models (pre-September 1974). For this kind of money a very sound example can be purchased, with relatively low mileage, probably with rebuilt sill sections and an excellent interior.

Buying between £1500 and £1000 is more difficult. These are the cars that tend to attract short cut renovation; attractive looking resprays can deceive. Cars around this price should be looked at very carefully, especially if work on the body has been carried out, so always check bills for specialist work.

Below £1000 and you could be asking for trouble. The cars are generally rough bodily and will soon require expensive restoration work. Unless you are an experienced buyer and very lucky beware of this region of the market.

Up to £500 will buy a good and generally viable restoration project, and many believe this to be the soundest way to buy an MGB. Careful costing will prove you need to budget for approximately £1500 to produce a very sound example, perhaps far superior to the type of complete car bought for this sum. Overall, roadsters tend to be more expensive than GTs, although there is seasonal fluctuation here, while extras such as overdrive and wire wheels enhance a car's value.

Rubber bumper variants are the younger cars and people seem to buy them mainly for that reason. We can't see them becoming as collectable as the earlier cars, and they will probably drop considerably in value in the future.

The best approach, then, is to go for a known history vehicle that's led a sheltered life, was built between October '72 and September '74 and is priced around the £2000 mark.

Life with an MGB has been rough for Assistant Editor Mike Walsh

Assistant Editor Mike Walsh and his troublesome 'B'

Affairs with motor cars are a strange business. I bought my MGB for all the right reasons – practicality, sturdiness, longevity. Very sensible, but uninspiring motives. However, my relationship with BAP 62K has contradicted all those qualities.

It began two years ago when I handed over cash for a 1971 (the wrong year), British Racing Green (the right colour) roadster in the late spring (the wrong season to buy any open sports car). Having missed a previous good example by 10 minutes, my frustration encouraged impatience and neglect on inspection and, as I handed over my precious savings, I had that uncomfortable feeling of regret, that second sense when you are about to suffer ownership of a genuine 'lemon' which no amount of physical grind and pounds sterling are going to improve.

That first summer was great and I actually began to enjoy the car. I wasn't particularly proud of buying a 'B' and found myself apologising to fellow enthusiasts, but those warm summer evenings with the top down chasing along rural roads were pure magic. With colder weather my enthusiasm began to wane, the slow heater and poor hood proving how dated the 'B' had become. The hood in particular is a disaster, taking days to lower and erect, especially compared to Italian counterparts. Then the engine started to overheat, mainly in traffic; quite welcome in the winter but when warmer times arrived the temperature gauge was doing battle with the oil pressure needle. A continuous process of elimination didn't cure the problem. First a new thermostat was fitted, then a new radiator, then new hoses, followed by a timing check, new head gasket and decoke – but still no cure.

And then disaster... Racing along the M25 to Brands last Easter, BAP 62K was converted suddenly to three cylinder specification. The long tour home was the most peaceful journey I have ever had in the 'B', cruising at a steady 70 in the slipstream of a friend's Talbot Samba – at the end of a tow-rope. At home the cylinder head was removed to reveal a chipped piston crown which gave rise to a new dilemma. Should I buy a guaranteed secondhand engine and sell the car quickly, rebuild the original block, or acquire a Gold Seal unit?

The latter was chosen as the safest and most straight-forward option – or so I thought. The following Bank Holiday – three days available just in case a small technical hitch presented itself – was set aside to complete the transplant. The exhausted block was removed and exchanged at the local Unipart store for a lurid gold unit – and naturally we hadn't removed all the necessary ancillary parts. By

Saturday afternoon the wooden crate was brok open and the new unit examined. Everything look all right at a glance so the new clutch was offe up – and there the trouble began. Two dowels w missing from the flywheel, and all possible sour were closed. The whole job was thwarted until Tuesday with the car in the street, engine on pavement, and the hoist to be returned. All affect for BAP 62K melted away. On top of the proble mentioned a plate was missing to blank the hea outlet, the mountings were for dynamo specificat and not alternator, and so it went on.

Finally the transplant was completed in embarrassing two weeks.

While running in the car two days later someb reversed heavily into the rear wing. I could see way of selling out now without more expenditure least the new wing could be replaced via insurance and while it was being done the other (which was rusty) could also be restored. These ta exposed desperate inner sill rot. The estimate pr too much, especially with the summer escape to I planned, so I took half measures restoring b wings but just one sill. The rest could wait until autumn, together with the repaint. The car looks like a camouflaged wartime edition! Basic that's the tale – except for an electrical rebuild, f suspension overhaul, and a change to the later g to improve that awful original nose styling.

A poor purchase

In general my MG affair proved an ordeal: alm everything has gone wrong, mechanically structurally, to a car I didn't passionately desir the first place. If I'd invested all that work in an or Fiat Spyder, it wouldn't have been nearl painful because of the pride of ownership.

On the positive side, I always enjoy driving the It's one of the safest cars I've ever owned, altho tyre pressures are absolutely crucial to the handl The basic oversteering characteristics can be ploited and enjoyed and I constantly look forv to roundabouts in wet conditions! The lac overdrive is intolerable on motorway journeys the gap between second and third can be emba sing when accelerating, but the gearchange is o and positive.

In conclusion, my particular 'B' experience is to forget, basically because too little care was t when buying. This is a great shame since, giv good specimen with the right specification, I th would have actually enjoyed ownership.

Out with the old, in with the new – a roadside swap